Saniye Dedeoglu is Marie Curie Fellow at the Centre for Research in Ethnic Relations at the University of Warwick, UK, and Assistant Professor in the Department of Labour Economics at the University of Muğla, Turkey. She holds a PhD from the Department of Development Studies at the School of Oriental and African Studies (SOAS), University of London, and is the author of *Women Workers in Turkey: Global Industrial Production in Istanbul* (I.B.Tauris, 2007).

Adem Y. Elveren is Assistant Professor of Economics at Sütçü İmam University, Kahramanmaraş, Turkey. He holds a PhD in Economics from the University of Utah, and has also studied at Ankara University and Boston University.

GENDER AND SOCIETY IN TURKEY

The Impact of Neoliberal Policies, Political Islam and EU Accession

SANIYE DEDEOGLU
and
ADEM Y. ELVEREN

I.B. TAURIS
LONDON · NEW YORK

Published in 2012 by I.B.Tauris & Co Ltd
6 Salem Road, London W2 4BU
175 Fifth Avenue, New York NY 10010
www.ibtauris.com

Distributed in the United States and Canada
Exclusively by Palgrave Macmillan
175 Fifth Avenue, New York NY 10010

Library of Modern Turkey 4

ISBN 978 1 78076 027 8

A full CIP record for this book is available from the British Library
A full CIP record for this book is available from the Library of Congress

Library of Congress catalog card: available

Printed and bound by CPI Group (UK) Ltd, Croydon, CR0 4YY
camera-ready copy edited and supplied by Fatma Çiftçi

To Ayşe and Asya

CONTENTS

List of Abbreviations   ix

List of Tables, Figures and Boxes   xiii

Acknowledgements   xvii

Foreword by Diane Elson   xix

Part One: The Welfare State, Labour Market and Gender in Turkey
1. Introduction: Gender, Society and the Welfare State
in Turkey   3
Saniye Dedeoglu and Adem Y. Elveren

2. The Changing Welfare Regime of Turkey: Neoliberalism,
Cultural Conservatism and Social Solidarity Redefined   15
Ayşe Buğra

3. Understanding Gender Equality Demands in Turkey:
Foundations and Boundaries of Women's Movements   31
Feride Acar and Gülbanu Altunok

4. The State of Female Labour in the Impasse of the
Neoliberal Market and the Patriarchal Family   47
Gülay Toksöz

5. Gender Aspects of Income Distribution and
Poverty in Turkey   65
Meltem Dayıoğlu and Cem Başlevent

6. Housewifisation of Women: Contextualising Gendered
Patterns of Paid and Unpaid Work   87
Emel Memiş, Umut Öneş and Burça Kızılırmak

7. Domestic Labour and Well-Being: A Case Study of
the Evlatlık Institution in Turkey   103
Hande Toğrul

**Part Two: The Effects of the Welfare Reforms on Women's Status
in the EU Accession Process**
8. Gender Equality Policies and Female Employment:
The Reforms in the EU Accession Process   125
Saniye Dedeoglu

9. The Social Security Reform and Women in Turkey   141
Mustafa Şahin

10. Gender and Health Sector Reform:
Policies, Actions and Effects   155
Tuba İ. Ağartan

11. Gender Gaps in the Individual Pension System
in Turkey   173
Şule Şahin and Adem Y. Elveren

12. Child and Elder Care Providers: Women
in the Informal Sector   189
Helga Rittersberger-Tılıç and Sibel Kalaycıoğlu

13. Women and Trade Unionism in Turkey:
The Impact of the European Union   205
Şerife Gözde Yirmibeşoğlu

Endnotes   223

Bibliography   239

The Contributors   277

Index   281

LIST OF ABBREVIATIONS

AKP	Justice and Development Party [Adalet ve Kalkınma Partisi]
Bağ-Kur	Social Insurance Institution for the Craftsmen and Artisans and Other Self-Employers [Esnaf ve Sanatkarlar ve Diğer Bağımsız Çalışanlar Sosyal Sigortalar Kurumu]
CA	Capabilities Approach
CEDAW	Convention on the Elimination of Discrimination Against Women
DC	Defined Contribution
DP	Democrat Party [Demokrat Parti]
DPT	State Planning Organisation [Devlet Planlama Teşkilatı]
ECD	Early Childhood Development
EU	European Union
ES	Retirement Fund [Emekli Sandığı]
ETUC	European Trade Union Confederation
GDP	Gross Domestic Product

HBS	Household Budget Survey
HSBS	Health Seeking Behavior Study
HSR	Health Sector Reforms
HTP	Health Transformation Programme [Sağlıkta Dönüşüm Programı]
ILO	International Labour Organisation
IMF	International Monetary Fund
IPS	Individual Pension System [Bireysel Emeklilik Sistemi]
İş-Kur	Turkish Employment Organisation [Türkiye İş Kurumu]
JIM	Joint Inclusion Memorandum
KEIG	Coalition of Women's Groups for Women's Work and Labour [Kadın Emeği ve İstihdamı Girişimi]
KSGM	General Directorate on the Status of Women [Kadının Statüsü Genel Müdürlüğü]
MDG	Millennium Development Goals
MEDA	Euro Mediterranean Partnership
MENA	Middle East and North Africa
MP	Member of Parliament
MPG	Minimum Pension Guarantee
NGO	Non-Governmental Organisation
OECD	Organisation for Economic Co-operation and Development

PAYG	Pay-as-you-go
PEA	Private Employment Agencies
RC	Regular Contributions
RHP	Reproductive Health Program
SAP	Structural Adjustment Program
SGK	Social Security Institution [Sosyal Güvenlik Kurumu]
SHI	Social Health Insurance
SSK	Social Insurance Institution [Sosyal Sigortalar Kurumu]
TGTV	Turkish Foundation of Voluntary Organisations [Türkiye Gönüllü Teşekkülleri Vakfı]
TEPAV	Economic Policy Research Foundation of Turkey [Türkiye Ekonomi Politikaları Araştırma Vakfı]
TİSK	Confederation of Employers' Associations of Turkey [Türkiye İşveren Sendikaları Konfederasyonu]
TL	Turkish Lira
TurkStat	The Turkish Statistical Institute
TUSIAD	Turkish Industry and Business Association [Türk Sanayicileri ve İşadamları Derneği]
UN	United Nations
UNDP	United Nations Development Programme
WHO	World Health Organisation
WTO	World Trade Organisation

LIST OF TABLES, FIGURES AND BOXES

Table 2.1   Historical trends in sectoral distribution of employment in Turkey in comparison with selected OECD countries   20

Table 2.2   Total public social expenditure in selected OECD countries   22

Table 4.1   1988-2007 Developments in sectoral distribution of employment   56

Table 5.1   Gender differences in the distribution of the sources of personal income   67

Table 5.2   Inequality in earnings by employment status and sex in 2008   73

Table 5.3   Inequality in non-labour income by type of income and sex   77

Table 5.4   Composite index values for men and women for average achievement   83

Table 6.1   Descriptive statistics of the data   93

Table 6.2   Mean time spent on unpaid and paid work   95

Table 6.3   Mean time spent on unpaid and paid work-married couples without children   96

Table 6.4   Mean time spent on unpaid and paid work-married
             couples with children   96

Table 6.5   Comparison of work burden of women and men   98

Table 6.6   Comparison of singles, couples without children,   99
             and couples with children

Table 6.7   Married-with-children phase households over the
             life course by the number of children   100

Table 7.1   The CA framework: summary of the capabilities
             through life cycle   115

Table 11.1   Source of social security for women and men   179

Table 11.A1 Women's yearly annuity benefit as a percentage of
             men's yearly annuity benefit according to education
             and age   186

Table 11.A2 Probability of guarantee payoffs   187

Figure 5.1   Share of females in income deciles   69

Figure 5.2   Female - male earnings ratio evaluated at various
             points of the respective distributions in 2008   70

Figure 5.3   Share of females in earnings deciles   72

Figure 5.4   Share of females in non-labour income deciles   74

Figure 5.5   Female - male income ratio evaluated at various
             points of the respective distributions   75

Figure 5.6   Cumulative distributions of household income by
             income status   78

Figure 5.7   Distribution of three groups of women by house-
             hold income   80

Figure 5.8   Cumulative distribution of household income
              excluding women's incomes   81

Box 7. 1   List of capabilities   120

ACKNOWLEDGEMENTS

This collective work has benefited from the help of different people and institutions. We would like to thank Ahment Makal and Gülay Toksöz for hosting our one-day workshop at the Faculty of Political Sciences of Ankara University. A warm thank you is due to Günseli Berik who read and commented on an earlier draft proposal of the book. We also would like to thank Christina Hammer for her hard work in editing our English and to Fatma Çiftçi for her fine work in copy-editing our manuscript.

Lastly, we thank our families for their support and encouragement they shared with us during the preparation of this book.
SD and AYE

FOREWORD

This is the first book to examine how gender relations are being reconfigured in Turkey through the intersection of neo-liberal social policies, political Islam and EU accession. It offers many original and well-researched insights into the paradoxes of a set of legal, economic and political changes that, on the one hand promote a formal equality between women and men in a 'marketized' social security system, and on the other, intensify the social norms that make unpaid care 'women's work,' and do nothing to enable more women to get decent paid jobs. It is a very valuable addition to the literature on gender, social policy and welfare states.

In the last ten years, in response to EU recommendations, there have been a number of important legal changes in Turkey that provide for formal equality between women and men. This book rightly insists that it is essential to look beyond these legal changes to examine whether progress towards substantive equality between women and men is being secured. Its findings reveal a persisting gap between formal equality before the law, and the realities of gendered poverty and income inequality.

This book highlights the importance of the low female labour force participation rate, and the important role of the family in the provision of social welfare. The latter has been strengthened by the policies of the AKP (Justice and Development Party) government, with the Prime Minister asking Turkish women to have at least three children. This book shows how the symbolism of the headscarf has been changed from 'religious obligation' to 'human right'. However, the evidence in the book points to continuing neglect of other aspects of women's human rights, such as the right to work.

The demands on women to provide unpaid care to their families are demonstrated in an innovative quantitative analysis of gender differences in time use, based on the Turkish national time use survey that was conducted in 2006. The state does little to provide public child care and elder care services, and women are left to manage as best they can. The book deploys fieldwork based evidence to show how women augment their own provision of care for their families with care provided by paid care workers supplied by private agencies, and on unpaid care provided by poor young rural women brought into middle class households in a form of quasi-adoption. Both of these additional sources of care often entail infringements of the well-being and rights of those providing the care.

In this context, the government has introduced reforms to the social security, health insurance and pensions systems, which entail a high degree of marketization and privatization. This book clearly demonstrates that although these reforms incorporate formal equality between women and men, they do not lead to substantially equal welfare provision because most women do not have the kind of jobs that are covered by these contributory systems. Most women will continue to be dependent on male breadwinners unless policy starts to address the provision of decent jobs for women.

This well-researched and well-argued book shows that while there have been some gains for women in terms of their legal status, there has not been a transformation of gender relations in everyday lived reality.
Diane Elson, University of Essex

PART ONE

THE WELFARE STATE, LABOUR MARKET AND GENDER IN TURKEY

1

INTRODUCTION: GENDER, SOCIETY AND THE WELFARE STATE IN TURKEY

Saniye Dedeoglu and Adem Y. Elveren

Gender has been the core theme of the Turkish modernisation project since the founding of the Turkish Republic in 1923. While women's issues have been the subject of heated political debates, women themselves have been absent from these circles. Women as 'symbolic pawns' of opposing political camps are brought into the fight of men's domination of political power. In recent years, the political fight for modernisation through secular or religious paths has become more visible in the issue of veiling. However, there has been little effort made to understand the gendered nature of the Turkish state or identify how its public provisions envision women's place in society, where indeed women stand at the junction of poverty and development.

Gender and Society in Turkey presents an overview of the gendered nature of the Turkish welfare state and also an account of how the current welfare reform process affects the nature of gender practices in Turkey. The Turkish welfare state has traditionally rested on the ideal of women's main societal role as mothers and wives because the family is an important source of security for the vast majority of the population. This, in turn, results in women's low involvement in formal social provisions and women remaining outside the formal health and social security systems as independent citizens. The current welfare reforms promise to grant women equal citizenship rights and to change women's role in society.

In investigating these objectives through a broad selection of articles from various fields, the book aims to contribute to the wider debates on gender and the welfare state in non-Western countries and to shed light on the changing nature of social policy and the consequent outcomes for women. This investigation will also show that these reforms, while promising equality for women, can in some cases protect traditional gendered roles while in others stigmatise women as a weaker, more vulnerable group in need of special protection. Therefore, we contribute that the changing nature of the welfare state may increase women's vulnerabilities by granting them legislative equality without sufficient policy measures or provisions.

Social Policy and Gender in the South

Social policy is a form of social contract between state and citizens and the result of a specific configuration of interests of power groups. Forming a general social policy frame is a mixture of public provisioning to eliminate the risks of market relations and the institutions of family and community to assure the economic security of members. In this regard, Esping-Andersen's well-known welfare typologies are formed on the basis of the notion of a welfare mix of state, market and household as well as a focus on political economy as an analysis of power structures and social clusters (Esping-Andersen 1990). The attention of the model to social clusters is seen as neglecting gender, ethnicity and religious influences on welfare. Even heavily criticised as being gender-insensitive, these typologies are, however, a reflection of the state of inequalities between women and men in any given society.

In building upon this neglect, the feminist analysis has integrated women and gender into the analysis of the welfare state, documenting inequalities between men and women as recipients of welfare benefits. Feminist analysis emphasized the nature of state, the market and the family as determinants of gender inequalities and public provisions of welfare. It is clear that the role of family and gender ideologies has an impact on the outcomes of state provisions, benefits, and services. Sainsbury (1994) highlights two important contributions of feminist research into the analysis of the welfare state. First, basic concepts of mainstream research are gendered to begin with. Second, alternative models and theories are developed on which different typologies of the welfare state can be based. Models identified as critical regarding gendered frameworks include the male breadwinner model, the welfare state type (which enables women to create their own home), in addition to typologies that recognise and treat women within limiting confines such as mothers, wives or workers.[1]

All the models and analyses of the welfare state are about Western countries, trying to evaluate their social order and social stability. However, where the spread of markets, the effectiveness of state and the sense of citizenship remain unstable outside the context of advanced countries it is difficult to apply the same models and arguments of the welfare regimes (Kabeer and Cook 2000). It is argued that needs satisfaction and self-sufficiency are more important for those countries in the South but the welfare regime model of Esping-Andersen focuses on de-commodification. This omits the central role of informal institutions in the provision of welfare in low-income countries. The informal institutions, such as family, religious organisations, community and kin-based relations are important in assuring the welfare of citizens and, of course, defining the role of women.

In this book, the primary focus is not to illuminate the role of informal institutions in providing welfare, but to highlight how the changes in the social policy frame in Turkey affect women's roles as the main actors of the informal welfare system. It is evident that there is a move towards more universalisation or a Europeanisation of social policy in Turkey. Thus, the aim is that while welfare state rights and benefits in conjunction with the operation of family units change dramatically, how do these affect the roles and positions of women as a response to social policy reforms.

Gendering Welfare State in Turkey

In Europe, the effects of welfare reforms on gender regimes is analysed in a framework of a gender transformation from a domestic to public form. This analysis developed by Walby (2004) offers an analysis of the effect of the EU gender policies on gender regimes that may take a different shape depending on which route is taken for the gender regime transformation. She offers three main types in the context of the EU and North America, which are market-led, welfare state-led and regulatory polity-led. The welfare state-led is presented through the social democratic public service route followed by the Nordic countries. In this system, the development of public services provided women with the capacity to increase their paid employment. The market-led route, followed by the United States, where provision of the service necessary to support women in employment, takes place through market mechanism. The regulatory policy-led route is developed by the EU, in which women's access to employment is facilitated by the removal of discrimination, regulation of working time so that it is compatible with caring, and policies to promote social inclusion. These different routes produce different outcomes in gender transformations that also depend upon the degree of gender inequality and the form of gender regime (Walby 2004: 10-11)

While Walby's analysis is more attuned to explain the effect of EU policies on gender regimes in Western countries, it is less helpful in explaining the gender implication of the EU gender policies in less developed countries, such as Turkey. Here, Molyneux's (1985) distinction of practical gender interests and strategic gender interests offers a way of analysing the effect of EU gender policies on women's interests in a given country. Practical needs relate to the immediate needs of women and do not entail a strategic goal such as women's emancipation or gender equality. Strategic interests aim to overcome women's subordination, such as abolition of division of labour by sex, the alleviation of the burden of domestic labour and childcare, mainly removing obstacles standing in the way of achieving gender equality (Molyneux 1985: 233-34). In some cases, strategic interests can be achieved at the expense of the short-term practical interests of some women and these interests produce different outcomes for women of different race, ethnicity and class. But Molyneux's concepts can be useful tools in the analysis of the effects of particular policy on women.

There are ongoing reform initiatives in Turkey which significantly affect the role of women. These reforms are implemented to meet the demands of the EU recommendations or as neo-liberal reforms of the AKP (Justice and Development Party) government. The main piece of legislation began with the Constitutional amendments in 2001 and 2004. In Article 10 of the 2004 amendment, the state was deemed responsible not only for ensuring non-discrimination between women and men, but also to take necessary measures for equality in practice in every field. The new Civil Code of 2001 abolished the head of family concept and equalised the status of husband and wife. Women's unpaid labour in the family was recognised as having a material value in the case of divorce by dividing the property acquired during marriage equally between spouses. The new Penal Code (2005) containing provisions in line with contemporary international standards constituted a paradigm shift with regard to gender equality and women's human rights in Turkish law. The Code recognised a woman's right to be the sole controller of her body. It classifies sexual crimes as against the individual and not as against 'public morality' or 'community order' (Acar et al., 2007:5). The new Labour Law of 2003 reinforced existing provisions such as prohibiting discrimination on the basis of gender and introduced some improvements for women workers by prohibiting discriminatory practices owing to marital status or family responsibilities such as prohibiting dismissal on grounds of pregnancy. It included for the first time provisions prohibiting sexual harassment in the workplace. However, many women remain outside its coverage as they are out of the labour market or informally working.

There are other policies abolishing the traditional social security system in which women were presumed to be dependants of men who were the breadwinners. A radical change took place with the new Social Security and General Health Insurance Law of 2006 with which ended some former entitlement enjoyed by women and introduced the equalisation of welfare policies for women and men. In the pension system, the equalisation of retirement ages at 65 is planned for 2048, and the gender-neutralization of welfare benefits, ending the former entitlement of dependent daughters of the insured persons to lifelong health insurance. There is also an equal treatment of survivor spouses, extending the marriage allowances to male survivors as well. These changes might signal a move from the ideal of 'male-breadwinner family' towards a model of 'universal breadwinner' (Kılıç 2008:493). However, it is important to see that the implications of these policy developments for women have been limited to those covered by a social security system and have right to pensions. Most women are employed in the informal sector or the few who have unpaid family workers, and are therefore covered as dependants through their fathers' or husbands' social security. Another issue to be raised here is the question of whether granting women with the same rights as men really brings equality for women or not. For example, the equalisation of the retirement age at 65 may end up discriminating against women as they tend to stay in the labour market for shorter periods and their social security contributions are not paid during unpaid maternity leave. On the other hand, different treatment of female children in the survivor's benefit is an encouragement for women to stay out of productive activities and focus on domestic roles, which strengthens traditional gendered roles in Turkish society. These policies, to a certain extent, abolish gender-differential treatments rather than introducing a positive discrimination policy which compensates disadvantages of both women and men.

Consequent to these realities, however, contributors of this book also recognise that women do not have independent status either in the labour market or at home. It is argued that neoliberal agendas of the recent Turkish governments, especially the AKP government, have impaired managed attempts to secure gender equality in the legal texts, without offering practical policy remedies to change women's position and role in society. We argue that the changing nature of the welfare state regarding promises of equality for women increases vulnerabilities by treating them equally without sufficient policy measures or protection. We make the case here that the current welfare reform processes are destined to remain ineffective for women as long as they are not backed by political willingness and commitment to promote gender equality. Such a process would involve challenging traditional gender norms and relations, such as setting employment quotas for women and increasing public child and elder care provisions, and is a necessary proactive step in balancing gender inequalities.

Gendered Nature of Welfare State in Turkey

In the first half of the book, the chapters contribute to a wider understanding of the gendered nature of the welfare state in Turkey. The opening chapter by Ayşe Buğra sketches an overview of the Turkish welfare regime, with an emphasis on the partnerships between the state and civil society actors in the provision of social protection. She discusses the determinants of the transformation taking place in recent years and how the main aspects of the regime have affected women's welfare. She points out the very low female employment rate in the non-agricultural sector and the fact that the traditional social security system was very inegalitarian, and forced many people, particularly during old age, to rely on the familial support, in which women play the primary role. This strong familial connection helped those immigrants from the agricultural sector, in which there is a high level of participation compared to the South European countries. By creating an extra rental income, *gecekondu*, a form of illegal or irregular type of low-income housing, has also played a crucial role in provisioning the social security in urban areas. Buğra states that apart from the male breadwinner model, the state indirectly contributed to the perpetuation of the traditional family through agricultural support policies and as well as the *gecekondu* settlements. However, she indicates, the commercialisation of agriculture and ongoing armed conflict in the southeast resulted in an increase in rural-urban migration. These developments as well as expanding flexible employment practices that cause the informality in the absence of supportive networks have created new poverty for which the current welfare regime was not able to address. She rightly points out that besides the lack of fiscal sustainability and administrative inefficiency, this was the main reason for social security reform. Buğra states that the welfare regime in the era of the current government turns out to be a synthesis of neo-liberalism and Islamic notions of social solidarity. The policy makers sustained fiscal discipline, strengthened the role of the family in social solidarity, and replaced the traditional modes of provision of the social aid and services with Islamic traditions of charity. Obviously, as she states, these new forms of familialism and clientelism reinforced the position of women as care providers. Buğra concludes that the compatibility of the existing welfare regime with policies aiming to increase the very low female labour force participation is questionable.

Following these remarks on the influence of Islamic values on the transformation of the welfare regime, Feride Acar and Gülbanu Altunok discuss the impact of Islamic conservatism on women's life in Turkey by comparatively analysing the political agendas of the feminist, Kemalist and Islamist branches of the women's movement. Taking gender equality as the main axis, they analyse the headscarf issue as reflecting the changing discourse of the politically mobilised conservative women from 'headscarf as a religious obligation' to 'headscarf as a human right'. The authors discuss how to forcefully argue for an independent gender equality agenda by reviewing of the existing literature, examining the recent public/media debates and public statements as well as the information they have from several interviews conducted with prominent figures in women's activism in various strands of the movement.

The low level of female labour force participation is one of the basic characteristics of the Turkish welfare state. Gülay Toksöz addresses this issue in detail in the context of the neo-liberal model. She identifies the characteristics of the capitalist mode of production in Turkey that lead to a low level of demand for female labour and the role of private and public patriarchy that restricts its supply. Toksöz discusses the three distinctive macroeconomic factors that contribute to the low level non-agricultural female employment in Turkey. First, the increase in investment of private sector was not large enough to compensate for the shrinkage of the public sector resulting from the adoption of an export-led growth model and the Structural Adjustment Programs. That is, she argues, limited industrialisation was one of the main reasons behind the low level of non-agricultural female employment. Second, this growth model until recently was deteriorating due to the low level of foreign direct investments. Finally, the economy could not create enough jobs to respond to increasing adult population, which in turn caused male dominance even in low-paid jobs. Discussing the conformity between the neoliberal market and private and public patriarchies which prevent women from participating in the labour market, Toksöz argues that unless there are sufficient public services and policies aiming to mitigate the care burden of women and promote an equitable share of care work, the exclusion of women from labour markets will continue. A crucial consequence of the lower female labour force participation rate is a substantial gender income gap and poverty.

Using micro data from a recent survey, Meltem Dayıoğlu and Cem

Başlevent provide a comprehensive picture of the financial vulnerability of women, which complements the previous chapter by deepening the discussion on the result of low female labour force participation. The authors state that the gap in income and poverty levels between men and women are remarkable. Women have both less labour and non-labour income and constitute a higher proportion of lower income groups. Also considering that income distribution among women is more skewed and men have greater control over assets, Dayıoğlu and Başlevent emphasise greater vulnerability of women beyond the average figures. Overall, the findings of the chapter provide some crucial facts about better possible outcomes for women in the labour market reform and point out the importance of a comprehensive employment policy that includes the target of income and education levels of women.

The real 'big picture' about gender gap can only be seen when one takes time use into account. This is crucial for seeing the gender based disparities and explaining gender differences in labour force participation. Using the first national time use survey conducted in 2006, Emel Memiş, Umut Öneş and Burça Kızılırmak provide a comprehensive analysis of gendered patterns of time use in Turkey. They examine the differences between women and men in time spent on unpaid and paid work over the life course, and how it changes with respect to some crucial factors such as household type, employment status of the adult female in the household, the number of children, and marital status. Their findings reveal a clear picture of the traditional gender division of labour in Turkey. Women spend most of their total work time on unpaid work activities in a range of family types. Even in dual earner families, women spend a lot more time than their spouses on unpaid work. Also, getting married and having children increases women's unpaid work and turns out to be the major cause for the lower female labour force participation. Memiş, Öneş and Kızılırmak's analysis provides a deeper understanding of the gendered division of labour and women's lower labour force participation. The analysis shows that social reforms to increase paid work opportunities for women should be supported by provision of care services for children. As stated above, as a result of the gendered division of labour, women are expected to shoulder domestic and care work. Particularly with an aging population and the changing nature of the social structure, there has been increasing demand for labour in this area.

A special form of unpaid domestic work in Turkey is called 'the *Evlatlık* Institution'. It is seen as a way to alleviate poverty among the vulnerable girls of poor rural households and provide a better future for them on the hand one, while providing urban middle class households with unpaid domestic labour and the opportunity to "fulfill their class identity by engaging in what appears to be charity and 'giving' at first sight." Hande Toğrul utilises the capabilities approach to examine the wellbeing of these vulnerable – mostly orphan and/or poor peasant – girls, who are brought into upper and middle class households under conditions of quasi–adoption. The *evlatlık* institution is a distinctive case since it stands at the intersection of child labour, migration and informality of domestic work relations. Making it visible, Toğrul, therefore, provides a crucial discussion in the context of the welfare regime in Turkey not just by simply broadening the analysis of the domestic labour carried out in the previous chapter but rather emphasizing the well-being, to enhance the approach to the welfare reforms.

All these chapters point to a common conclusion that the desired and actual role of women is as homemaker and care providers for their families and communities. The Turkish welfare state rests upon a normative model of family in which women are care providers while men are the principal breadwinners. In this system, women receive benefits like healthcare on the basis of the labour market status of fathers or husbands. This is not an exceptional situation as so many women worldwide are dependent welfare beneficiaries. However, the Turkish case still stands as an exception as its minimalist corporatist structure is maintained through strong family ties and the important domestic role played by women. Family is the crucial element in coping with social risks and in the provision of social assistance where there is no fully fledged social assistance scheme and social aid takes the form of charity and is distributed mostly in kind.

Women and Welfare Reform in Turkey

Turkey's EU candidacy has opened new doors in the areas of social policy and gender equality. This change, brought about largely by the AKP government, has included a series of legislative changes in which the perception of women was shifted from being dependent citizens to independent participants in society. Even though these reforms have occurred, the pro-Islamic stance of the AKP leaves doubt as to the sincerity of the party in promoting gender equality and raises questions about the possible future ramifications of the reforms. With these reforms in place, the Prime Minister, Recep Tayyip Erdogan, publicly directed each woman to have at least three children with no accompanying political commitment to increase public childcare facilities.

In the second half of the book, the chapters focus on analysing the effects of these reforms on women. This analysis starts off with Saniye Dedeoglu's article that discusses the potential of gender equality policies lately implemented as the partial requirement in Turkey's EU accession process, to promote female employment. Until now, the Turkish welfare state has rested on the idea of women's main role in society being mothers and wives. This manifested itself in low female labour force participation and other structural inequalities between women and men. Depending on their conceptualisation, equality policies can bring the ultimate sameness of women and men, or the equal valuation of different contributions, or the transformation of gender relations. In the EU level practice, equality policies are instrumental in channelling women's labour into employment rather than transforming traditional gender divisions. In Turkey, where the welfare state conceptualises women as homemakers, Dedeoglu shows that gender equality polices are not alone sufficient to promote female employment, and even in some cases work against women. So, they are destined to remain in the legal texts or reach only a small fraction of women if they are not supported by sufficient policy measures to improve women's position in the society.

Mustafa Şahin examines social security reforms. The structure of the social security system is the key point in the determination of the role and wellbeing of women in society. The ongoing social security reform over a decade in Turkey is a typical neoliberal restructuring program in the sense that it is retrenchment of the welfare state. The reform involves three elements. First, it has several measures to reduce the deficits of the system which have increased since the early 1990s. Second, it is a move toward a more market oriented public health service. Third, it promotes the private pension system. Şahin focuses on the compulsory coverage, social benefits, and entitlement conditions of the Social Insurances and General Health Insurance Law which came into effect in 2008. By examining these aspects Şahin reveals the impact of the reform on women's wellbeing in Turkey. The social security reform unifies the institutional structure for various groups, including agricultural workers, tightens the linkage between social protection and premiums paid, and treats all insurance holders equally, including setting the same higher retirement age for both genders. Additionally, some aspects of the reform simply carry over the male bread-winner model rooted in society. Further, he argues, despite some gains, by making it harder for farmers to have social security and leaving more working people out of the coverage, widen the existing gender gap. Also, he adds that the new regulations of the reform tend to discourage women from participating in the formal labour market.

Tuba İnci Ağartan deals with another key component of the social security reform, the Health Transformation Project (HTP), which was introduced in 2003 in the era of the current ruling party. She examines precisely how gender-sensitive the HTP is and whether it can improve women's welfare. By taking a closer look at the three major aspects of the reform in the health sector – namely financing, provision and regulation –, Ağartan discusses the conflicting outcomes for women. Although, as she states, the policy agenda of the government involves the concept of gender mainstreaming, it is not likely to be implemented fully because it has no strong linkage to the reform package, the HTP. The author argues that some elements of the major health care reform such as 'making provision of health services conditional on the payment of premiums and introducing user fees at all levels of service provision' are detrimental for women. She emphasises that there is a clear gender bias both in the program itself and its implementation, where women are considered as dependants.

Another crucial element of ongoing reforms in the social security system was the introduction of the Individual Pension System in 2003 alongside the pre-2003 social security system. Analysing the gendered nature of this private pension scheme Şule Şahin and Adem Y. Elveren complete the big picture drawn in the previous two chapters. The article responds to three main questions: Are there actual gender gaps in the system? Is there an inherent gender gap in the system? And, what can be done against gender gaps? Şahin and Elveren raise two crucial issues in this context. First, considering the system as a part of the ongoing commodification process of the welfare regime in Turkey, they argue that the current private system is a potential threat to the pre-2003 social security system, contrary to the claims of the government officials. Second, they show that while there is no significant difference in the regular contribution rates between females and males currently, the system inherently involves a substantial gender gap, to a greater extent for those in rural areas, for those with lower education and the elderly. Because the potential earnings of women in retirement years would be highly dependent on their contributions to the system, life expectancy and the length of working time, women with intermittent work life and lower earnings will be worse off in the private system. Although they propose and discuss minimum pension guarantee implementation as a way to reduce this gap, they point out that the implementation only addresses the result of the disparities rather than the sources, which is the current disadvantageous position of women in socioeconomic life discussed throughout the book. The authors argue that, on top of the current discrepancy in the labour market, the extension of the private pension system would deepen the inequality between men and women in terms of retirement income.

Helga Rittersberger-Tılıç and Sibel Kalaycıoğlu examine domestic and care work by means of two field studies conducted a decade apart. With the changing welfare regime in Turkey, families rely more on women's labour for all kinds of care work. Due to an aging population and a tendency towards the privatisation of care work, the increasing need for paid domestic labour has been filled in the informal sector by women with low education and low skills who migrated from rural areas. The authors analyse both the social dynamics of the development of elder care and the role of Private Employment Agencies that have emerged in line with the EU accession process in the early 2000s. These agencies aim to organise informal employment and reduce unemployment. However, the authors argue that due to the high degree of informality in the labour market, these establishments can have only a modest impact in creating decent work if at all. Indeed, the authors state that the agencies just transform exploitation in the labour market.

Finally, Şerife Gözde Yirmibeşoğlu deals with the reflection of the patriarchal ideology of the government in the public sphere. She examines the low participation and secondary position of women in trade unions based on two sets of interviews conducted a decade apart. The comparative dimension of the chapter clearly presents the changes in both the public and private sphere for women in the context of the rising influence of Islam and the neo-liberal era. She reveals the conflicting approach of the current ruling party in the context of trade unions: On the one hand, this approach puts women in a secondary position (i.e. expecting women only be wives and mothers) as a natural result of basic Islamic ideology of the party, and on the other hand, it claims to be the defender of women's rights in the context of the EU accession. She points out that women's familial role is the biggest obstacle preventing women from getting involved in the public sphere, which has not changed. However, there are some improvements in terms of women's greater awareness of sexual harassment and the negative effects of globalisation.

2

THE CHANGING WELFARE REGIME OF TURKEY: NEOLIBERALISM, CULTURAL CONSERVATISM AND SOCIAL SOLIDARITY REDEFINED

Ayşe Buğra

In this chapter on the Turkish welfare regime in its recent, and still incomplete, transformation, the term welfare regime is used to denote the society-specific articulation between the state, the family and the labour market regarding the provision of social protection for the individual. In the original typology introduced by Esping-Andersen (1990), we find three welfare regime types: (1) the conservative corporatist regime, of which Germany is the most typical example (2) the social democratic type exemplified by Scandinavian countries, Sweden in particular and (3) the liberal residualist type found in the USA and UK. The first model is characterised by a stratified system of social protection where benefits reflect the status-at-work of, basically, the male breadwinners. In their role as providers of care for children and the elderly, women's access to social protection is mainly through male relatives. Universalistic benefits, based on citizenship status rather than status-at-work, are central to the social democratic model. As for the liberal model, it is market-based in which social policy intervention is supposed to provide residual benefits to the excluded.

In the 1990s, the South European system of social protection began to be discussed as a distinct model to be added to the three original ones (Leibfried 1993; Ferrera 1996). Some writers, including Esping-Andersen (1999: 90-94) himself, argued against a distinct South European model. In fact, the most important characteristic attributed to the model, namely* the centrality of the family as the primary locus of solidarity, seemed to be largely in line with the corporatist conservative typology. Protected jobs and incomes for adult males along with more limited and precarious employment opportunities for women and youth could also be said to constitute another aspect of the familial character of the corporatist model. However, the South European welfare regimes also had distinct characteristics seemingly too important to overlook, and the fourth model maintained its place in the literature. These distinct characteristics pertain, first, to labour market structures given the significance of self-employment, small and medium enterprises and the informal sector. The rudimentary character of unemployment insurance or social assistance schemes also required the family solidarity to substitute for the absence of a strong welfare state. In spite of this weakness of social safety nets, 'welfare clientelism' also appears in the list of specific features of the South European model and the type of state-society relations it incorporated (Ferrara 1996; Karamessini 2008).

As Mingione (2002) argued, much of the South European specificity could be analysed from a historical perspective with reference to the experience of late industrialisation as the basis of the shared labour market characteristics of Italy, Spain, Portugal and Greece. This historical perspective is highly useful in accounting for the similarities between the South European model and the social protection systems in other late industrialising countries such as in Latin America or Turkey. In fact, both the Latin American welfare regime (Barrientos 2004) and the Turkish one (Eardley et.al. 1996; Gough 1996 and 2001; Saraceno 2002) have been compared to the South European model. However, one should be cautious when using the welfare regime analysis in the context of late industrialisation where it might be difficult, first, to assume the generalised validity of contract-based employment relations. Second, rule-based state intervention reflecting the principle of redistribution might not be a typical element of the institutional settings where state-society relations are marked by different types of clientelism. Outside Europe, both labour market informality and clientelism are particularly salient features of a context where personal and informal relations of reciprocity acquire a central significance in determining the economic and social coordinates of an individual's position in society. In such a context, not only the modern nuclear family but also ethnic or religious networks of reciprocity may be important in providing employment and social protection to the individual. In a parallel vein, reciprocity relations might permeate the realm of state-society relations and replace the logic of redistribution in certain areas where 'gifts' from political authorities (which are, of course, never free) substitute for formal social policy intervention.

It is against this analytical backdrop that I will discuss what the Turkish welfare regime before and throughout the recent transformations has been undergoing during the last two decades or so. Welfare regime change in Turkey is situated in the context of the global transformations that the social protection systems have been undergoing. In this regard, it can be observed that the "welfare state retrenchment" that neoliberal globalisation could be expected to bring cannot be said to have materialised, especially in the European context. In countries without mature welfare states, too, we see more rather than less emphasis placed on welfare provision by the state and social policy intervention now has become more important in these countries. However, among the distinct features of the contemporary patterns of welfare governance, we also find a new tendency that modifies redistributive action by the state through diverse partnerships between the state and civil society actors regarding the provision of social assistance, care and public services (Jessop 1999; Bode 2006). Hence, terms such as "social entrepreneurs" enjoy widespread popularity as designating those engaged in different forms of philanthropy, assuming quasi-public functions in different fields of social policy. In the contemporary international environment of social policy, this new tendency takes place alongside the significance now attached to non-contributory social assistance in the attempts to combat poverty.

The ways in which these new forms of welfare governance manifest themselves in late industrializing countries whose social protection systems have been analysed with reference to the South European model depend on both domestic and international factors. The influence of European integration has played a crucial role in welfare regime change in the South European members of the European Union (EU). In Latin America and in Turkey, on the other hand, the change was triggered by the developments toward economic liberalisation and deregulation as well as the changes taking place in the political environment. The transition to electoral democracy was a significant factor in many Latin American countries. In these countries, the formal social security system which excluded a large part of the population has come to be complemented by a series of non-contributory systems including social pensions and different types of targeted cash transfers, leading to a dual system with mixed corporatist and liberal residualist features (Barrientos 2004; Ferreira and Robalino 2010).

• In Turkey a market-oriented and outward looking economic strategy was implemented after the military intervention in 1980. Yet, after 1987 when the political ban on former political leaders was lifted, Turkey, too, returned to electoral democracy, albeit with the mark of the military regime still observed in several areas including the labour union legislation (Adaman et al. 2009). One significant distinctive feature of the environment in which the welfare regime change has been taking place in Turkey is the rise of Islamic conservatism in the country. We observe, in this context, the appeal to traditional Islamic forms of charity articulated with the globally observed emphasis of non-state actors and their collaboration with the state in welfare provision and it appears to be in harmony with policy instruments endorsed by international financial institutions. At least for the time being, this particular policy orientation is not counterbalanced by the influence of the relations with the EU which could lend support to both those groups who try to defend their rights entrenched in the formal security system and to the articulation of political demands in favour of a rights-based policy intervention to combat poverty and social exclusion.

In the following, I will discuss the evolution of Turkey's welfare regime by examining the developments both in the social security system and in the realm of social assistance in its formal and informal components. I will highlight, in this discussion, the elements of continuity and change observed in two characteristics of the social policy environment, familialism and clientelism, which remain important albeit in different forms.

Turkish welfare regime as a variant of the South European social model?

The South European model constitutes a useful analytical perspective in the discussion of the Turkish welfare regime. Turkey's formal social security system introduced in the aftermath of the Second World War was a corporatist one, with a fragmented and inegalitarian structure of benefits as observed also in the South European model. Originally, this system was composed of two organisations providing combined old age and health benefits to civil servants (Retirement Fund, ES) and formally employed workers (Workers' Insurance Organisation). The Workers' Insurance Organisation was later reorganised as the Social Insurance Institution (SSK). As the system was taking shape, some writers had remarked that these two institutions could cover only a limited portion of the working population, large segments of which remained outside formal social protection (Talas 1955).[1] In the period that followed, successive governments tried to expand the coverage of the system. A third social security organisation, Bag-Kur, was established to incorporate the self-employed in the 1970s and then independent farmers in the 1980s.

Social security coverage reached, according to the official figures, well over 80 percent of the population either as contributors or dependants in the 1990s. However, these official figures should be interpreted carefully by taking into account several factors. One such factor is the high dependency ratio, which indicates the significance of family ties in determining access to social protection. This ratio of the total number of pensioners and dependants to active insured people was close to 4:1 in Turkey by the year 2000 (Adaman 2003). This conforms with the very low female employment rate in the non-agricultural sector, which was 12.7 percent in 1988, 15 percent in 2000 and still remains around 17 percent today (TurkStat 2008; Buğra and Yakut-Cakar 2010). In fact, the assumption that women would remain outside the labour market and depend on male relatives was central to the corporatist social security system which was clearly protective of women. Women received privileged treatment through gender-differentiated benefits for survivors as well as health and old age benefits (Kılıç 2008).

Moreover, the social security system was highly inegalitarian with significant inequalities in old age and health benefits of the people covered across the three different organizations. Given this unequal corporatist character of the social security system, access to health services remained problematic for many people, especially for the self-employed who would, at times, fail to pay their contributions and consequently lose their entitlements. In periods of economic crisis, this problem could become especially severe.[2] Except for civil servants, old age pensions, too, remained far short of assuring a decent livelihood for people in retirement. Many people had to rely on family support mechanisms to avoid destitution in old age.

The importance of family support could well be observed in the wording of a means-tested social assistance program with very limited coverage and very low benefits introduced in 1976. The target population was the elderly and the disabled with no source of income or social security coverage and without close relatives to take care of them. The fact that social assistance would not be available to those with close relatives clearly indicates the strength of the familalistic outlook dominating the welfare regime of the country.

So far, this overview of the Turkish welfare regime can be said to reveal many of the characteristics of the South European model. There is, however, one difference to consider specific to the Turkish case. For an incomparably longer period than any other South European country, peasant agriculture and, consequently, employment in the agricultural sector has remained important in Turkey. In 1988, agricultural employment as a share of total employment was 46.5 percent in Turkey while it was 14, 26.6 and 9.9 percent in Spain, Greece and Italy, respectively. In 2007, the agricultural sector still accounted for about 23 percent of total employment in Turkey, while welfare regime change has been taking place amid the rise of Islamic conservatism in the country.

Table 2.1: Historical trends in sectoral distribution of employment in Turkey in comparison with selected OECD countries (percent)

	Share of Agricultural Employment in Total Employment			Share of Services Employment in Total Employment			Share of Industrial Employment in Total Employment		
	1988	2000	2007	1988	2000	2007	1988	2000	2007
Spain	14,0	6,7	4,6	53,1	62,2	66,1	32,9	31,2	29,4
Greece	26,6	17,4	11,6	46,2	60,0	66,0	27,2	22,6	22,4
Italy	9,9	5,4	4,0	57,7	62,2	65,5	32,4	32,4	30,5
Turkey	46,5	36,0	23,5	31,2	40,0	49,8	22,3	24,0	25,5
Portugal	11,5	12,8	11,7	55,3	52,5	57,6	33,2	34,7	30,7
OECD Total*	8,8	7,0	6,0	62,9	66,1	70,2	28,3	26,9	26,3

Source: OECD (2008)

In fact, it has been remarked by several writers, including E. Hobsbawm (1995:291), that Turkey constitutes a rare example among countries at similar levels of industrialisation and development in maintaining peasant agriculture for an extended period of time. It would not be possible to account for this historical specificity of Turkey without considering the role of the state in maintaining peasant agriculture through economic change. In this regard, agricultural support policies that remained unchanged under successive governments until the 1980s have undoubtedly played an important role. Also important, however, was the fact that in Turkey immigration to the city did not constitute a total rupture from the countryside and multiple strategies of livelihood that combined earnings from peasant agriculture with urban sources of income could be pursued by many families (Buğra and Keyder 2006). The remittances immigrants sent to family members who remained in the village contributed to the survival of the family farms and these remittances would be reciprocated by the in kind or in cash support received from the peasant economy.

Employment opportunities in public and private enterprises, which, in the context of the Import Substituting Industrialisation strategy, operated in a protected economy with heavy state intervention, were important in the integration of immigrants from rural areas in the urban economy. There was yet another aspect of the economic opportunity space that owed its existence to forms of state intervention or non-intervention. In this regard, *gecekondu*, the Turkish version of irregular housing, is of particular significance. Like many similar forms found in Asia, Africa and Latin America, the Turkish *gecekondu* constituted a form of illegal or irregular type of low-income housing. However, due to two factors specific to Turkey, the form acquired a unique economic and social significance for the population until the recent neo-liberal transformation of the urban economy. One of these factors has to do with the characteristics of the urban land market. In this regard, the historical significance of publicly owned land in the cities and their vicinity was instrumental in the relative ease with which land invasions took place and led to the development of irregular settlements. While a very important percentage of *gecekondu*s were built on public land, the hazy boundaries between urban plots and surrounding agricultural land eventually integrated into the cities also contributed to the mushrooming of irregular settlements where houses were built on plots with title deeds but without construction permits. The second factor which was important in determining the economic and social significance of these settlements on invaded public land or on subdivided agricultural land was political. Irregular patterns of access to urban land provided an unusual opportunity to government authorities to engage in clientelistic politics. Hence, *gecekondu* owners acquired title deeds through periodically enacted amnesty laws and the irregular settlements were regularised through the provision of municipal services, usually around elections as favours granted in exchange for votes. What is important to underline here is that through these processes of regularisation, the *gecekondu* became not only a dwelling for the urban poor, but also a mechanism of integration to the urban society through rental income generated by the new floors added to the original building and through the economic activities developed around the settlements (Öncü 1988; Buğra 1998; Işık and Pınarcıoğlu 2001).

In this brief overview, it is possible to point out several factors which account for the familialistic character of Turkey's former welfare regime. Apart from the male breadwinner model that characterised the formal social security system, the state indirectly contributed to the protection of the traditional family in its economic significance. Agricultural support policies and the toleration of informal access to urban public land or land without proper building permits together shaped a rural-urban opportunity space to which kinship ties remained central. Family farms survived and *gecekondu* settlements enabled the family members to remain together in space and often in economic interest.

It is clear that in this Turkish context the role of personal and informal relations in providing economic and social protection to the individual was of crucial significance. These relations were important not only for that portion of the population excluded from the formal social security system but also for those whose entitlements did not provide adequate protection in situations of unemployment, ill health, disability or old age. In the absence of a formal social housing policy, different networks of reciprocity operated also in the housing sector. Along with the family, the state, too, was important in the context of the strategies of life and livelihood pursued outside the formal labour market and rights-based social policy relations. While the effectiveness of these strategies has been seriously undermined through the recent developments in economy and politics, informal relations of reciprocity, which involve the family but also extend to state-society relations, have remained important in Turkey's changing welfare regime.

Table 2.2: Total public social expenditure in selected OECD countries (% of GDP)

	1980	1985	1990	1995	2001	2002	2003	2004	2005
Turkey*	4,3	4,2	7,6	7,5	10,4	10,5	11,5	12,2	13,7
Greece	10,2	16,0	16,5	17,3	20,6	20,0	19,9	19,9	20,5
Portugal	10,2	10,4	12,9	17,0	19,9	21,3	22,9	23,1	n/a
Spain	15,5	17,8	19,9	21,4	20,4	20,8	21,5	21,6	21,8
OECD Total	16,0	17,7	18,1	19,9	19,8	20,3	20,8	20,7	20,6

Source: Data for countries except Turkey are taken from OECD (2008), Social Expenditure Database (SOCX), 1980- 2005, http://stats.oecd.org/WBOS/index.aspx.
*As the OECD database does not include statistics on Turkey for the period 2000-04, Turkish data in this table are based on the estimations made by Boğaziçi University Social Forum by using SOCX methodology. See Buğra and Adar (2007). Data for Turkey for 2005 is taken from OECD database.

Social Security Reform, Poverty and Social Assistance Through the Transition to a Market Economy

The significance of the informal component of the Turkish welfare regime went together with the low level of public social spending. In 1980, public social expenditures merely constituted about 4 per cent of the GDP, which was much lower than not only the average figure for the OECD region (16 per cent), but also the comparable figure for South European countries (10.2 per cent for Greece and Portugal, 15.5 per cent for Spain and 18 per cent for Italy). In 1995 the figure for Turkey had reached 7.5 percent, but the difference from the OECD average (now 20.6 per cent) and the South European countries remained: In 1995, public social expenditures accounted for 17.3 per cent of the GDP in Greece, 17 per cent in Portugal, almost 20 per cent for Italy and over 20 per cent in Spain (see Table 2.2).

Nevertheless, it was with the objective of alleviating the burden of social security on the public budget that social security reform came on the agenda in the 1990s, mainly through pressure from international financial institutions. The reform attempt also aimed to improve administrative efficiency by unifying different social security organizations within the Social Security Institution under the jurisdiction of the Ministry of Labour and Social Security. Apart from the fiscal and administrative concerns, the reform was also motivated by the inability of the existing system, with its formal and informal components, to provide protection against the higher risk of unemployment and poverty associated with economic liberalisation. In the post-1980 period, Turkey had opted for an outward-looking, market-oriented economic strategy. Hence, agricultural subsidies were gradually eliminated, public enterprises began to shed labour, and, with enhanced competition in the private sector, there were pressures to also reduce labour costs in private enterprises. At the same time, urban developments associated with the country's insertion in the global economy had begun to challenge the former real estate property regime and the irregular settlements that were part of that regime. Within the formal legal framework of a market society, private property had to have a more solid foundation.

One outcome of these developments was the commercialisation of agriculture and the associated increase in rural-urban migration. In the mid-1980s, the urban population came to equal the rural population and even surpass the latter at an accelerating pace. Although it is still very high in comparative terms, the share of agriculture in total employment too has been rapidly declining since the 1980s (Table 2.1). At the same time, the urban opportunity space open to immigrants from the countryside had become much more limited than it was in the pre-1980 period. In other words, multiple strategies of livelihood that combined rural and urban resources and opportunities had come under pressure in the new political economy, with a newly emerging form of poverty as a result. The emergence of new poverty in the 1980s was also associated with the armed conflict in the southeast between the Kurdish separatist movement and the Turkish security forces, which had produced patterns of rural-urban migration radically different from previous ones. Unlike the previous waves of migration, the Kurdish migration resulted almost exclusively from push factors, rather than the attraction of a better life in the city, in the absence of supportive networks of relatives or co-locals that had already moved to the city. With the conspicuous deprivation of these Kurdish migrants, poverty has also acquired a distinct ethnic dimension (Buğra and Keyder 2006; Buğra 2007).

With almost no social assistance component except for the above mentioned program targeting the elderly and the disabled introduced in 1976, Turkey's welfare regime was hardly equipped to deal with these new forms of poverty. The Fund for Social Solidarity and Cooperation, established in 1986 more as a philanthropic foundation administered by the state than a formal welfare institution, constituted an early attempt to keep poverty under control. In 1992, the formal health system was complemented with the Green Card scheme introduced to provide means-tested access to health care for the poor population outside social security coverage. Both the Green Card scheme and the assistance provided by the Solidarity Fund have become important especially after a major economic crisis in 2001, which was instrumental in clearly exposing both the dimensions of poverty and the inadequacy of the existing mechanisms of social protection to help the destitute. It was during the crisis that the World Bank sponsored program of Social Risk Mitigation was introduced to provide conditional cash transfers[3] and support for local initiatives. The program was administered by the Solidarity Fund, through over 900 local foundations situated in all provinces, along with other programs, mainly involving in kind emergency aid.

Welfare Governance under a Socially Conservative and Economically Liberal Government: New Forms of Familialism and Clientelism

Under the socially conservative and economically liberal Justice and Development Party (AKP) which came to power in 2002 in the aftermath of a major economic crisis, the previous trends in social security reform and welfare provision have continued. In an economic conjuncture marked by the impact of the economic crisis of 2001, the new government had little choice but to comply with the financial austerity measures imposed by the IMF and the World Bank, and the AKP set out to implement the reform program more willingly and with more determination than any other Turkish government had done before. The unification of the three social security organisations under the jurisdiction of the Ministry of Labour and Social Security was completed. Although there were certain changes in the conditions of access to health and old age benefits, the system has maintained its corporatist character and funding still continues to be based on contributions by employers and employees. All beneficiaries, whether in formal wage employment or not, are expected to pay their social security premiums, and individuals whose incomes remain below one-third of the official minimum wage have means-tested access to health services through the Green Card scheme which has remained in implementation after the introduction of the new so-called General Health Insurance system.[4]

Organised labour was able to resist some of the changes that involved a retrenchment of the existing benefits. In fact, in spite of the emphasis put on fiscal restraint, the share of public social spending in GDP reached over 13 per cent in 2005, with old age benefits constituting the largest item in total social spending (see Table 2.2). As far as the formal social security system is concerned, one might argue that the developments where in line with P. Pierson's (1996) analysis of the politics of social policy in countries with mature welfare states where organised action of the beneficiaries could, to a large extent, prevent a significant welfare state retrenchment. However, independent of how social security reform proceeded, there was another development which led to a major change in the socioeconomic coordinates of the formal sector. With the advent of flexible employment practices, of subcontracting relations in particular, the boundaries between formal and informal employment have begun to blur. In many enterprises, production activity has begun to be carried out both by formally employed core workers and by informally employed workers through subcontractors. Outsourcing and subcontracting have also become the rule in the public sector; municipal governments, in particular, have outsourced many activities from garbage collection to public transportation. This has made informal employment emerge in areas where it was hitherto absent and has rendered unionisation extremely difficult among the formally employed who have found themselves under the ever present threat of having their work outsourced. The fear of outsourcing indeed appears as an important deterrent to unionisation and seems to be a major factor behind the falling rate of formal sector workers under collective bargaining coverage, which is estimated to have declined from 46.9 in 1985 to less than 15 per cent in 2003 (Adaman et al. 2009). Whatever portion of the previously acquired rights could be protected by formal sector employees now concerned an ever shrinking part of the working population.

As to the disadvantaged groups excluded from the formal system, their problems and needs were not part of the agenda of labour unions or other organised groups and, given the historical absence of non-contributory social assistance in the Turkish social policy scene, vulnerable groups facing the threat of poverty were not really in a position to demand what they never had. Nevertheless, the undeniable significance of poverty has created pressure on both the government and the international actors to take policy action in this area. In this regard, Turkey's relations with the EU were especially significant. Turkey became a candidate country at the Helsinki summit of 1999 and the EU accession process involved the preparation of a Joint Inclusion Memorandum (JIM) as a background to participation in the European social inclusion policy platform. The preparation of Turkey's JIM began in 2004 with the collaboration of several ministries and state administrative organs. Turkey could not complete the process and proceed to the preparation of a National Action Plan for social inclusion, but the initial effort has made an invaluable contribution to a clear exposition of the dimensions of the problem of poverty and social exclusion in the country in a comparative perspective. It was shown that relative poverty, measured by the percentage of population living on an income less than 60 per cent of the country's median income, was 26 per cent, and it was the highest figure among all European countries. Until recently, the TurkStat did not publish similar, internationally comparable data on relative poverty, but the statistics published last year show that, in 2006, relative poverty was 22.8 per cent, lower than in 2003 but still the highest figure in Europe (TurkStat 2009; EuroStat 2009).

The EU accession process required Turkey to take policy action to combat poverty and social exclusion, but, along the lines of the Open Method of Coordination used in the field of social policy at the European level, the institutional mechanisms and instruments to be employed to this end were not specified. Hence, the policy environment could continue to be shaped by the culturally conservative and economically liberal outlook of the government, which reflected a harmonious synthesis of neo-liberalism and Islamic notions of social solidarity. The resulting social inclusion approach had three components. It was made clear, first, that social spending had to be limited by the imperative of budget discipline, which Turkey has managed to maintain to this day even through the recent crisis of 2008. Second, the central significance of the family as the pillar of social solidarity was strongly asserted. In fact, in the program of the first AKP government formed in 2002, it was explicitly stated that the strength of the Turkish family was the main reason why social cohesion could be maintained in spite of severe economic difficulties faced by the country.[5] Third, Islamic traditions of charity were remembered and reintroduced in forms that were also informed by the contemporary emphasis on partnerships between public authorities, civil initiatives and the private sector in the provision of welfare, social assistance and social services.

Although fiscal restraint was an important element of the social policy orientation under the AKP government, the latter has also introduced a series of policies for the protection of vulnerable groups. Among the latter, the disabled had a particularly privileged position since the conservative worldview clearly situated them in the category of 'deserving poor'. Perhaps the most extensive institutional and financial social policy efforts were directed at the disabled.[6] Here, as well as in the realm of child protection and elderly care services, the preferred policy option was to financially support the family and to minimise the role of institutional care seen to be clearly inferior to care provided within the family (Yazıcı 2008). Cash transfers provided to biological or foster parents to take care of children in need of protection, along with transfers made to the disabled, introduced a new form of familialism to the country's welfare regime. Thus, positing the family as the primary unit of care, the new system implicitly but obviously reinforced the position of women as care providers.

The resulting situation was somewhat paradoxical because the changes in social legislation introduced by the AKP had undermined most of the privileges that women had in the former system reshaped to conform to the international labour trends. On the one hand, the changes made to eliminate the advantages women had in access to health, old age and survivor benefits seemed to indicate that women were now expected to participate in the labour market on equal terms with men. In fact, the government has recently taken certain policy measures to encourage female labour force participation.[7] On the other hand, the new regime of care placed the female members of the family in the position of care providers which, along with the general inadequacy of child care and early childhood development services, now constituted an important obstacle to women's increased labour force participation.[8] Not only policies of social care but also social assistance policies currently have a gendered character. Like the disabled, women have a privileged status as the 'deserving poor' in their relationship with welfare administrators. More or less formal instruments of poverty alleviation such as conditional cash transfers are specifically provided to women. The myriad of, often in kind, benefits provided through different mechanisms and institutions that involve central government and municipalities as well as voluntary associations and benevolent individuals also target women. In the context of the current welfare regime of Turkey, we thus observe a situation which is reminiscent of the one problematised by C. Pateman (1988) in her seminal criticism of the welfare state as a gendered institution where the citizenship status of women comes to be defined in the realm of social assistance.

As to the relationships that characterise the realm of social assistance in contemporary Turkey, they do not seem to be dominated by the formal logic of state redistribution.[9] In the context of the society specific manifestation of the global trends in contemporary welfare governance in Turkey, voluntary associations have proliferated and private benevolence has become very important in the social area. For example, the umbrella organisation TGTV (Turkish Foundation of Voluntary Organisations) now brings together about one hundred NGOs that use religious references in their organisational strategies[10] Along with strictly philanthropic associations, these NGOs also include business associations and think-tanks which also engage in charitable activities. While religiously inspired charity constitutes an important aspect of a social environment marked by the resurgence of Islam, the AKP government also attempts to integrate benevolence and philanthropy into formal social policy processes. In 2004 for example, a special project, known as One Hundred Percent Support to Education (Eğitime %100 Destek), was initiated by the Ministry of Education under the leadership of the Prime Minister and aimed, as the Minister of Education put it, at 'bringing the social state and social society (sic.) together' through private donations to schools which were one hundred per cent tax deductible. In 2005, a similar project, Project Rainbow (Gökkuşağı Projesi) was launched by the General Directorate of the Disabled and the Ministry of Education to raise donations for the financing of rehabilitation and labour market integration services to the disabled. These two projects, which initially received extensive media coverage, were nevertheless not very long lived. Information on the first one, available at the website of the Ministry of Education, was not updated after 2004.[11] As for the second one, it seems to have ended in 2007, around the time when some news about the misuse of donations by the public officials in charge appeared in the media.[12] However, such public-private collaboration in the realm of social policy has continued and become especially salient at the local level where benevolent individuals participate on the boards of trustees of local foundations for the

Directorate of Social Solidarity, and municipal governments have 'social funds' to raise donations for the financing of assistance provided to the poor. It is, of course, difficult to tell whether these donations are reciprocated in the form of privileged treatment in economic activities that require regulating or enabling the intervention of local public authorities.

It would be wrong to think that it is only the religiously motivated charities or individuals and their collaboration with the government through special projects and institutional arrangements which are present in the scene of social assistance. There are also many well established, secular NGOs, including the ones that work with disadvantaged women and children and provide certain social services. The activities of some of these NGOs received special mention and praise in a recent World Bank report on child poverty and its implications, where the importance of early childhood development (ECD) is highlighted. In the report, we find references to 'Turkey's innovative and inspirational experiences of ECD service delivery through non-governmental channels [which are] looked at across the globe with admiration' (World Bank 2010: 26). Nevertheless, the report in question admits that the coverage of such service delivery remains very low and it suggests, albeit timidly, that more serious public funding and provision might be necessary for the availability of quality services for disadvantaged children.

Independent of the nature of the outcomes attained, the new model of welfare governance, with the blurring of boundaries between philanthropy and state redistributive policy as one of its distinct characteristics, remains very popular in Turkey. While this particular social policy orientation conforms with globally observed trends, it also has certain implications which tend to sustain the clientelistic trends in state and society relations, albeit in new forms. These new forms of clientelism have been reinforced in a context where the logic of charity has begun to permeate the activities of public welfare institutions not only in the patterns of fund raising but also in determining the 'deserving poor' and providing assistance in a discretionary manner that lacks transparency and regularity. The political implications of this state of affairs became quite clear in the period before the municipal elections of 2009 when the radically increasing magnitude and changing form of assistance distributed by the local foundations of the Directorate of Social Solidarity generated widespread concern in public opinion.[13] The Turkish public had been long accustomed to see, before each election, the proliferation of state favours, like the granting of title deeds to *gecekondu* owners or the provision of municipal services to irregular settlements, which were expected to be reciprocated with votes. People could now see that social policy had become an important arena where clientelistic relations would hitherto take place.

Conclusion

Turkey's welfare regime, which consisted of a formal corporatist component and a set of informal relations encompassing both the family and state, was situated in the context of a protected economy where state intervention was important. In the post-1980 period, with the transition to a market economy integrated in the global system, both the formal and the informal components of the former system of social protection have come under pressure. While fiscal concerns have brought social security reform onto the agenda, problems of poverty and social exclusion have come to be perceived as problems that require systematic policy intervention. Current mechanisms of social care and assistance, introduced by the economically liberal and socially conservative AKP government, incorporate a strong emphasis on the family as the primary locus of social solidarity as well as persistent references to traditions of Islamic charity. However, the social policy orientation of the government also appears to be in harmony with the global trends in welfare governance, in particular with the salience of public-private-NGO partnerships within these trends.

In Turkey, this new policy outlook has brought along new forms of familialism and clientelism, which currently appear as the source of major socioeconomic and political concerns. The compatibility of the existing regime of social care and assistance with policies which aim to increase the extremely low female labour force participation has recently emerged as a pressing question. At the same time, the increasingly visible political implication of a social assistance system that reflects the logic of charity has begun to undermine trust in the democratic process. The existing model of social solidarity is, therefore, hardly a stable one. It is increasingly challenged by the political opposition and organised groups, which includes women's organisations such as KEIG (The Platform for Female Labour and Employment). Whether the current social policy orientation could be consolidated and made permanent constitutes, therefore, a question that will be answered by the political developments in the country.[14]

3

UNDERSTANDING GENDER EQUALITY DEMANDS IN TURKEY: FOUNDATIONS AND BOUNDARIES OF WOMEN'S MOVEMENTS

Feride Acar and Gülbanu Altunok

Recent political history shows that all over the world movements striving for the recognition of different political identities and social, cultural, and sexual existences have come to occupy a prominent place on the political stage. Iris Marion Young (1990; 2007) called these new forms of activism 'politics of difference' and argued that they can constitute a good source for a discussion-based politics. Participants in these movements aim to cooperate, reach understanding and do justice to those who suffer from disadvantageous social positions, division of labour, normalized legal, cultural and historical standards, and thus feel alienated and excluded from the political system. In exploring the impacts and meaning of 'politics of difference', Young also noted that one has to distinguish between 'politics of positional difference' and 'politics of cultural difference'.

'Politics of positional difference' is related to structural inequality and injustice and has been central to the arguments of feminist, anti-racist, and gay liberation activists of the 1980s who have argued for equality and inclusion. 'Politics of cultural difference', on the other hand, has gained increasing currency in the 1990s, focusing on differences of nationality, ethnicity and religion and has emphasized "the cultural distinctness". Both forms of politics, it is argued, challenge the vision that tend to identify equality with 'sameness' and both require moral intervention from "public and civic institutions to take into account individual or group differences, treat them differently for the sake of promoting equality and freedom" (Young 2007: 62-63).

There are some drawbacks of the 'politics of cultural difference', Young argues. First, "structural injustices do build on perceived cultural differences; a 'politics of cultural difference' and its emphasis on liberty does not make visible enough issues of structural inequalities" (Young 2007: 86) such as gender and class. Secondly, "the politics and political theory of cultural differences tends to focus on what state policy properly should allow, forbid or remain silent about... [therefore they]... tend to ignore civil society as a crucial site for working on injustice" (Young 2007: 89). Since the 1980s, there have been increasing political demands for the recognition and extension of political, cultural and religious rights in Turkey. Those demands have effectively challenged the conventional equality approach of the state. The secular and unitary character of the state and the meaning of Turkish national identity and citizenship have come to be questioned by different movements. Among these, 'political Islam', putting forth policy demands articulated with reference to a religious identity and a 'conservative' way of life, has been a major force. Women's movements, in their feminist and other veins, have also carved a significant niche for themselves – albeit often with contradictory demands – in the ongoing equality and identity debates in the country.

The present chapter aims to analyze some of the issues pertaining to women and gender equality in Turkey where the intersection of gender as 'politics of structural inequality' and religion, i.e. political Islam, as 'politics of cultural difference' unfold to reveal deep-seated cultural and social tensions.

The Turkish Context

In the ongoing debates on political Islam in Turkey much emphasis has been put on culture and life-style differences. A myriad of forces ranging from international politics to demography, rural-urban migration, skewed income distribution and electoral politics have been identified as root causes of the Islamist movement in Turkey. Yet today many perceive the movement's distinguishing feature as a rising 'social conservatism' that is reflected mainly around gender equality and women's rights issues symbolized by the controversy over the women's 'headscarf'.

In Turkey a state-centric approach, which conceptualizes the state as the main regulator of all things social and political, has generally characterized both the political arguments of different groups and the analyses in the literature. A reference to the state, (capital "S") as the source of values and norms related to the economic and socio-political order, including those of gender equality, has long dominated the political and intellectual scene.

One strand of this perspective, mainly represented by the so called 'secularist' or 'Kemalist' view, has traditionally given exclusive credit for the advancement of gender equality and improvement of women's status in Turkey to the Republican reforms and hailed them unconditionally for their modernizing impact on society and institutions.[1] Since the 1980s this perspective has been increasingly challenged by the arguments that blamed the Republican state for having been inadequate, if not reluctant, to recognize and respond to the demands of groups with differing cultural, religious, ethnic or sexual identities. To the extent that these arguments, too, were based on a critique of the state's acts of commission or omission, they remained state-centric. While the preoccupation with the state and its role in Turkish society can be justified by reference to the historical realities of the country, it has also carried the risk of leaving civil society, as a locus of explanation, out of most analyses. The role of civil society in rendering or legitimizing existing inequalities as well as its potential as a force in eliminating them was, for a long time, unexplored by analysts and untapped by activists.

In the Turkish context, the risk 'politics of cultural difference' carries in obscuring and normalizing gender inequality can be easily observed at the intersection of gender and religion. For instance, while 'religious' or 'Islamic' men could freely attend universities, and enter into civil service, due to the ban on 'headscarves', women of similar identity and choices have been relatively disadvantaged. In the recent past, this situation has often been criticized as an erroneous state policy by many including the Islamist and other women's groups in the country. While most have agreed on the gender discriminatory impact of the 'headscarf ban', the meaning of the 'headscarf' itself was not much discussed. A gender-equality-based discussion of the so-called 'obligation to veil',[2] made almost untouchable by reference to divine ordinance, led to a skeptical silence on the part of most feminists and did not at all constitute an item on the agenda of Islamist politics.

The first part of the paper, attempts to provide a review of the construction of the gender regime of the Turkish state and the challenges this regime has faced the emergence of women's movements since the 1980s. In this context the 'radical' but 'public-sphere-limited' nature of Republican reforms and their impact on the lives of different groups of women in Turkey are explored. The challenges expressed by the latter day women's movements (in their various forms) will then be explored against this background.

The Republican Gender Regime

Women's integration into modern nationhood, as feminist scholars point out, has always played an important role in the formation and reproduction of national identities.[3]

The early period of the Turkish Republic was an era of major reforms aiming to create a modern and secular nation-state. A radical socio-political and cultural rupture from the heritage of the Ottoman Empire was perceived as a necessary condition for the establishment of this new order. In this process, particular emphasis was placed on the secular and unitary character of the state. Secularism was the foundation of modernization and unity was the main pillar of national identity.

Numerous reforms such as the abolition of Islamic educational and religious institutions, introduction of Western legal codes, particularly in the area of civil law to replace the Shariat-based personal status codes of the Ottoman Empire, Western forms of dress, adoption of the Gregorian calendar and the Latin alphabet were all aimed at a wholesale transformation of the social, political and cultural premises of the country. Weakening the impact of religion on social and political life and relegating it to a personal and private sphere served to bring about the rational individual as the new citizen of the Republic. In the effort to create a Turkish national identity, religious and ethnic identities were treated as tangential, primordial and even dangerous attachments. The ideal of modern citizens enjoying equal rights was presented as the new reality. Existing differences or continuing inequalities in terms of gender, religion, ethnicity or class were conceptualized mainly along urban-rural axes and perceived, at best, as differences between city folk and peasants; essentially a transitional problem of development.

It is within this context that the idea of 'gender equality' effectively became part of what defined the Turkish Republic as a 'modern' country. A women's empowerment discourse was often used by the Kemalist elites as a means of dismantling the old order. Women were defined as the group most oppressed through Islamic practices such as veiling, seclusion and polygamy (Tekeli 1981). The idea of the Turkish woman was also invoked for the creation of a national consciousness. Women were depicted as courageous, altruistic heroes of the Turkish War of Independence and hailed for their active support of the national liberation movement. Most importantly, women's emancipation from traditional role expectations, their increased education and active participation in public life became symbols of the place the Republic was aiming to take among Western nations. In this context, the 1926 Civil Code replacing Shari'at-based personal status laws of the Ottoman Empire was the most noted reform advancing women's rights. Abolishing polygamy and giving women equal right to divorce, child custody and inheritance accorded Turkish women a truly progressive status at the time. In 1930 and 1934, women were granted suffrage and the right to stand for election, at local and national elections respectively, an accomplishment for which the Republic has since been credited.

In this early Republican period, Turkish women not only gained access to social, civil and political rights but were also encouraged, by the state and public authorities, to use and enjoy their rights. Women figures that excelled in education and in unconventional professions such as science, medicine, and law were used to promote the ideals of the Republican regime of women and men working side by side to elevate the country to the "level of the contemporary civilization".

Although veiling was not legally forbidden in the country, the image of the ideal Republican woman was unveiled and this image was openly endorsed by the political leadership at all levels of society and strongly promoted through the media, and the education system. Pictures of women in Western attire and with fancy hair-do's active in work life or social gatherings were published in newspapers and magazines to promote the new woman (Arat 1998). Wives of political leaders and civil and military officials as well as women professionals, (especially teachers) acting as role models to school girls, were expected to conform to the image of the modern woman. This modern woman was also expected to be modest in the way she dressed in public life. Her caregiver role in the family was also always emphasized. While educated women were expected to be the enlightened mothers, perfect homemakers, dutiful and loyal wives and raise healthy children for the Republic (Bora, 2001), the Republican gender equality policy, as distinct from conservative ideologies, insisted and actively encouraged the public sphere presence and professional achievement of women (interalia, Acar 1983; Durakbaşa 1998; Kadıoğlu 1998; Arat 1998; Toktaş and Cindoğlu 2006).

Thus, parallel to the dominant approach at the time, the 'gender equality' notion of the Turkish Republic was mostly limited to the formal equality of women and men. It assumed an imagined 'sameness' of all the citizens, including women, so far as the public sphere was concerned and was blind to cultural, religious or social class differences and identities. Yet, it also promoted, in unprecedented manner, progressive legal equality standards of spouses in marriage and family matters through civil law reform. In this approach, the modern Western appearance of women was promoted and perceived as a sign of the achievement of gender equality and modernity claims of the regime, thereby attaching a critical, symbolic meaning to women being unveiled in the national psyche.

Despite the presence of a rather muted disapproval, particularly among conservative religious groups in the country, up until the 1980s the Republic's gender equality approach was not actively and effectively challenged by any women's movement.[4] Nor did it receive any significant public criticism from different political parties in the country for a long time. This has generally been attributed to the fact that Republican reforms indeed, promoted a very significant number of women in public life through education and public employment (inter alia, Öncü 1981; Acar 1991b; Günlük-Şenesen and Özar 2001). Analysts of the latter day women's movement in Turkey have generally conceded that as the early goals of feminism were accomplished by the state's proclaimed gender equality commitment a feminist awareness was redundant for many professional and academic women. In Turkey generations of urban, middle class, professional women who benefitted from the positive impact of Republican reforms, became ardent supporters of these reforms and used their voice to endorse the Republican ideology. In the 1960s and 1970s when some of these educated women were politicized in leftist circles and engaged in the criticism of the capitalist system, they still defended gender equality principles of the Republic as compatible with their overall objectives. By not including in its political agenda a critique of patriarchy, the socialist activism of 1960s and 1970s that invited women and men to the public sphere in the name of a class struggle also affirmed the Republican gender equality approach (Tekeli 1990; Berktay 1990).

The Post 1980s Era

In Turkey, the 1980s corresponded to a rapid transformation of the socio-economic landscape in line with economic and political liberalisation and the opening of Turkish politics to international influences in ways and degrees unseen before. Turkey's accelerated integration with global capital via implementation of neoliberal policies and the political transition to parliamentary democracy after a period of authoritarian military rule characterized the 1980s. In this period, seemingly new actors that often represented existing centers of power in society appeared on the political scene. Economic liberalisation gave way to the shrinking of the state's regulative power in the economic domain, and political liberalisation opened the way to what has been termed "a shift of state power from the state elite to political elite". The new political elite tried to reconstruct national identity by synthesizing Islamic values with a pragmatic rationalism (Göle 1994; Acar 1991a; 2002).[5]

It is against this background that new political oppositions such as political Islam, Kurdish nationalism and an independent feminist women's movement emerged in the 1980s.[6] Although these movements have followed differing trajectories in terms of their interaction with the state, their political strategies, and their achievements and/or failures, they shared the common characteristic of challenging the basic pillars of Turkish modernization; secularism, and the conception of Turkish national identity.

Feminist movement
In understanding and explaining the rise of the feminist movement in the Turkish context, several factors are noted in the literature. It is well-conceded that the second-wave Western feminist movements had an impact on Turkish women of the educated strata, enlarging their political horizons and directing them to pay attention to patriarchy and the functioning of its mechanisms in different contexts (interalia, Kandiyoti 1987; Tekeli 1981 and 1986; Sirman 1989; Acar 1983). It is also often noted that the accumulated knowledge and experience of political activism in leftist organizations led women to a critique of these movements from a feminist perspective. The political conjuncture in the 1980s facilitated their organisation on the basis of their identity as women and act with an agenda of women's problems (Tekeli 1990; Berktay 1990).

The feminist movement in the 1980s questioned and challenged the long existing Republican conception of gender equality. The feminist critique which took shape in academic and civil society circles approached gender inequality as based on structural characteristics of patriarchy and criticized the Kemalist modernization project from this perspective. Some analysts have held the Republican state responsible for practicing a kind of 'state feminism' that resulted in the extended dependence of the women's movement on the state (Tekeli 1986; White 2003). The Republican 'gender equality' perspective that was based on the assumption of the 'sameness' of women and men as agents of the modernization project and as the dutiful citizens of the Republic, also came under criticism (Arat 1990). It was argued that the most crucial areas of gender relations, i.e. private sphere matters such as the double standard of sexuality, stereotyped domestic division of labour, have remained unquestioned and unchallenged (inter alia Kandiyoti 1987; Arat 1990; Arat 1998).

The feminist scholarship of the 1980s and 1990s, in keeping with the true colours of the Second Wave Feminist movements, thus brought into discussion new areas of concern hitherto untouched in the Turkish context. Drawing attention to the gap between what existed in laws and what was practiced in the real life feminist movement questioned and challenged the essence of the Republic's gender equality understanding. Through its strong critique of the state's limited gender equality approach the feminist movement has contributed to expanding the notion of gender equality. In its attempt to gain public attention and raise consciousness and mobilize for political action on women's rights issues this movement came to develop successful strategies and tactics for civil society activism in Turkey. Street protests, sit-ins, public campaigns were organized to protest age-old, well-internalized patriarchal values and everyday inequalities and violations such as domestic violence, sexual harassment and virginity testing, experienced by women in public and private settings. Legal provisions such as the Civil and the Penal Codes were publicly criticized for confirming and reinforcing discriminatory traditional gender roles.[7] Women activists and academics worked, with considerable success, to increase familiarity with and awareness of international standards of women's human rights in the Turkish political scene.[8]

Islamist /conservative/religious[9] women's movement

The visible and active presence of groups of Islamist women has also become a part of the women's movements in Turkey in the recent past.[10] Since the 1990s different elements in the Islamist women's movement have put their mark on Turkish politics in various contexts: as visible actors of the street protests against 'the headscarf ban' in the universities; as chief mobilizers of the support behind various Islamist political parties' rise to power (Arat 2005; Ayata and Tütüncü 2008); and as significant contributors to the Islamist cultural-intellectual front's critique of the secular regime in Turkey. In general, political sensitivities based on religious identities have been the distinguishing mark of the activism of these groups, and the 'headscarf' issue played a pivotal role in the Islamist women's political activism.

In Turkey, political dissatisfaction of religious groups has been the basis of an ever-present opposition, albeit to different degrees and expressed in a variety of ways, since the establishment of the Republic in 1923. Attempts to challenge the secular character of the state openly in the form of rebellions received harsh responses from the state in the early years leading to the covert organizations of some radical Islamist groups.

With the transition to the multi-party system in 1946 and with the rise of the Democrat Party (DP) to power in 1950, despite the fact that the secular nature of the state remained uncontestable, some groups with

Islamic sensitivities found new opportunities to move into different parts of the state structure. They were able to form some partial alliances with the state elites, giving way to transformations in the state's until-then radically secularist policies. Some analysts have labeled this process the incorporation of the "elements of Islamism into the ideology and practice of the Kemalist state" (Gülalp 2001: 434). The running theme of Turkish politics in the years since has been the continuing confrontation between the so-called 'secularist' and 'Islamist' groups over the extent to which the state was able to control religion as opposed to the extent to which Islamist perspectives infiltrated the state's mentality and actions.

From the 1980s on, groups with religious identity began to enjoy considerable autonomy in Turkish society diffusing into economic and political spheres in hitherto unseen forms and degrees. Official state and critical political and bureaucratic decision-making positions were occupied more than ever before by individuals displaying religious identities; religious businessmen, accumulating capital, started to expand their commercial weight in the country and at the global level (Ayata 1996; Narlı 1999; Göle 1997; Öniş 1997).

In the 1990s Islamic parties widened the bases of their ideological appeal beyond their religious constituencies and successfully increased their support bases. Their conservative discourse increasingly offered a political invitation to all those who were dissatisfied with the existing economic conditions and/or political and social governance. The Welfare Party, successfully articulating the people's mundane discontent into a critique of the modernist/Kemalist/secularist regime thus became a powerful voice in Turkish politics.[11]

It is against this background women with conservative sensibilities mobilized within Islamic political movement since 1980s. They had gathered at "house meetings" where they exchanged religious knowledge, conversed about religious issues and (in their own terms) "raised consciousness" about Islam (Şişman 2000: 155-165). They also worked in the local branches of the Islamist parties to expand the latter's electoral base, established and maintained networks with people in local settings and engaged in fundraising activities for charity (Arat 1999; Ayata and Tütüncü 2008). Thus, the existential call that conservative women had answered in the 1980s turned into a 'political vocation' (Beruf in Weberian sense) in the 1990s when women assumed the duty of delivering the Islamic message to the masses. Throughout this evolution the 'headscarf' became an identity marker of the Islamist women's movement.

The 'Headscarf' Controversy

Any attempt to analyze the meaning and functions of the 'headscarf' issue and the controversy that has developed around it in Turkish society needs to look at this phenomenon in its multiple and multilayered meanings. At the risk of oversimplifying the complex social, economic and cultural reality one could state that women's headscarf, in the Turkish context, is many things to many people. It is both 'tradition' and 'modernity'; it is both 'social pressure' and 'individual choice'; it is both 'women's pass to public life' and 'women's way to marriage'; it is both 'women's modesty' and women 'being fashionable'. But perhaps most significantly, it has been a salient site of national political debate and contestation that fed into the political activism of some conservative women, although they could hardly be considered the main actors on the scene.

In the early years of the Republic the 'headscarf' was associated with a rural and traditional lifestyle and somehow romanticized as a folkloric aspect of the Turkish culture (White, 2003). Yet, in time, it also came to take on a class dimension. As White (2002) noted, with the migration from rural areas that started in the 1950s and became extensive and large-scale in later periods, the 'headscarf' came to denote a class distinction more than anything else; it became a symbol of the rural-lower class inserted into the urban context.

Along with increased urbanisation, capital accumulation by the Islamist groups and their integration into the economic and political system, the 'headscarf' gained new meaning in Turkish society. Middle or upper-middle class women, who did not reflect the qualities associated with the Republican image of ideal women, were now using the 'headscarf'. Thus it started to be associated with the alternative elite status that also denoted to some an 'enlightened' Muslim consciousness (Saktanber 2002; Saktanber and Çorbacıoğlu 2008: 526; Göle 1996; White 2002). It acquired a different meaning as an expression of Islamic subjectivity that was 'constructed' and 'lived' as opposed to the Republican one. In a way women's rights rhetoric of the modernist elites was turned upside-down with its promise of emancipating women from the superficiality, problems and complexities of modern/working/city life via Islam (Acar 1991c; 1995). For some, the 'headscarf' became a symbol of an authentic relationship with God and an alternative modern life-style (Göle 1996). By wearing the 'headscarf' women were expressing their will to dedicate themselves to their families and to God.[12]

The conservative/Islamist women's movement, thus, transposed the 'headscarf' – a symbol of rural womanhood – to a signifier of the new urban woman in her religious identity. In the process, the multicoloured kerchiefs turned into the uniform-like, drab-coloured, large- 'headscarves' and loose, full coat outfits of religious women of the 1980s, which were then also replaced by the brightly coloured, fitted, fashionable pantsuit and matching headscarves that are tightly wound around the neck of many contemporary urban women.[13] In the 1990s the public activism of some well-educated women and female university students who insisted on expressing their religious identity by using the 'headscarf' and demanding that they be allowed to attend the university in such garb became increasingly visible. These women were almost always publicly supported by significant numbers of Islamist men in their street demonstrations, an exceptional case vis-à-vis women's rights demands in Turkey. Their cause, the 'headscarf' constituted one of the most ardent demands of the Islamist political parties in the country.

The development of civil society platforms such as NGO's, (replacing the private home meetings of the 1980s) further enabled conservative/slamist women to come together in the public arena to formulate collective action strategies (Göle 2002; Kadıoğlu 2005). The political activism of these associations continued to be based on the headscarf dispute.

Islamist women claimed that the 'headscarf' ban in the universities and state institutions was a form of discrimination against them as religious women. Over time, the 'headscarf' issue in Turkey came to be debated within the liberal framework of human rights that considers this ban a violation of women's right to education and work. Along with the transformation seen in the appearance and meaning of the 'headscarf', the bases of the arguments in its favor also shifted from 'religious obligation' to 'personal choice'. Landmark political events and judicial decisions at both the national and international levels guided this evolution.[14]

The political and legal struggle for lifting the ban on the 'headscarf' in the universities and civil service was instrumental in consolidating the conservative women's movement. This struggle also contributed to the construction of a legitimate political identity for Islamist women in Turkish society at large. Simultaneously, among different segments of population ranging from secular traditionalists to Islamists and from liberal democrats to feminists an increasing support for the matter developed over time.[15]

On the other hand, many in Turkey continued to see the headscarf as a symbol of political Islam and judged the struggle for the political recognition of such Islamic identity to be incompatible with the institutions and practices of a secular state.

In this regard, particular opposition from Kemalist women needs to be noted. Mainly constituted of middle-class, middle aged, educated women, they displayed a strong loyalty to the secular nation state and an equally strong commitment to the Republican reforms. They had long advocated the role of education in women's empowerment and liberation. Having country-wide organizations, they also engaged in activities to that end. To them, the headscarf represented an anti-modern stance, and was seen as an expression of a movement working to re-create a social order in which Islamic laws (shariat) would regulate life.[16]

While the most visible and most widely shared 'cause célèbre' of the Islamic women's movement was the 'headscarf' issue, some groups within this movement also engaged in activism around other issues. For instance, several Islamist women's groups took part in protests against Israel for the Palestinian cause or organized aid campaigns for victims of natural disasters such as the Malaysian and Indonesian victims of the 2004 tsunami or those of the 2011 earthquake in Pakistan. Notably, the focus and beneficiaries of these activities were almost always exclusively Muslim populations indicating the religion-defined sphere of activism of the conservative women's movement.

Only a few conservative women's organizations[17] took part in activities and engaged in collaborations with secular women's groups (particularly feminists and/or feminist-leaning secular groups) most notable among such cases was the broad-based women's coalition advocating for reform of the Civil and Penal Codes, in 2001 and 2005 respectively, and the women's human rights activism around preparation and presentation of shadow reports to CEDAW (2004 and 2010). It is interesting in this context that, during the Penal Code reform process, when an MP from the ruling AKP proposed an amendment to re-criminalize adultery, feminists and secular women's groups harshly criticized the government for being regressive on the issue (İlkkaracan, 2007) Islamist women refrained from taking a manifest stand on the matter and broke ranks from the coalition (Acar and Altunok 2009).

Some Concluding Remarks on State, Women's Movements and Gender Equality

The conventional approach in the mainstream academic analyses of the women's movement in Turkey has always placed Republican reforms at the foundation of the gender equality regime in the country (inter alia Abadan-Unat 1981; Arat 1986). It has regarded the secular state as the main change agent and chief benefactor of women, a perspective that has also been shared by the Kemalist and secular women's movement in the country. This meant that responsibility for unsatisfied ambitions and thwarted goals was attributed to the state both by stakeholders at the political level and by analysts in the literature. To the extent that the image of an 'unveiled woman' was regarded as validation of the secular Republic and 'the headscarf' was viewed, by many, as the primary symbol of political Islam the latter was perceived as a threat to the regime (Saktanber and Çorbacıoğlu 2008). In the recent political history of Turkey, not only the political system and such state institutions as the military and the judiciary, but also a significant part of civil society, including the Kemalist, secular women's NGOs, reacted to this threat defensively and forcefully.[18]

Those who have long expressed their pride in the Republican policies and addressed their demands by appealing to the state, once again, searched for ways to deal with the challenges originating from political Islam in the same way.

A seemingly different approach, however, was the hallmark of the political activism of the contemporary feminist movement. Along with their critique of the Republican policies these groups have targeted the civil society, were engaged in consciousness-raising and bottom-up activisms on hitherto untouched issues (such as violence against women, sexual division of labour, virginity) of women's human rights.

In the 1990s and the early 2000s some Islamist women's efforts to assert their individualistic rights and demands, and "extend the private sphere" in this way, were evaluated by some analysts (Arat 1999; 1990) as signs of these movements' potentially liberating impact on women. In this regard, attention was drawn to the beginnings of a 'rapprochement' between some Islamist and feminist groups as both appeared to struggle for recognition of individual liberties by the state and the civil society at large. Thus, they were viewed as contributing to the transformation of the strong state tradition and to the political liberalisation process in Turkey (inter alia, Arat 1999; Göle 1996; Özdalga 1998). These Islamist and feminist women's movements were seen, as sharing an opposition to the state and its definition of the common good in denial of women's subjectivity, choices and preferences (Arat 1995; 2008).

Criticizing the existing state-dominated and exclusionary conception of politics, this perspective reflected a trust in bottom-up movements and their political agency as essentially democratic and liberating. However, such analysis also tended to homogenize many forms of "politics of difference" under the common banner of being 'against the state'. It thus tended to overlook the variation in the grounds on which each activism had been built and how it compared to the universal standards of women's human rights and gender equality. The fact that "politics of cultural difference" demands recognition of cultural distinctiveness for the group, whereas "politics of positional difference" demands justice for 'structural group differences', is very salient here (Young 1990). Structural differences of gender, race or class cut across ethnic, national or religious categories regardless of whether these are majority or minority cultures. Therefore, analyzing 'politics of cultural difference' as 'politics of positional difference' would mean disregarding structural inequalities and specific forms of group based injustices (Young 2007). This is particularly relevant for religious groups as religious adherents often take doctrine and ceremony not to simply help define their identities, but also as obligations (Young 2007).

Consequently, in the Turkish context, a mere focus on the 'headscarf' as a religious liberty to be enjoyed by conservative women carries the risk of not only failing to assess the very nature of this obligation as 'patriarchal community control over women's sexuality' but also of overlooking other forms of injustices that are produced and circulated by patriarchy or social class differences. In this context, for instance, some recent studies that argue against the ban on the 'headscarf' have also pointed to the debilitating impact of the conservative worldview on women's chances in the employment market.[19] Women's own religion-inspired values and constant valorization of motherhood and homemaking as women's primary roles in the society[20] (Acar and Ayata 2002; Acar 1990; Arat 2010) combine to exploit the headscarf ban for discrimination against women in employment (Cindoğlu 2010).

Conservative women in Turkey have been conspicuously silent on some issues such as women's sexuality and homosexuality. They have been very careful not to overstep the limits of religious dictates on these matters. The boundaries of their conception of women's freedoms and gender equality have been mostly defined by these dictates. It has also been argued that the 'equality' demand voiced by the Turkish Islamist women differ from their counterparts on important accounts. Different from most of their sisters who live under Islamic laws, Turkish Islamist women did not have to engage in a struggle for equal legal rights (Merçil 2007; Tekeli 1980). In fact, they are implicitly, if not openly, supportive of the fundamental gender equality gains of the Republic.[21] However, differing from the feminists, they do not insist on furthering such equality to the de facto level and do not dwell on participation of women in all the public sphere activities equally. While women's participation and non-discrimination in education and political participation has been emphasized (albeit, with reference to the 'headscarf'), employment has not received much attention. Subscribing to the Islamic insistence on 'complementarity of sexes' and 'gender equity' rather than 'gender equality', the Islamist women's movement in Turkey has been selective in its support of different equality issues.

As the conservatism in Turkey has been increasingly shaped by the decade-long political rule of AKP, the Islamist women's movement has refrained from challenging the main premises of this worldview from a gender-equality standpoint. It has been argued that an AKP style of social conservatism has been imposing notions of common or individual good with 'explicit moral tones' in Turkish society, giving way to everyday 'social pressures' and lack of tolerance for the 'other' and 'other's life-styles (Toprak et al. 2009) with negative implications for gender equality.

Also, with the transformation of the image of conservative women from rebellious protest agents to docile and content wives of political and public leaders (Cindoğlu and Zencirci 2008) the Islamist women's movement has been alienated from the realm of oppositional political activism.

In Turkey women have been at the center of the main political divide between secularists and Islamists for a long time. They have been used by both political camps to define, defend and propagate opposing conceptions of subjectivity, life style and common good. They have also often been used as 'objects' of analysis and as concrete representations of abstract ideologies by students of the political and social scene in the country. Women's movements in Turkey have, on the other hand, hardly been considered agents or 'subjects' of change by actors, including women themselves, or analysts until recently.

With the emergence and increasing activism of an independent women's movement with strong feminist overtones, in the post 1980s, secular women were able to effectively challenge the patriarchal premises of the Republican gender equality order. As such they put forth a woman-centered opposition to the order of which they were a part. Secular women's rejection of their 'emancipated but unliberated' (Kandiyoti 1987) status helped define this movement as an autonomous women's movement and an agent of social change in its own right. Despite the presence of some exceptional voices among them, a similar reflection of autonomy is yet to be seen among Islamist women.

4

THE STATE OF FEMALE LABOUR IN THE IMPASSE OF THE NEOLIBERAL MARKET AND PATRIARCHAL FAMILY

Gülay Toksöz

The female labour force participation and gender composition of employment are the result of complex compounds of demand and supply factors. The supply of female labour and women's working conditions in different countries of the developing world depend largely on the patriarchal system prevailing in the country and on the way it is articulated with the capitalist mode of production. In countries where private patriarchy has been strong, a man as husband or father, benefiting from the maintenance of the gender-based division of labour at home, has decided whether or not women may work outside the household. In this system, women have been excluded from the public sphere, and women's participation in employment has been very limited and/or in forms non-threatening to men's authority. Within the concept of public patriarchy, women are not excluded from public arenas but join it through subordinated positions. The household continues to be the important site of private patriarchy but women are no more confined to it. The state as the main representative of the public patriarchy, with its regulations and practices reinforcing women's secondary status in the labour market, reduces women's bargaining power not only against employers but also against men, and supports private patriarchy pertaining to its power.[1]

In countries where private patriarchy historically loses power due to strong demand for female labour, participation in waged labour can have an emancipatory aspect for women. However, the state can still adopt policies and practices for the continuation of women's secondary status in the labour market which favors capital. The struggle of a women's movement forcing the state toward policies and programs of gender equality can cause the weakening of public patriarchy. The conditions contributing to the weakening of public patriarchy depend a lot on the capitalist mode of production in a particular country and the forms of its integration to the global markets. The articulation among capitalism and patriarchy can emerge in very different forms as the wide range in the employment rates of women in developing countries of the southeast Asian and the Middle East and North Africa (MENA) shows. Although the expansion of female employment in deregulated labour markets in precarious and unprotected forms of employment may undermine the emancipatory dimension, women can still be active agents engaged in changing the unfavourable conditions of their employment even when the achievements are very restricted (Lim 1990; Lie 1996; Wolf 1997; Kabeer 2004).

Keeping in mind the general characteristics of export-led industrialisation triggering female employment in the majority of the developing world in the last quarter of the twentieth century, the feature that distinguishes Turkey from the majority of the middle income developing countries is the huge gender gap and women's declining trends of participation in employment and the labour force. The aim of this article is to explore the factors that theoretically should have led to similar expansion in Turkey, but did not, despite Turkey having adopted a similar development strategy. What are the characteristics of the capitalist mode of production in Turkey that lead to a low level of demand for female labour? What type of a restrictive role does private and public patriarchy play on the female labour supply? Under which conditions do macro economic factors challenge private and public patriarchy or comply with them? In other words what influences do the neoliberal labour market and patriarchal family structure, society and state exert on the female labour force? How influential are the male family members' negative attitudes toward women's income earning activities? Can the gender equality rhetoric of the governments be interpreted as a sign of weakening public patriarchy?

To find answers to these questions the determinants of the macroeconomic strategies influencing the low level of demand for female labour will be discussed within a comparative framework. Subsequently, the patriarchal family structures as an expression of private patriarchy and the State's role in the continuation of gender inequalities as a manifestation of public patriarchy will be examined.

Export-Oriented Industrialisation and Female Labour Force
The growth model based on export-oriented industrialisation has led to different trajectories in different regions and countries of the developing

world. As the demand for female labour has varied greatly, women's labour force and employment participation rates have been increasing at different rates, fastest in Asia and lowest in Latin America. (UN 1999:27; Joekes 1999). Southeast Asian countries are considered to be the most successful examples of export-oriented development and there is a wide spread debate on the determinants of Asian growth. Different approaches emphasise different factors such as economic openness, the active role of facilitating state institutions, technical progress, investment in human capital and income equality. They agree, in general, on the positive role of exports enabling access to foreign technology. Seguino (2000:51) points to the neglect of gendered characteristics of Asian growth in these approaches and to the vital role of female workers' low wages employed in export industries in this process. The low wage levels of women made these countries competitive, promoted their export sales, contributed to the provision of foreign exchange necessary for modern technologies. However women's bargaining power has been limited through patriarchal gender norms sustained by the state in these countries where rapid growth depends on cheap female labour.

In spite of changes occurring in the gender composition of labour force demand, east and southeast Asia are renowned as successful examples of export-led industrialisation. The high share of women in the industrial workforce still continues to be the distinctive feature of the countries in the region compared to the rest of the developing world. Karshenas and Moghadam's (2001) work comparing MENA region with east and southeast Asia, with respect to female participation in labour force and employment, points to the role of relative high per capita income and wage levels in MENA countries supported by oil revenues in the transition period to market economy in the 1960s and 1970s. They assert that in the societies with relative high per capita income in non-agricultural sectors during the transition period the restrictive elements of the traditional culture gain weight, whereas in other societies with low income levels, one breadwinner cannot ensure the family subsistence and new cultural norms emerge allowing women to participate in the labour force to greater extents. The relative high level of income in MENA countries enabled the preservation of patriarchal family structures in which only men work and women did not participate in waged work which results in a very low female labour force participation rate. However, Morocco and Tunisia are exceptions in that they have no or limited oil revenues and adoption of export-led industrialisation caused an increased share of women in manufacturing. Within this economic context, Moghadam (2001) refers to a 'patriarchal gender contract' in MENA countries, according to which men are held responsible for the subsistence of the family and women take care of children and domestic chores; women are economically dependent on men. The patriarchal gender contract determines which jobs and professions are suitable for women entering the labour market. This contract is systemised through the laws and particularly through the family laws in the region. Moghadam criticises approaches only providing 'culture' as explanation and shows how women's employment patterns are largely shaped by the macroeconomic factors and limited industrialisation in the region. In her comparative analysis of MENA countries with respect to economic development and women's employment, she explains the low level of non-agricultural employment of women in Turkey, being the most industrialized MENA country, in the context of limited industrialisation (Moghadam 2003).

Macroeconomic Strategies and Demographic Trends Affecting Demand for Female Labour in Turkey

Transition from agricultural to semi-industrial society in Turkey

Women's labour force participation and employment patterns in Turkey resemble the other countries in the MENA region, although Turkey does not have oil resources. After the import substituting industrialisation period in the 1960s and 1970s, Turkey adopted the policies of export-oriented industrialisation in the 1980s, a growth process which has not lead to a significant increase in women's labour force participation. Another major difference of Turkey from other MENA countries is in its laws and regulations pertaining to gender equality as part of a westernisation process begun with the foundation of the Republic in 1923. Further, during the current process of accession negotiations to the EU, all laws and institutional structures have been changed to adjust to the EU acquis. However, gender equality in legal settings falls short of automatically bringing gender equality in labour markets and employment. The realisation of equality depends on the paths chosen for economic and social development and the type of welfare regime, namely, integrating to the world markets through a 'high road' strategy based on the production of high value added products and availability of decent jobs, not only for men but also for women, and provision of infrastructure for public care work.

Looking at the impact of macroeconomic strategies and policies on employment in Turkey, we observe that, starting from the 1950s parallel to the process of capitalist development, market relations and mechanisation have gained ground in agriculture, where subsistence production prevailed, reducing need for agricultural labour, which has also affected female labour. Intensity in the use of female labour in agriculture depends on such variables as patterns of land ownership, level of mechanisation, crop type and the need for manual labour in the process (Kandiyoti 1997). Especially in areas where mainly cereals are grown, spread of mechanisation displaced surplus labour, and large masses now facing difficulty in subsisting on crop farming started moving to urban areas. In line with the ideology of private patriarchy, males in their new urban settlements joined the labour force as 'breadwinners' while women were expected to stay home to undertake domestic chores and care for children and the elderly. This is the major factor explaining why, in the second half of the twentieth century, women remained mostly out of the urban labour force and why their labour force participation kept falling. On the other hand, when it comes to industrial and labour-intensive cash crops such as cotton, tobacco, tea and sugar beets, women as a cheap source of labour continued working either as unpaid family workers in small family holdings or as wage labourers, if they had no land.

In the new millennium, however, agricultural policies imposed by international finance institutions have had the effect of reducing agricultural production and employment rather sharply, as a result of which female labour has been pushed out of production more rapidly than male labour. With the new policy line envisaging the reshaping of national agricultural policies in line with those of the World Bank, European Union and World Trade Organisation, development plans in Turkey included reducing the agricultural population while enhancing productivity and competitiveness as priority targets. Consequently, support to growing domestic crops was curtailed; subsidised inputs and credit to farmers were abolished; crop farming areas were narrowed; and price support policies were abandoned. The new policy line envisaged direct income support to farmers on the basis of the size of land owned irrespective of output, input, use, or income level. This policy caused significant falls in both output of and employment related to such crops as sugar beet, tobacco, tea, cotton and hazel nut (Gulcubuk et al 2005). Consequently, the need for female labour for all these labour intensive crops diminished substantially.

Nevertheless household based agricultural enterprises currently continue to have the largest share of female employment in Turkey as there are only limited non-agricultural employment opportunities for female labour. In the manufacturing industry, it is not possible to speak about any significant female employment, neither in undertakings of multinational companies nor in establishments mainly producing for such companies. Likewise, even in smaller enterprises in the manufacturing industry, where informal employment is predominant or in various branches of the services sector, it is not possible to talk about any significant level of female employment. Hence, while female participation in the labour force and female employment are both on the rise worldwide, Turkey is one of the few countries remaining outside this trend. Now we can take a closer look at factors giving rise to this state of affairs.

State of Industrialisation

The first factor related with industrialisation is the limitedness of productive investments generating employment. In the 1980s, Turkey, in line with advice of the IMF and World Bank, abandoned the import substitution model and adopted an export based growth model and Structural Adjustment Programs. Pushing free market economy to the fore in line with neoliberal policies led to the shrinking of the public sector and many public enterprises were privatised. While fixed capital investments by the public sector receded, increase in investment by the private sector was far from closing the gap, which is one of the factors contributing to a widening gap between labour supply and demand for labour (Şenses 1996). In spite of various measures adopted by governments, including ease in both foreign and domestic investments, various legislative arrangements to reduce administrative and bureaucratic formalities in enterprising and other incentives mitigating tax burden, investments still failed to generate sufficient employment. This can be explained by the emergence, especially in the 1990s, of an accumulation model mainly based on rent. In this process income distribution further worsened, economic priorities drifted away from the real sector while priorities of speculative and rent earning sectors gained importance. Instead of helping investments financed by the real sector, banks acted as intermediaries for the public sector whose means of getting direct loans from abroad have weakened and financed the debts of this sector. Like the banking system, even real sector enterprises shifted to speculative accumulation and preferred short-term financial investments rather than long-term fixed capital investments (Yeldan 2001:144-146). Historically leading the 'low road' strategy and articulating to the world markets through labour intensive products, Turkey has not been successful in acceding to the 'high road' strategy. However even in the 'low road' strategy, the limited level of investments in industry brought along limited demand for female labour in labour-intensive branches of manufacturing industry. The table in the following section on developments in sectoral distribution of employment shows that women's share in total industrial employment, increasing only from 19 per cent to 23 per cent in the period 1988–2007, can be taken as an indicator of this situation. So Moghadam's (2003) consideration about the limited industrialisation of Turkey holds true in explaining the low level of non-agricultural employment of women in Turkey.

A second factor, related with the first one, is the recent low level of foreign direct investments in Turkey. One of the most important criteria of success in export-based growth is the intensity of foreign direct investments. In the period 1975-2001, foreign direct investment in Turkey totaled $14 billion. Following the enactment of legislation pertaining to foreign investment, the value of foreign investment in Turkey climbed to $34 billion in the period 2002–05. Although foreign capital may have its preference for Turkey as a result of cheap labour and a rather large market, it is stated that in this respect Turkey still lags behind some new EU members including Czech Republic, Poland and Hungary (Sak and Acar 2007, TEPAV 2007). Moreover, it is well known that a considerable part of foreign capital inflow is related to the undertaking of newly privatised public enterprises or to that part of the shares of banks sold to foreigners rather than being new investments in a proper sense. Limited investment of foreign capital in the manufacturing industry and the present status of export-oriented free trade zones, far behind in economic activity and level of employment compared to similar ones in southeast Asia are factors explaining why a high level of demand for and employment of female labour observed elsewhere does not take place in Turkey.

At the same time, informal economic activities in Turkey gained further impetus in the period following 1980 within the framework of neoliberal policies as the public sector withdrew from the economy, and subcontracting and outsourcing became the norm in both public and private enterprises. Large enterprises, for whom to move out of the formal economy is quite difficult, find their solution by assigning labour-intensive components of their production to smaller firms. Smaller firms, in hot competition among themselves for taking work from larger ones, push their costs down by employing workers informally, which means work without social protection, that is, employment without social security coverage and protection of fundamental legislation governing working life. In association with these developments, employment grows in the informal economy rather than the formal. A striking indicator is the fact that within the period 2000–06 the rate of growth of non-agricultural informal employment was double the rate of growth of non-agricultural employment in general (Toksöz 2007:37).[2] In terms of both sector basis and status at work, informal work is much more common among females than among males.[3] Unqualified women joining the labour force have almost no other chance but to work in informal jobs. These types of jobs usually do not have any empowering economic impact.

Another factor contributing to the low level of demand for female labour is in the demographic structure. In Turkey, the rate of population growth is falling parallel to the decrease in fertility rate.[4] Still, according to demographic projections, the share of adult population will continue to increase until 2025 due to the fact that population in this group were born in a period in which fertility had yet not fallen (TUSIAD 1999). This means a rising potential supply of labour and, unless employment is provided, high rates of unemployment. In Turkey, the rate of population growth of working age people and of population participating in the labour force have so far been higher than the rate of growth in employment. The reason this situation has not yet led to striking increases in unemployment is associated with the fact that young girls and women of working age mostly remain out of the labour market. As will be addressed in more detail under the heading on the influence of private and public patriarchy on the supply of female labour, the gender-based division of labour in Turkey and the associated burden of domestic chores and child care on women as well as a lack of sufficient public care services all largely prevent women's job seeking and entrance into labour markets.

At this point we can ask the question as to whether the level of female workers' wages are not low enough to offer an adequate incentive for employers as in other developing countries. As the manufacturing industry permanent wage data of the Turkish Statistical Institute is not disaggregated by gender so as to enable the calculation of gender wage differentials, we have to rely on some individual surveys pointing to the gender gap in earnings in specific years. According to the 1994 Income Distribution Survey both the public and private sectors monthly earnings of males are higher than those of females irrespective of educational status, professional group and economic branch of activity, and this difference is wider in private sector. In the manufacturing industry, males earn twice that of females.[5] According to another study based on the 1994 Survey of Employment and Wages, which investigated wage differentials in the manufacturing industry, mining, electricity, gas and water works, the wage differential between males and females amounts to 24 per cent even when such factors as education and experience are excluded. Isolating other factors including occupation, branch of industry, collective agreement, etc., the remaining difference of nine per cent can be attributed solely to gender discrimination (Ilkkaracan and Selim 2007). In the Turkish Labour Market Report of the World Bank (2006:54) too, it is stated that average earnings of male wage and salary earners have increased by 22 per cent in the period 1988–2002, while this increase remained at 12 per cent for females. According to this study, females earn 78–83 per cent of what males earn. Although various calculations differ from each other using different data bases it is common to all that females earn substantially less than males. However, the gender gap in wages does not seem to be effective in favour of women's recruitment.

In countries where the labour market is tight, that is, where labour supply is limited, women's participation in the labour force is encouraged and supported. The attitude of the State as the representative of the public patriarchy loosens due to the employers' demand for female labour and women's struggle for gender equality. Given that the State has developed public policies for care services and demand for labour is high enough to push wages up, patriarchal structures that keep women at home tend to dissolve, and women become essential actors in labour markets (Pearson 1992). In Turkey, on the other hand, existence of a large mass of males ready to work under any condition leads employers with a patriarchal mentality to prefer male labour. In this way they can also avoid all expenses related with child bearing and rearing, responsibilities connected with women workers. Consequently, males constitute the major source of cheap and long-term labour in Turkey.

Gender Composition of Employment

In Turkey from October 1988, the date in which the Household Labour Force Surveys were started, to October 2007, the number of people of working age increased by 19 million while the increase in employment remained at 5 million. Of this total figure, 4.5 million are males.[6] These sheer figures reveal the limited employment creation capacity of the process called 'growth without employment' and the male predominance in new jobs. On the contrary, an overwhelming majority of women of working age remain out of the labour force. During this period of 19 years, the labour force participation rate decreased from 34.3 percent to 24.4 percent of females and from 81.2 percent to 71.8 percent of males. The employment rate of females fell from 30.6 percent to 21.7 percent. According to the ILO's Global Employment Trends for Women 2009 report, even in the Middle East region, the employment rate in 2007 was

24.3 percent higher than that of Turkey. There is an increasing trend in the region as the rate was 20.5 percent in 1998 (2009:38).

Table 4.1: 1988–2007 Developments in sectoral distribution of employment (thousands)

	Total employment		Males		Females	
	Oct 1988	Oct 2007	Oct 1988	Oct 2007	Oct 1988	Oct 2007
Total	17,755	22,478	12,519	16,708	5,235	5,771
Agriculture	8,219	5,881	4,231	3,156	4,019	2,728
Percent	46,5	26,2	33,8	18,9	76,8	47,3
Industry	2,806	1,332	2,357	3,517	448	815
Percent	15,8	19,3	18,8	21,1	8,6	14,1
Construction	1,012	1,419	997	1,382	15	37
Percent	5,7	6,3	8,0	8,3	0,3	0,6
Services	5,687	10,843	4,935	8,653	752	2,191
Percent	32,0	48,2	39,4	51,8	14,4	38,0

Source: TurkStat, Household Labour Force Statistics, http://www.tuik. gov.tr (Accessed: 23.05.2009 and prepared by the author)

The sectoral distribution of employment shows that total agricultural employment decreased sharply by 2.4 million during the period 1988–2007. Although women comprise more than half of this reduction, agriculture still constitutes the most important domain of employment for women. Agricultural employment represents 47.3 per cent of working women. Total employment in industry increased only by 1.5 million from 2.8 million in 1988 to reach 4.3 million in 2007. Such a meager increase in industrial employment within a period of 19 years clearly points to the limited employment generating capacity of this sector. Only one quarter of the growth in employment belongs to female workers. In the manufacturing industry, branches such as garment and leatherworks, textiles, metal, metal items and machinery, food and beverages stand out as traditional branches with relatively more females employed.[7] But, in none of these branches do females constitute the majority of employees.

While employment growth in industry remains constrained, employment in the service sector is growing more rapidly, reaching 10.8 million constituting an almost twofold increase from 1988–2007. Within the sector, wholesale and retail trade, restaurants and hotels come to the fore as fastest growing sub-sectors in terms of employment. This growth is also associated with the fact that many people unable to find any other employment join these sub-sectors as own account workers. Female employment in the services sector grew about threefold in the period mentioned and reached over 2 million. This situation indicates that services offer the main area of recruitment for women in non-agricultural employment.

Female Workers in Different Branches of Manufacturing and Services

Studies on gendered aspects of employment in the manufacturing industry in Turkey are very few. Macro data on the manufacturing industry not being disaggregated on the basis of gender plays an important role in the lack of surveys. According to a 1980 study based on enterprise level information, more export-oriented enterprises tend to employ more female workers (Ozler 2000). However, technological changes in a given enterprise may reverse this tendency and push the proportion of female workers down again. According to another study on the effects of technological renovation on female labour conducted in textiles and electronics both in three plants, new technologies used in export-oriented enterprises reduced the demand for unskilled female workers leading to an overall decline in their employment, while fewer in numbers, increased the number of females working as technicians or engineers (Ansal 1998). Another study on the impact of export-based growth on female labour maintains that a positive effect of export orientation can be observed in the case of single and/or younger women, and there is no influence on the participation of married women. This difference indicates the importance of gender-based division of the household. In an economy with low performance in investment and growth, export-oriented policies *per se* do not guarantee expansion in employment, and thus, any positive and sustained impact on female employment. Under conditions in which low wage, flexible labour market and high profit margins are accompanied by low rates of accumulation, stagnating employment also means a barrier to the feminisation of the labour force (Baslevent and Onaran, 2004:1390).

Limited expansion of female employment in the manufacturing industry can be associated with developments in the garment sector. Studies on the garment sector, which has its significant share in exports, reveal that this branch competes in world markets mainly over cheap and invisible female labour in subcontracting firms and shows similar patterns of female employment with other developing countries. (Eraydin and Erendil 2000; White 2004; Dedeoglu 2008). According to a survey conducted in

...anbul in the mid-90s, women join employment in the garment industry through various modes of production organisation. This encompasses qualified or unqualified jobs in large scale enterprises in line with labour legislation, largely informal work in small scale enterprises and workshops, and finally fully informal and unprotected work at home. Women working in large factories and workshops gradually adopt working out as a mode of life, and while their earnings contribute to the family budget, women gain more ground in decisions related to the disposal of the family budget. On the other hand, earnings of women engaged in home-based piece work are much lower and irregular without any similar empowerment. Traditional family enterprises can survive on the basis of family and community solidarity mechanisms and the unpaid labour of female family members plays a vital role in the survival of such enterprises (Eraydin and Erendil, 2000). Both engagement in family workshops and piece work at home are preferred by many since these forms of employment reconcile traditional roles that keep women at home, preventing contact with other males, and not threatening the male's role as the breadwinner in the family and the need to obtain additional income. In families from low income groups where working out of home with strangers is considered at odds with the concept of 'good' Moslem woman, this practice can be ethically and socially accepted so long as women's earning is regarded not as 'work', but as an expression of group identity and solidarity. However, association of woman's labour with 'role identity' rather than anything else leads to its low remuneration or no remuneration at all (White 2004).

Women's employment in the garment sector without pay, at a very low wage, or status as reserve labour mobilised only when needed within the framework of family relations make them 'invisible' workers of totally informal enterprises. When women work in family workshops or at home, this form of employment is largely unrecorded and it is therefore argued that this situation leads to the understatement of the number of actually working women (Dedeoglu 2008:56). In sum, due to the informal nature of work, it is quite difficult to measure the share of family-based, small scale production in the garment sector as a whole, or the number of women employed in this way. It is obvious that there is a need for more detailed studies focusing on the gender composition of employment with respect to enterprise scale and characteristics.

Based on the findings of studies conducted so far, it is possible to assert that female employment in manufacturing remains limited as employers can easily find male workers even in those sectors considered fit for female employment. The 'nimble fingers' of women seem to be substituted with the tough hands of men! Only those forms of female employment that do not pose any threat to patriarchal family structure are relatively more common. Work in family enterprises without remuneration or home-based work at very low wages can be taken as the concrete manifestation of the conformity between the neoliberal market and private patriarchy.

The services sector, being very heterogeneous in character, offers women employment opportunities in very qualified occupations as well in unqualified jobs. For female employment wholesale and retail trade, restaurants and hotels are the fastest growing sub-sectors. The thriving tourism sector is the driving force behind the increase in number of hotels, restaurants and other similar trades. However, the potential that the tourism sector presents for female employment is restricted to large metropolis and tourism areas. In many other Anatolian cities striving for development through tourism, employment in such places as hotels and restaurants mainly serving males is not considered appropriate for women under existing patriarchal norms; private patriarchy has its imprint on the labour market. Consequently, jobs in these sub-sectors are mostly filled with men.

Community, social and personal services, which together represent more than a half of all women employed in the services sector, grew to a lesser extent. This can be associated with the demands from international finance organisations to decrease public expenditures, including the sectors of health and education, consisting of the major areas of qualified work for women. On the other hand, as the share of elderly in the total population gradually increases and as women in professional occupations face difficulty in performing their expected roles in sick and elderly care, demand for people to take up such work is increasing. Given the lack of availability of public services in the fields of child, health and elderly care, the market comes to the fore and the number of profit seeking firms acting as intermediaries in finding caregivers is rapidly increasing. Although there is no available data concerning the increase in the number of women employed in care services, it is safe to say that there is an increase. Domestic and care work is an important employment area for unskilled women migrating from rural to urban areas and finding jobs only in domestic services. Due to its informal character, this work is invisible and precarious (Kalaycıoğlu and Rittersberger-Tılıç 2001). A factor which contributes to this 'invisibility' is the existence of irregular migrant women working in this sub-sector. As a result of expectations stemming from the gender-based division of work and the patriarchal family structure, even women from low income families who work in domestic services can rarely consider working as a live in caretaker in others' homes.

Consequently, demand for such services is met mostly by migrant women from the countries of the former Eastern Bloc and Turkic republics (Kaska 2009). In this form of employment, which is entirely informal and based on the 'invisible' labour of migrant women, service providers are without any protection at all and they can rarely show up in the public without the fear of being deported if spotted.

In short, Turkey, with a rapidly increasing working age population, can be considered a developing country with a limited industrialisation process generating insufficient employment. 'Growth without employment' actually means women's inability to join the labour market as a gendered institution in Elson's term (1999) giving priority to men. Although the services sector acts as the most important area of non-agricultural employment for women, it is far from compensating for the reduction in agricultural employment. The low level of demand for female labour lies behind the decreasing female labour force participation rates in Turkey.

Private and Public Patriarchy Affecting the Supply of Female Labour Force

Private patriarchy in the household and public patriarchy at the societal level determine gender relations in Turkey. The impact of private and public patriarchy on female labour force participation shows variations at the intersection of class, religious belief, and ethnicity. Private patriarchy based on the gender division of labour prescribes women domestic chores and care work and men the livelihood of the family. Control of female labour determines if women can participate in the labour market, when, and under what conditions. Although there are important differences among various socio-economic classes in the attitude toward female employment, women's out-of-home work for pay is accepted by tradition-led, religious sections of society only in cases where men cannot provide for family subsistence. Due to the spatial distinction shaped by Islamic values and the prevalence of single gender socialisation in conservative and traditional circles, working life, besides education, is the area allowing combined socialisation of both sexes. Even men who allow their wives to work have a negative attitude to their working in places with other men and regard their paid employment as something that threatens male authority in the household and hegemony over women. Thus many men either keep their wives from working, unless it becomes absolutely necessary, or approve employment only at home or in places where all other employees are women. These ideas and convictions are also behind girls' limited access to education and training. Women's and young girls' participation in out-of-home income generating activities depends not on their own will but on decisions taken by men.

Why an overwhelming majority of working age women remain out of the labour force can only be understood in their confinement to house-wife status as determined by the decisions of men.[8] According to the find-ings of a survey in Istanbul covering unemployed women, 74 per cent of women graduated from primary school think their husbands' permission is necessary before they can work. As level of education increases, the pro-portion of women who regard their husbands' approval as necessary decreases. However, even among university graduate women, 19 per cent still think that this permission is necessary. Despite the fact that a large majority of women (73 per cent) state they will try to convince their hus-bands, two-thirds of female respondents still say they will forget about working out of the home if they cannot get their husbands' permission (Demirel et al. 1999:211-214). Hence, it is observed that private patri-archy constitutes a decisive factor on the labour force participation of mar-ried women. In urban areas, participation of unmarried women in the labour force is much higher than their married counterparts.[9]

It should also be noted, however, that private and public patriarchy has developed some cracks within it throughout the twentieth century as the Republican project of making women visible in the public sphere created the possibility of access to education and working life for girls and women in Turkey. On the one hand, middle and upper class families in urban areas have encouraged their daughters' education and employment in profes-sional fields. For women holding professional jobs, marriage does not lead to withdrawal from work. In lower classes, on the other hand, lack of opportunities for higher education after primary and secondary enrolment means early marriage and housewife status for many girls. While rural women take part in agricultural production as unpaid family workers irre-spective of their educational status, urban women with lower levels of edu-cation remain out of the labour market. In cases where they have to work for reasons such as men's failure in ensuring family subsistence, women concentrate mainly in low paid jobs requiring no qualification.

Education is a domain where private and public patriarchy intersects. Low levels of education-training and qualification are salient features of the labour supply in Turkey. In 2006, 80 per cent of working age females and 70 per cent of males in the same age group had an educational level lower than high school, including those with no school enrolment at all (TurkStat 2006). Turkey has yet to reach universal coverage even at the primary school level. Hundreds of thousands of children, many of whom are girls, miss even this most fundamental opportunity.[10] Causes for non-enrolment or non-attendance in the first place include school costs (Sahabettinoglu et al. 2002). The fact that this impediment is stated more frequently in the context of the female children in both rural and urban areas reveals that priorities work against girls in lower income group households when it comes to the disposal of scarce resources. Similarly, more frequently stated factors such as 'helping in domestic chores,' 'having to take care of younger siblings,' 'denial of schooling by family,' etc. in the context of girls indicate that a gender based division of labour and a patriarchal mentality prevent girls, starting from early childhood, from equally benefiting from the social opportunities that education may bring. Low level of education of women is effective in keeping their labour supply limited. While men join the labour force countrywide irrespective of their educational status, women with low levels of education can only have limited participation and reach similar levels with men only at higher levels of education. Due to the coercive neoliberal policies in downsizing public expenditures in Turkey, the State cannot make adequate investments in education. Besides deficiency in expenditures for education, lack of comprehensive policies to overcome the gender gap in education can be interpreted as an expression of public patriarchy.

Another expression of public patriarchy is the insufficiency or, more appropriately, total absence of public services and policies aiming to mitigate the care burden of women and promote an equitable share of care work. Absence of such public services means, especially for women in low-qualification and low-paid jobs, returning home for child care with the exception of those who can solve this problem with the help of female family elders or relatives, since it is virtually impossible for them to pay for high cost private services. In Turkey, three-fourths of working urban women with children younger than six years of age try to solve the problem of child care at home individually or with the help of family elders and other family members. While eight per cent of working women pay for private child care services, 10 per cent of women make use of institutional services. Those who can benefit from private or institutional services are the highly educated, urban women that can afford the prices (HUIPS 2008:194-5). Likewise, both the number and capacity of existing service facilities for sick and elderly care are extremely low and this situation poses serious difficulty for working women leaving them with the alternative of either withdrawing from working life or, if they are in well paid professional jobs, hiring migrant female labourers.[11] The existence of a rather wide female population in urban areas who want to work without looking for jobs indicates that they may shift from passive to active job seeking, and a significant increase in female labour supply will take place if care services expand, especially through local governments.

Government Policies and Some Concluding Remarks

Differing from many other developing countries, the process of industrialisation and development in Turkey provided relatively few employment opportunities, and female employment in particular remained at rather low levels. As the demand for female labour has not reached a level sufficient to challenge the patriarchal control on the supply of female labour, the transformation of gender relations toward equality takes place at a modest level. Although gender based division of labour is a distinctive feature of all classes in society, class origin acts as the determining factor in terms of access to education and paid employment opportunities which enable women's participation in the public sphere. Women from low income families with low level of education have the least chance of joining the labour market. Governmental agencies, employers' and workers' organizations, as well as other professional organizations, have consensus that this situation poses serious handicaps for democracy and social progress. Women's organizations, too, have been drawing attention to this problem, struggling for equal rights and asking for concrete steps to be taken (KEIG 2007).

Turkey has acceded to the UN Convention on the Elimination of All Forms of Discrimination against Women (CEDAW), many ILO Conventions on gender equality, and many other arrangements in the context of the EU acquis targeting gender equality as required for the status of a democratic and social state under the rule of law. Official documents including development plans and annual plans and programs point to the necessity of measures geared to enhance women's participation in the labour force and employment. Can the gender equality rhetoric and some implementations in this direction be evaluated as signs of diminishing public patriarchy?

Governments so far taking office in Turkey have opted for the continuation of the division of labour within the framework of the patriarchal family structure whereby men undertake family subsistence while women are occupied with household chores and care. It can be interpreted as the conformity of public patriarchy with private patriarchy. The last development plan prepared by the present government for the period 2007–2013 includes two packages of measures under the pressure to increase female labour force participation rates, namely the promotion of flexible forms of employment and encouraging women to these forms; as well, supporting female entrepreneurship can be evaluated within the context of this conformity.

Promotion of flexible employment models for women, including part-time or temporary work, means supporting the types of female employment which do not interfere with household obligations. The same holds true for encouraging female entrepreneurship.

> The encouragement of women to own account work is seen as a way of avoiding the task of creating decently paid jobs for women in both the public and private sector and ensuring a balanced distribution of employment with regard to gender. Own account working is only a form of employment, and in present day Turkey it is one of the forms that is accorded the least protection, remuneration and stability. Own account working may doubtlessly be supported when there is failure in creating new jobs in industry and services, but the task of enhancing female employment can by no means be limited to it (Toksöz 2007:52).

When the employment policies determining the demand for female labour offer growing possibilities of recruitment for women under favourable conditions we can expect women to become permanent participants of labour markets through an empowering dimension. However the development trajectory of Turkey within the framework of neoliberal policies where the potential for the generation of decent employment is very weak, only a limited number of women join the labour market and mostly under precarious conditions. So we can speak of an articulation of capitalist mode of production with neoliberal economic policies and private and public patriarchy restricting women's access to labour markets and remunerative activities. The state, represented by governments adopting neoliberal policies continues to be the main actor in terms of public patriarchy in that the measures it takes reinforce forms of vulnerable employment for women. Unless macroeconomic policies in Turkey are redesigned to combat unemployment, poverty, regional development disparities and especially the problem of employment without social protection, and unless these policies target gender equality in education-training, employment and care responsibilities, there is no way to prevent the exclusion of women from the labour market. Reaching the goal of gender equality, in turn, requires a concerted political will ready to take special measures to support women in cooperation with women's organisations.

5

GENDER ASPECTS OF INCOME DISTRIBUTION AND POVERTY IN TURKEY

Meltem Dayıoğlu and Cem Başlevent

• Despite considerable improvements during the past decade, income distribution is still very unequal in Turkey with the Gini coefficient estimated at 0.41 in 2007 (TurkStat, 2009). Expressed differently, while individuals in the bottom 20 per cent received 5.8 per cent of the total income, those in the top 20 per cent received 48.4, which is almost 2.5 times their population share. In the face of such high income inequality, the incidence of poverty is expected to be high as well. Indeed, most recent estimates from the Statistical Institute of Turkey, TurkStat, put relative poverty (at half the median income) at 18 per cent.

An interesting question in the context of income inequality and poverty is whether notable gender differences exist. There are reasons to believe that women are concentrated at the lower end of income distribution in Turkey, and that distribution is worse among women than men. The significantly lower labour market participation of women, their lower labour market earnings and more heterogeneous skills compared to men are among the key predictors of their likely positions in the income distribution. Another contributing factor is the concentration of wealth mainly in the hands of men. Of course, lower incomes and worse income distribution do not necessarily mean a lower standard of living and higher poverty among women if income is shared equitably within households. Based on household consumption expenditures, TurkStat estimates the incidence of (absolute) poverty to be only slightly higher among women (at 21 per cent in 2006) than men (at 20 per cent). However, this finding is likely to be an artifact of the methodology used to arrive at individual consumption expenditures. In the absence of information on personal consumption expenditures, each individual in the household is assigned equal consumption based on total household expenditures corrected for household size and composition. Since neither single parenthood nor female headship, which are likely to pose additional poverty risks to women, are common household structures in Turkey, female poverty measured using TurkStat's methodology cannot deviate from household poverty.

In this paper, we work with micro data drawn from the 2008 round of the annually conducted Household Budget Survey to draw attention to the greater financial vulnerability of women by demonstrating that (1) women's earnings are lower and more unequal than men's, (2) women receive substantially less non-labour income, and this is more unequally distributed among women than men, and (3) transfers accrue mostly to men. By examining the role of transfers from public sources in determining the position of women in income distribution, we also attempt to understand how far the State is able to redress the problem of the greater financial vulnerability of women. In the subsequent poverty analysis, we uphold the conjecture that women with limited access to the labour market and lower financial resources face a higher poverty risk than men.

The remainder of the chapter is organized as follows. In the next section, we describe the data used and provide basic descriptive statistics on personal incomes. The subsequent section looks at personal income distribution and its components (i.e. earning and non-labour income) to show the position of women in various distributions and identify the income sources from which women do not benefit as much as men. We then take a closer look at women who do not have any income and compare this group to others who have either labour or non-labour income. Before concluding the chapter, we assess the relative well-being of women through a composite measure that takes into account their educational achievement, access to labour market, and income. We argue that, given the nature of household-based data sets, this measure provides a better way of showing the relative poverty risk of women.

Data

The empirical work is based on the 2008 round of the Household Budget Survey (HBS) conducted by the Turkish Statistical Institute (TurkStat). The HBS surveyed 33,287 individuals from 8,549 households nationwide, and collected information on both household consumption expenditures as well as income accruing to individual members of the household. The income data collected include earnings from primary and secondary jobs over the year, as well as non-labour income and transfers from public and private sources. All income figures are net of taxes and contributions. In the present study, we restrict our analysis to individuals of prime working ages, i.e. 25-54 years, who constitute 58.3 per cent of all individuals (57 per cent of women and 59.6 per cent of men) above the age of 15. The lower age cut-off point is chosen so as to exclude children and students[1], while the upper age limit is set at early 50s because of the early retirement tendency in Turkey, which has been partly to do with the generous retirement opportunity available until very recently, especially favoring women.[2]

Table 5.1: Gender differences in the distribution of the sources of personal income (25-54)

	Total income	Wage & salary earnings	Self-employment Earnings	Returns from assets	Retirement benefits	Other transfers
	% Female share among...					
Non-recipients	92.0	70.6	56.2	52.3	51.9	59.4
Recipients	28.3	23.3	17.2	24.8	24.8	24.9
	% Share of recipients among...					
Men	94.6	67.1	27.0	11.7	11.2	41.5
Women	37.5	20.4	5.7	3.7	3.7	13.8
Overall	66.1	43.8	16.4	7.5	7.5	27.7
	% Share of source in total income					
Men	100.0	55.9	30.5	4.1	7.0	2.5
Women	100.0	58.6	12.1	3.4	11.3	14.6
Overall	100.0	56.3	27.6	4.0	7.7	4.5
	Ratio of the average amounts received by males and females					
Including non-recipients	5.16	4.93	13.07	6.25	3.17	0.89
Excluding non-recipients	2.05	1.50	2.74	1.49	1.05	0.30

Note: About 3.5 per cent (6.3 per cent among men, 0.6 per cent among women) of the sample is recorded both as a wage/salary earner and self-employment income recipient as a result of different work statuses for current primary and secondary and/or former jobs.

In Table 5.1 we provide information on the distribution of the different sources of income accruing to women and men aged 25-54 years. Total personal income is divided into five categories; labour market income from wage and salary work[3] and from self-employment,[4] returns from financial and physical assets, retirement benefits, and transfers other than retirement benefits. Annual labour income includes cash and in-kind earnings from primary and secondary jobs held over the year, including any irregular payments due to work performance or jobs assigned. Asset incomes include interest, rent and dividends from real and financial assets. Despite being a flow variable, we also think of this income source as a proxy for wealth. As mentioned above, within the category of transfer incomes, we distinguish between retirement benefits and other transfers. It makes sense to treat retirement benefits separately, not only because they account for a large part of transfer payments, but also because they indicate a regular income flow and reflect labour market activity in the past. The subcategory of 'other transfers' includes social assistance from public sources, unemployment benefits, survivor's benefits, transfers to farmers within the framework of agricultural reform policy, and transfers from individuals and private institutions.

• Perhaps the most striking observation in Table 5.1 is that 62.5 per cent of working age women – as opposed to 5.4 per cent of men – do not have any personal income. This finding stems mainly from the fact that the majority of women in Turkey do not participate in the labour market – only 35.4 per cent do – and when they do participate, a significant proportion (about 30 per cent) works as unpaid family workers. As a result, about 75 per cent of women, as opposed to 12.3 per cent of men, have no earnings. These findings alone imply a greater financial vulnerability of women. Furthermore, the proportion of women receiving income from real and financial assets is quite low as well at 2.8 per cent as compared to 11.7 per cent of men. Due to their lower labour market participation, a smaller proportion of women than men receive retirement benefits. This is despite the fact that they retire earlier than men. Indeed, while 3.7 per cent of women receive retirement benefits, the corresponding figure among men is 11.2 per cent. Women fare worse also in terms of the other transfers category. Only 13.8 per cent receive transfers (other than retirement income, but including survivor benefits) while the corresponding rate among men is 41.5 per cent.

Despite the fact that less than a third of women are gainfully employed, labour market earnings – in particular, wage income – constitute the largest source (70 per cent) of income for women. Returns from assets account for 3.4 per cent while retirement and other transfers constitute 11.3 and 14.6 per cent of their personal income, respectively. Although a much smaller proportion of women receive transfer incomes other than retirement benefits, they constitute a larger share of women's total income. This has to do with the fact that women's total income is considerably lower than men's, but the amount received in transfers is higher for women. While, on average, men's personal income is twice that of women, the amount they receive in transfers (other than retirement benefits) is only 30 per cent of women's income from this source.

Figure 5.1: Share of females in income deciles (among recipients only)

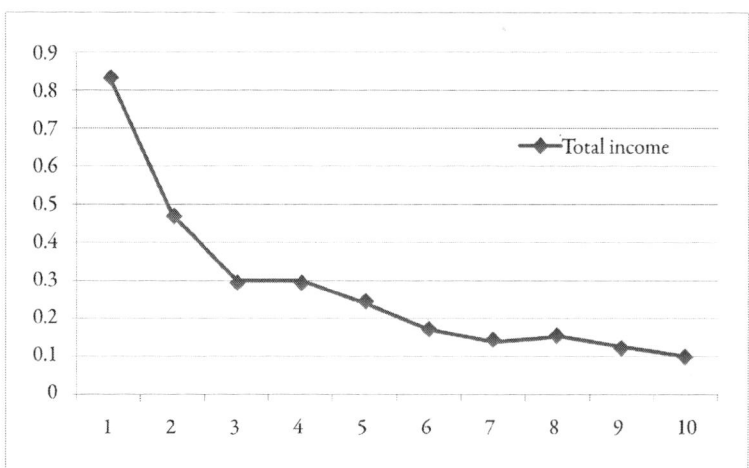

The consequence of the considerably lower incomes of women is their heavy representation at the bottom of the income distribution. Figure 5.1 shows that women constitute over 80 per cent of the lowest income decile, defined according to total annual personal incomes. Their share falls almost monotonically as personal income increases, declining to a mere 10 per cent among the top group of income recipients. In the next section, we take a closer look at the different sources of income accruing to women and the distribution among the recipients of those sources.

Income Inequality
Inequality in personal earnings
As noted earlier, a sizeable proportion of working age women (25-54 years) do not enter the labour market. In this section, we focus on the earnings of those few who do and their position in the earnings distribution vis-à-vis men.

• On average, women's annual earnings are about 55 per cent of men's earnings. Furthermore, women at the bottom of the earnings distribution suffer from significantly lower earnings vis-à-vis men (See Figure 5.2).[5] For instance, while at the bottom 25 per cent, women's earnings are less than 20 per cent of men's earnings, the female-male earnings ratio increases to over 80 per cent in the 90th percentile (Figure 5.2). As earnings increase, the gender earnings gap tends to improve, though the real boost comes only beyond the 25th percentile. Notwithstanding the general conclusion that higher earning women generally fare better, those at the very top (highest 10 per cent) experience wider gaps between themselves and their male counterparts. At the 99th percentile, the earnings of women are less than 60 per cent of men's earnings.

Figure 5.2: Female - male earnings ratio evaluated at various points of the respective distributions in 2008

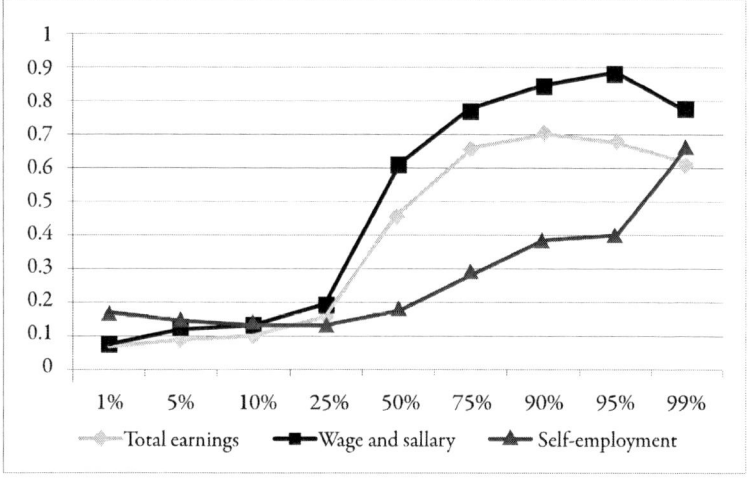

The gender earnings gap also shows variations by employment status. While wage/salary incomes of men, on average, are 1.5 times that of women, the corresponding income ratio for the self-employed is 2.7 (see Table 5.1). Figure 2 shows that wage/salary earners experience a lower gender earnings gap not only on average, but throughout the earnings distribution as well, except at the very bottom. Owing to their high share among the gainfully employed, the gender earnings gap for wage-earners follows a similar pattern as described above for the total of the gainfully employed women; the female-male earnings ratio improves gradually as earnings increase, the rate of improvement picks up beyond the 25th percentile, reaching its highest value in the 95th percentile at 85 per cent and declines thereon. In the case of the self-employed, the female-male earnings ratio actually declines until the 25th percentile, improves beyond that point and achieves its highest value of 60 per cent in the top 1 per cent. The rather significant improvement in the female-male earnings ratio observed among the self-employed at top end of the distribution is not enough, however, to prevent the overall gender earnings gap from increasing from the 90th percentile onwards. This is due to two reasons: (1) The self-employed women with top earnings (placed in the 10th percentile of their distribution) constitute only 4.4 per cent of gainfully employed women; and (2) the earnings of self-employed men at the top end of the distribution are distinctly higher than that of female wage earners similarly positioned in the earnings distribution. Self-employed men at the 95th (50th) percentile earn 2.3 (1.6) times higher than similarly placed female wage-earners.

A whole host of factors might be responsible for the observed gender earnings gap. For instance, women, on average, work fewer hours over the week and fewer weeks over the year. Among the gainfully employed (excluding unpaid family workers), weekly hours of work between men and women differ by 12 hours and the duration of employment over the year by three weeks. However, it is not clear whether the chosen work hours represent the actual preferences of women. Given the traditional division of labour, where much of unpaid household services (i.e. household chores) are regarded as 'women's work' and are carried out by women, it is not hard to imagine that hours of work outside of the household will in part be determined by the workload at home.[6] Besides the supply side factors, demand side factors might also be at play in determining both the hours as well as the amount of remuneration. Indeed, empirical evidence shows that differences in years of education and experience and occupation held to explain only a small part of the wage gap (See, for instance, Kasnakoğlu and Dayıoğlu 1997; Ercan and Tunalı 1998; Tansel 1994, 1999; Dayıoğlu and Tunalı 2003; Kara 2006; Ilkkaracan and Selim 2007). It should also be mentioned that although women are less educated in general, those entering wage employment are, on average, more educated than their male counterparts. Lower incomes of self-employed women,[7] on the other hand, possibly also reflect their lower use of capital, lesser opportunities to employ unpaid family workers, as well as less access to marketing and finance opportunities. While the HBS data set does not include any measure of capital, it does report the size of the establishment run by the respondent, which reveals a heavier concentration of women in micro-enterprises (i.e. establishments with less than 10 employees). Although the proportion of men heading larger businesses (with more than 25 employees) is also quite low (1.5 per cent of the self-employed), it is, nonetheless, revealing that there are no self-employed women in this category, indicating that it is too rare an event to be captured by household surveys. However, there is also evidence that part of the earnings gap might have to do with productivity differences. Examining wage earners and self-employed women, Tunali and Baslevent (2001) conclude that in Turkey, wage labour attracts the best workers. Indeed, self-employed women are, on average, less educated than wage-earner women and self-employed men (see Table 5.2).

Figure 5.3: Share of females in earnings deciles (among recipients only)

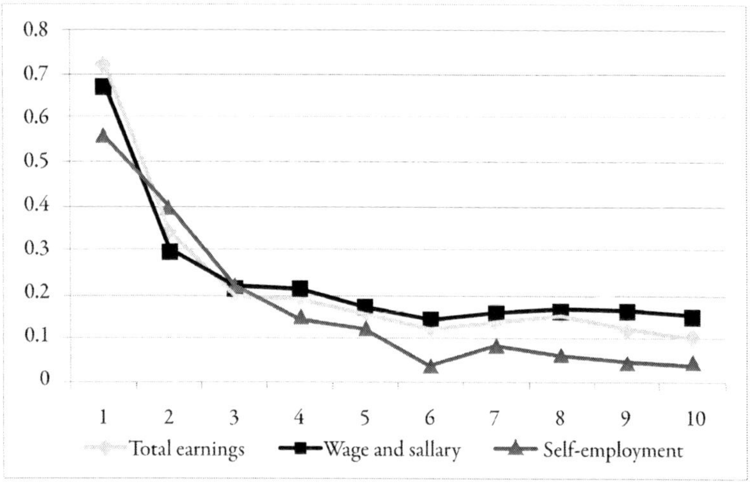

Figure 5.3, which shows the shares of women in various earnings per-centiles, makes it more apparent as to where women stand in terms of the earnings distribution.[8] Given our earlier findings, it is perhaps not surpris-ing that gainfully employed women are over-represented in the lower ranks of the earnings distribution. However, the finding that women con-stitute 72 per cent of those in the lowest earnings decile is shocking, espe-cially given that women constitute only 22.4 per cent of the gainfully employed workforce. As earnings increase, the share of women in each decile decreases, attaining a value of 10.3 per cent in the top decile. When the position of gainfully employed women is analyzed by employment sta-tus, women's over-representation continues in the bottom deciles for both

the wage/salary earners and the self-employed, attaining values of 67 per cent for the former and 56.2 per cent for the latter. In the case of wage/salary employment, the share of women falls rapidly as earnings increase, especially from the bottom to the second decile and stabilizes around 15 per cent in the upper half of the distribution. In the case of the self-employed, the decline continues until the 70th percentile, reaching values as low as 5 per cent in the top three deciles.

Table 5.2: Inequality in earnings by employment status and sex in 2008

	Men		
	Total Labour market earnings	Wag and salary income	Self-employment income
Share of recipients (%)	87.7	67.1	27.0
Gini coefficient (among recipients)	0.42	0.37	0.56
Mean years of schooling	8.2	8.4	7.5
	Women		
	Total Labour market earnings	Wag and salary income	Self-employment income
Share of recipients (%)	25.5	20.4	5.7
Gini coefficient (among recipients)	0.57	0.54	0.70
Mean years of schooling	8.1	8.7	5.7

Note: The total share of recipients may surpass the sum of wage/salary and self-employment income recipients since individuals may derive income from both sources.

The finding that the gender earnings gap varies by level of earnings and employment status, points to the presence of a rather diverse workforce. In fact, a simple distributional analysis of male and female earnings reveals a

higher inequality among the latter: the Gini coefficient is estimated at
0.42 among men, but 0.57 among women (See Table 5.2). The distributions of the components of labour earnings, wage/salary and self-employment income, are also found to be considerably more unequal among
women. While the Gini coefficient for wage/salary income is estimated at
0.54 for women, the corresponding figure for men is 0.37. In the case of
self-employment income, the Gini estimates are 0.56 and 0.70, respectively. Another indication of the more diverse nature of the women's workforce is the gap in the mean years of schooling between wage/salary earners and the self-employed. While in the case of men, there is less than one
year of difference, in the case of women, this figure rises to three years.

**Figure 5.4: Share of females in non-labour income deciles (among
recipients only)**

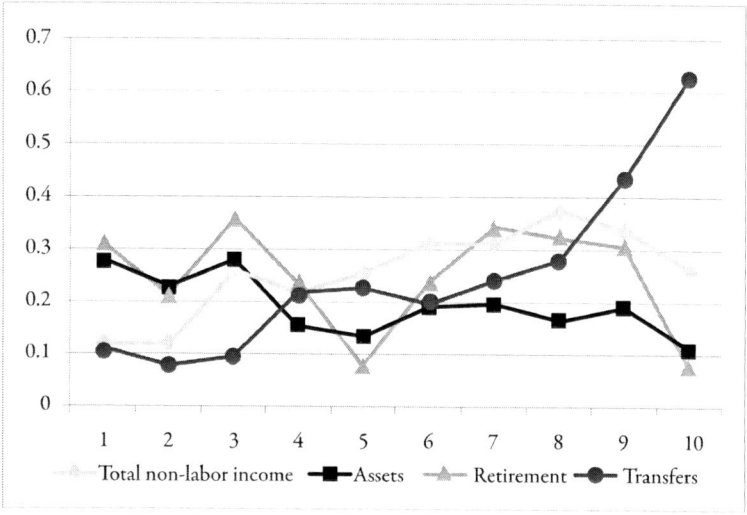

These findings not only point to the disadvantaged position of women in
terms of labour market access and earnings but also draw attention to the
more vulnerable position of women at the lower end of the earnings distribution, who not only fare considerably worse than their male counterparts but also as compared to their female counterparts higher up in the
earnings distribution.

Inequality in non-labour income
In this subsection, we repeat the exercises of the previous section using non-

labour income and its components. The proportion of women receiving non-labour income is limited to 23.5 per cent, as opposed to 51.6 per cent of men (see Table 5.3). Put differently, women constitute only 25.5 percent of non-labour income recipients. When the components of non-labour income are analyzed separately, the share of women among asset income recipients drops to 19.1 per cent, but increases to nearly 25 per cent for retirement benefit and other transfer recipients (see Table 5.1).

Unlike their heavy representation in the lower levels of the earnings distribution, women's share among non-labour income recipients tends to increase with income. For instance, while women constitute about 12 per cent of non-labour income recipients in the bottom 20 per cent, their share reaches 37 per cent in the 8th decile. Although women's share falls in the top two deciles, it, nevertheless, remains above 25 per cent.

Figure 5.5: Female - male income ratio evaluated at various points of the respective distributions (Total and transfers measured on the right axis)

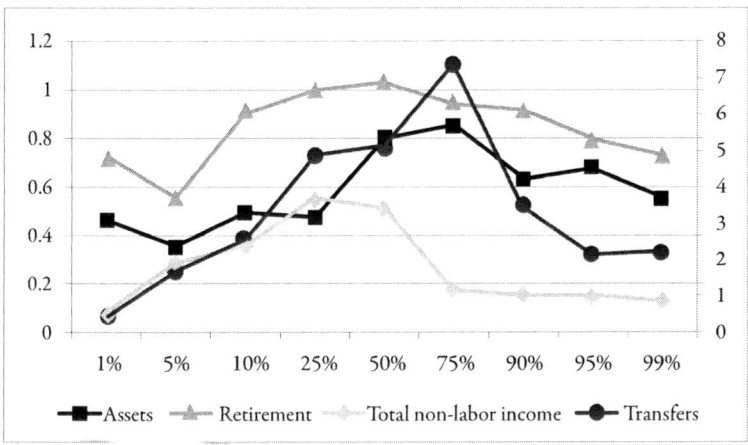

The female share of recipients not only shows variations in the level of non-labour income, but also amongst its components. The female share among the recipients of retirement income – the biggest component of non-labour income – follows an M-shaped profile, attaining a peak at both the 3rd and 7th deciles. Even at the peak though, women's share does not surpass 35 per cent. The share of women among asset income recipients tends to decline with income. While in the bottom 30 per cent of asset income recipients, the share of women fluctuates around 20-30 per cent, in upper deciles the share of women varies between 10 to 20 per cent, attaining its lowest value among those at the top decile. This is a surprising finding, which goes to show that the top asset income recipients are predominantly male. The share of women among transfer recipients, on the other hand, increases with income. While in the bottom three deciles, the share of women recipients is less than 10 per cent, this figure increases to 62 per cent in the top decile. The increase is mainly to do with survivor benefits, discussed more fully below, and their relatively high average values among transfer income recipients.

Although a smaller proportion of women receive non-labour income, the amount they receive is higher, on average, than men. In 2008, the average annual non-labour income received by women was 20 per cent more than the average amount received by men. This result is mainly driven by transfers, which are, on average, 3.3 times higher than those received by men. Since retirement benefits have been treated as a separate category, transfer incomes do not include retirement benefits but do include survivor benefits, which accrue primarily to women. Unmarried women, irrespective of age, for instance, can receive pensions from their deceased parents, while widowed women (with some exceptions) can receive their husband's, as well as pensions through their deceased parents. Having labour income or retirement benefits due to own contributions does not preclude the receipt of survivor benefits.[9] Technically, widowed men can claim survivor benefits as well, though this occurs rarely given the longer life expectancy of women and the fact that very few women participate in the labour market. Unmarried adult men, irrespective of employment status, are not entitled to receive survivor benefits.[10] However, the rather generous social security clauses for women do not mean that all unmarried or widowed women with deceased parents or husbands receive survivor benefits. The large informal economy in Turkey means that a sizeable proportion of men and women work without any social security coverage, and therefore, their survivors cannot claim benefits. Indeed, only 3 per cent of women and 0.2 per cent of men are estimated to receive survivor benefits. The gender gap is a reflection of the 'protective' social security legislation towards women.

Figure 5.5 shows female-male non-labour income ratios by subcategory. The gender gap in asset incomes and retirement benefits are generally in favor of men in all parts of the distribution, though the gap is smaller in the middle of the distribution than at either end. It is also interesting to note that the gender gaps reported for asset incomes and retirement benefits are much narrower than the gaps reported for earnings. The gender gap in transfer incomes, on the other hand, is in favor of women in all parts of the distribution except the bottom 1 per cent. The gap that is in favor of women is highest at the 75th percentile, where transfers accruing to women are 7.3 times higher than those accruing to men. The inverted U-shaped profile of female-male income ratio in transfers must have to do with the lesser importance of survivor benefits in the bottom and top parts of the distribution. Indeed, at the bottom 20 per cent of the distribution of transfers, the proportion of women claiming survivor benefits is limited to 0.3 per cent. At the top 20 per cent, on the other hand, 48.3 per cent of women claim survivor benefits. Despite the fact that the proportion of women claiming survivor benefits increases with transfer income, the female-male ratio in the top 10 per cent declines as a result of faster increases in other transfers accruing to men. Finally, the female-male income ratio for the total of non-labour income also follows an inverted U-shaped pattern, with the ratio increasing first, reaching a peak value of 3.6 at the 25th percentile and declining thereon. From the 75th percentile onwards, non-labour income accruing to men and women are near parity.

Table 5.3: Inequality in non-labour income by type of income and sex

	Men			
	Total non-labour income	Assets	Retirement	Other transfers
Share of recipients (%)	53.7	11.7	11.2	41.5
Gini coefficient (among recipients)	0.69	0.59	0.19	0.75
	Women			
	Total non-labour income	Assets	Retirement	Other transfers
Share of recipients (%)	18.5	2.8	3.7	13.8
Gini coefficient (among recipients)	0.59	0.57	0.19	0.64

We end this section by quantifying the degree of inequality among the recipients of non-labour income, which is summarized in Table 5.3. In line with previous empirical work on income distribution, we find that non-labour income in Turkey is more unequally distributed than labour income. Our calculations also show higher inequality among men than women, which is contrary to our results on earnings. The main reason for

this outcome lies in the distribution of transfers. Although the Gini coefficients for asset incomes and retirement benefits are quite similar
between the two groups, they diverge for transfers, for which the Gini
coefficients are estimated at 0.75 for men and 0.64 for women.

Household incomes of women with and without personal incomes

We have so far focused on personal incomes with the idea that what determines the fallback position of women is their personal income, i.e. what
they can take away with them should they leave the household.[11] However,
as noted earlier, 62.5 per cent of women do not have any income. To provide an indication of the living standards of these women (considering the
drawbacks identified earlier) as well as to paint a more complete picture for
others, we now turn to women's household incomes.[12] For the purposes of
this section, we group women into three categories: women with no personal income, women with non-labour income only and women with
earnings, some of whom may also have non-labour income. While those
with no personal income make up the majority, the latter two categories
constitute 12.1 and 25.4 per cent of women, respectively.

**Figure 5.6: Cumulative distributions of household income by income
status**

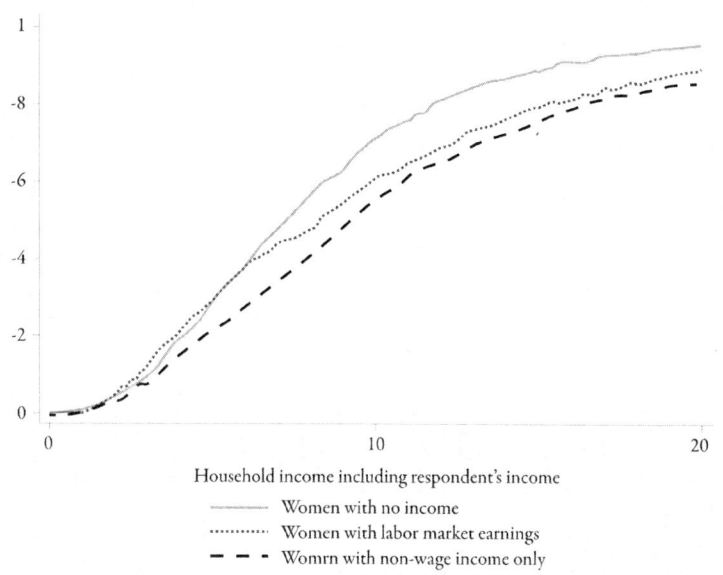

Household income including respondent's income

——— Women with no income

·············· Women with labor market earnings

– – – Women with non-wage income only

Figure 5.6 shows the empirical cumulative distributions of equivalent household incomes for women belonging to the three categories identified above. Women without any personal income clearly fare worse than women with labour market earnings; at any income level, the proportion of women receiving this income or something less is higher among women with no personal income as opposed to women with personal earnings. To given an example, while 28.5 per cent of women with no personal income have equivalent household incomes below TL 5,000, the figure for women with labour market earnings is much lower at 21.4 per cent. The same general result would follow regardless of the income level chosen for comparison purposes. In fact, the distribution of the equivalent household incomes of women with earnings dominates the incomes of those without any personal income in the first order, i.e. the cumulative distribution function of the former takes on smaller values at all income levels. One implication of this finding is with regard to poverty: regardless of the choice of the poverty line, there will always be a larger proportion of women without any personal income who will be classified as poor.[13] In terms of averages, the equivalent household income of women with labour market earnings is 37 per cent higher than the household incomes of those without any personal income.

When we turn to the comparison of women with no personal income with those with non-labour income only, we obtain mixed results. At very low income levels (up to around an equivalent household income of TL 5,100), women without any personal income fare better than women with non-labour income only. However, at higher income levels, we again observe that women without any personal income fare worse than other women. The comparison of average incomes of the two groups reveals a higher income for the latter. The gap is in the order of 20 per cent. However, as is apparent from Figure 5.6, the gap is much larger at higher income levels.

Figure 5.7 shows the distribution of women by household income more explicitly. Since the majority of women (62.5 per cent) do not have any income, they naturally have a clear dominance in all income groups. However, what is interesting to note is the tendency for the share of women with no income to decline with household income. While, in the bottom decile the share of such women is on the order of 64 per cent, this figure drops to 41 per cent in the top decile. The share of women with labour market earnings, on the other hand, increases with household income. While they constitute about 21 per cent of all women in the bottom decile (which is lower than their average share of 25.5 per cent), their share increases to over 40 per cent in the top decile. The share of women with non-labour income decreases gradually until about the fifth decile, only to increase again reaching a peak of 17 per cent in the top decile. If we look at the lowest two deciles, we note that women with no income and women with non-labour income only are over-represented (in comparison to their average shares), whereas women with labour market earnings are under-represented.

Figure 5.7: Distribution of three groups of women by household income

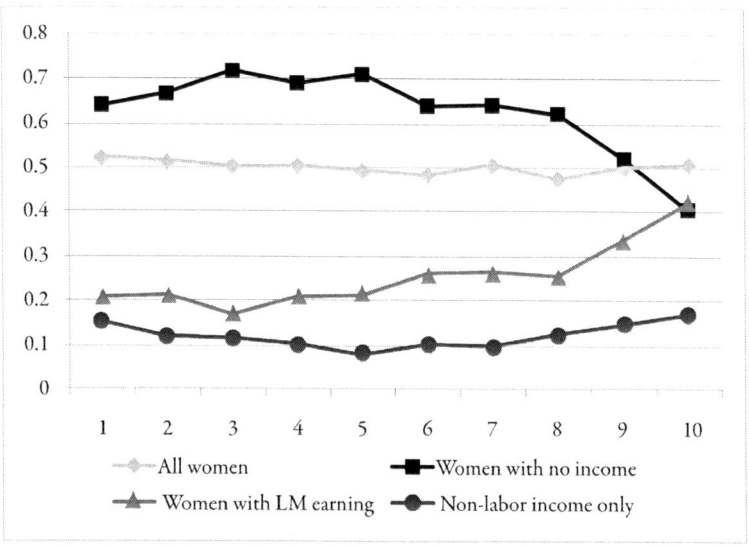

Another noteworthy point is the rather unequal distribution of (equivalent) household incomes for women belonging to the three categories. This is evidenced by the shapes of the cumulative distribution functions given in Figure 5.6. In comparison to women with no personal income, household incomes of women with labour market earnings and those with non-labour income only are found to be less equally distributed. While the Gini coefficient for women with no personal income is computed as 0.361, it is found to be 0.404 and 0.403 for the latter two groups, respectively. The rather unequally distributed earnings and non-labour income among women, illustrated in the previous section, no doubt contribute to the inequality in household incomes as well.

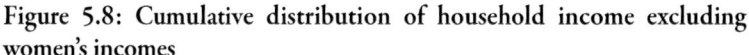

Figure 5.8: Cumulative distribution of household income excluding women's incomes

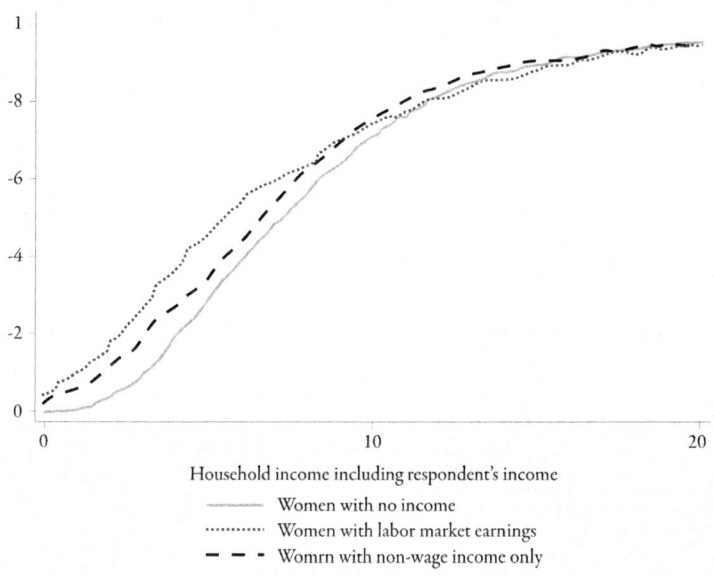

Household income including respondent's income

——— Women with no income
············ Women with labor market earnings
— — - Womrn with non-wage income only

Figure 5.8, on the other hand, shows how the cumulative distributions of household incomes of women change when all of the respondent's income is excluded from the household income figure. The finding of this exercise is that the position of women with non-labour personal income only and that of women with labour market earnings deteriorates vis-à-vis women with no personal income. The extent of the fall is especially noteworthy. The household incomes of such women drop so drastically that at lower household income levels, both groups fare worse than women with no personal income. The fall is especially dramatic for women with labour market earnings, who now have lower household incomes than women with no personal income. In fact, for almost the entire income range (except at the very top), the distribution of household incomes of women with no personal income first order dominates the distribution of income for women with labour market earnings. The high share of women's earnings in total household income (on average 26.7 per cent) must in part be responsible for this dramatic change.[14] This share – despite the gender earnings gap – is consistent with the narrower gender education gap noted earlier, as well as the higher tendency of more educated women to participate in the labour market. Another possible reason for the high share of women's earnings in household income can be assortative mating. If education level is taken as an indicator of such unions, there is evidence in the data that assortative mating takes place; the correlation between husband and wife's schooling (at 0.69) is higher for couples in the labour market than among those where the wife does not work (at 0.46).[15] It is also interesting to note the importance of women's earnings at the lower end of the distribution, where the deterioration of the relative position of women is the greatest when their personal incomes are excluded. This exercise – albeit with broad assumptions – may be interpreted as evidence for the ability of women to improve their positions in the income distribution by participating in the labour market. However, it also gives support to the theory that women who do not participate in the labour market are those with higher reservation wages, which in part are determined by household income.

In the case of women with non-labour personal income only, the deterioration in their position following the deduction of their income from household income is more pronounced as compared to women with labour market earnings at lower income levels. However, their position improves gradually and surpasses that of women with earnings at higher income levels. On the whole, this exercise illustrates the importance of non-labour income for women coming from households with low household incomes. Nevertheless, it is worth noting that non-labour incomes are by no means as effective as labour market earnings in uplifting the position of women in the income distribution.

Poverty

The literature on the gender aspect of poverty is quite vast. However, the debate on whether the incidence of poverty is higher among women than men is far from being resolved. The main reason for this lies in the lack of appropriate data to test this conjecture. The overwhelming majority of surveys around the world collect information on consumption expenditures by taking the household as a unit. In the absence of information on individual consumption or the allocation of total household income or consumption expenditures among household members, it is difficult to distinguish between household and individual poverty unless one is prepared to make assumptions about the latter. Indeed, women are not generally found to be over-represented in consumption-poor households (see Lipton and Ravallion (1995) for evidence from many developing countries). To circumvent the problem of distinguishing between individual and household poverty, while still addressing the gender aspect of the issue, some researchers have compared the incidence of poverty between female and male-headed or maintained households. The empirical findings in this line of work have been mixed as well (see, for instance, Bibi and Chatti, 2010; Buvinic and Gupta, 1997). However, as the findings of the current study have so far demonstrated for the case of Turkey, there is reason to suspect otherwise: fewer women participate in the labour market and those who do earn less than males and have less productive assets (as evidenced by lower asset incomes). There is also evidence from other countries based on nutrition and health surveys that women in poorer households suffer more from poverty-related health problems (Lipton and Ravallion, 1995; Strauss and Thomas, 1995). In the absence of information on personal consumption expenditures, it becomes imperative then to take a different approach in assessing female poverty.

Table 5.4: Composite index values for men and women for average achievement

Dimension	No weights		With weights	
	Index value for men	Index value for women	Index value for men	Index value for women
Education	70.3	61.2	58.9	48.9
Access to labour market	83.0	46.2	81.1	41.2
Income	66.7	50.7	63.3	37.7
Composite index	73.3	52.7	67.8	42.6
Index based on household income only	81.1	80.4	81.1	80.4

In this section, we adopt an approach developed by Amartya Sen and made operational by the UNDP's Human Development Reports and use a composite index to assess women's position. Sen sees human development as an enhancement of freedoms and capabilities – 'the range of things that a person can be and do, such as to be healthy and well nourished, to be knowledgeable, and to participate in community life' (Fukuda-Parr, 2003, p. 303). In the spirit of the Human Development Index[16] (UNDP, 2007) – the main index used in Human Development Reports – and the theme in this article, the composite index we employ takes into account three aspect of men's and women's lives: education (or being knowledgeable), access to the labour market, and income status. The educational achievements of men and women are measured via two indicators: literacy rate and mean years of schooling. Access to the labour market is measured through participation in the labour market, participation in gainful employment and in jobs that offer social security. Finally, the income dimension of the index considers the proportion of women receiving non-labour income, the amount of earnings, non-labour income, and household incomes (per adult equivalent), on average, for income recipients. In the construction of the index, continuous variables needed to be converted into indices taking values between 0 and 100. For mean years of education, we have used the minimum and maximum values observed in the data. For income figures, however, we have employed the values observed for the 1st and 75th percentiles.[17] In arriving at the final index value, all dimensions of the index are given equal weight.

If we were to base the well-being of men and women on their household incomes, women would only fare slightly worse than men – the index would have taken the value of 81.1 for men and 80.4 for women (see Table 5.4). However, when other aspects of men's and women's lives are taken into consideration, i.e. education, access to labour market and personal income, women's average achievement falls considerably behind men's. While the composite index takes the value of 73.3 for men, the corresponding figure for women is 52.7 (See columns 2 and 3 of Table 5.4). The individual components of the composite index show that women lag considerably behind men, primarily with respect to access to the labour market. While in terms of the overall index, women's average achievement is 72 per cent of men, in terms of access to the labour market their average achievement is only 56 per cent of men's. They fare better in terms of educational achievement – their average achievement being 87 per cent of men's – thanks to decades of educational drives to provide basic education for all. In the income dimension, women's average achievement - 76 per cent of men's – is better than their achievement in access to the labour market, possibly because, as discussed earlier, positive sorting occurs at labour market entry.

As noted above, these achievement estimates are based on simple averages that gave each component of the index equal weight. If, on the other hand, the computation of the index is changed such that more weight is given to areas where men and women lag behind, the gender gap in average achievement would increase: women's average achievement would be 63 per cent of men's average achievement.[18] While women's position would deteriorate in all three dimensions of the index, the biggest drop would take place in the income dimension, which is indicative of the rather heterogeneous achievements in this area. Although the choice of appropriate weights to employ – and therefore, the size of the resulting gender gap – is open to debate, it should be clear from our previous discussions as well as the discussion in this section that the choice of weights in obtaining index values would not change the conclusion that women's average achievement is lower than men's, i.e. they are over-represented among the poor.

Conclusion

We began the chapter by asking whether notable gender differences exist in income distribution and poverty in Turkey. Using a representative large household-based budget survey, we have arrived at the conclusion that gender differences are not only real, but that they are also quite sizeable. In particular, we have shown that (1) a significant proportion of women (62.5 per cent) do not receive any personal income, meaning that women constitute over 90 per cent of working age adults with no personal income; (2) women lag considerably behind men in terms of labour market earnings and, as a result, are over-represented at the lower end of the earnings distribution; (3) women's earnings are more unequally distributed compared to men's, illustrating the need to look beyond averages; (4) the majority of non-labour recipients (74.5 per cent) are men; (5) women's representation among asset income recipients is especially low (at 19.1 per cent) and declines with income deciles suggesting a greater control of assets by men; (6) women's representation among retirement income and other transfer recipients is somewhat higher (at about 25 per cent) on average, and increases with income; (7) the distribution of the (adult equivalent) household incomes of women show that gainfully employed women fare better in all parts of the distribution compared to women with no personal income, while women with non-labour income only fare better in higher income brackets; (8) reducing the household income of women by their personal incomes affects the position of gainfully employed women the most, placing them below women with no personal income; and finally, (9) a composite index that measures the achievements of men and women in education, access to the labour market, and income, shows women lagging considerably behind men, especially in their access to the labour market.

As discussed in the text, women's limited access to the labour market is related to several issues ranging from protective legislation, social values, and the large household sector (hence, the high reservation wage) to low labour market earnings. Identifying the low labour market participation of women as a problem, the government of Turkey has recently taken steps to alleviate it. The new employment package that went into effect in May 2008 aims to ease women's entry and integration to the labour market by subsidizing social security contributions of newly hired women. The gradual elimination of protective legislation such as early retirement and the right to receive survivor benefits from multiple sources is expected to increase women's attachment to the labour market as well. Expanding the opportunities of women, however, should not be limited to cost reduction policies at labour market entry but extended beyond it to include income and education policies that increase the rewards for employment. While education inequalities have received the most public attention, the gender pay gap, concentration of wealth in the hands of men, and inequalities in transfers have received the least attention. Future academic work could be instrumental in raising the level of public awareness in relation to these topics.

The needs of women at the lower end of the income distribution require special attention. As discussed in the text, women with no personal income and those with non-labour incomes only constitute the main groups with low household incomes. Based on the relatively better position of women with earnings, the gainful employment of women may be considered a remedy that can raise the position of these women as well. However, the high earnings inequality among women acts as a warning sign that gainful employment alone may not be the answer, especially considering that women in the labour market are positively sorted. Policies that aim to increase female involvement in the labour market need to take into consideration the various demand and supply side factors so that they do not result in greater income inequality.

6

HOUSEWIFISATION OF WOMEN: CONTEXTUALISING GENDERED PATTERNS OF PAID AND UNPAID WORK

Emel Memiş, Umut Öneş and Burça Kızılırmak[1]

Studies have established that across the world, while men's work is highly associated with paid market work, women devote the majority of their work time to unpaid work[2] (Gershuny 2000; Beneria 2003). Gender differences, in allocation of time between paid and unpaid work, not only inform about women's and men's daily experience of time, but also have important implications in terms of the well-being of the society as a whole, including all women, men, children, sick and the elderly (Floro 1995; Elson 2005; Antonopoulos and Hirway 2010; Kizilirmak and Memis 2009). The increased segregation of unpaid work and paid work according to sex in the transition between critical life course phases, i.e. singlehood, marriage, and parenthood, particularly pushes women into social and economic vulnerability (Elson and Cagatay 2000; Elson 2009) as well as time poverty (Bittman and Folbre 2004; Antonopoulos and Memis 2010). Given the importance of the gendered patterns of work time allocation, a large literature has been built up to explain existing differences and how they change over time. While some focus on individual decision-making processes and consider specialisation an efficient outcome of rational choice (Becker 1981), others focus on institutions (Hartmann 1979; Jaggar 1988; Brines 1993; Coltrane 2000) or provide an integrative approach focusing on the linkages between the two domains given that the individual decision-making process cannot be isolated from the complex social context (Bittman et al. 2003; Hook 2010, 2006; Fuwa 2004; Geist 2005).

The data from, which is the first national time use survey, in Turkey reveals that unpaid work comprises more than half of total working time even for employed women in the labour market. Participating in the labour market brings a much higher total workload (total sum of unpaid and paid work time) for women in comparison to both their spouses and other women who are economically 'inactive'. This result highlights one of the underlying reasons behind the low level of labour force participation of women in Turkey. Binding amounts of unpaid work of women shift them away from doing paid work. We argue that neither the supply side arguments nor the demand side arguments introduced to explain gender differences in labour force participation can provide a complete understanding of gender-based inequalities if they focus only on the revealed outcomes in the labour market without taking gender differences in unpaid work time into consideration.

In this study, we aim to examine women's and men's time-use in Turkey specifically focusing on the impacts of employment of women on their time use patterns under current conditions. Evidence we have found points to the housewifisation of women in Turkey observed through transitions between critical phases in the life course, specifically the one between marriage and having children. Our main research questions are: Are there differences between women and men in their time spent on unpaid and paid work? Do these differences vary across households? How does the picture change when the female adult is employed in the market/is a housewife? Does marital status have an impact on the gender division of labour? What is the impact of having children? For our purposes, first, we analyse within and across households differences in mean duration of time spent by women and men on paid and unpaid work. Then we adopt a life course approach[3] to explore patterns of unpaid and paid work defining three critical stages in the lifetime of a household, namely: (a) singlehood, (b) marriage/cohabitation without children, and finally (c) marriage/cohabitation with children.

The gendered patterns of time use obtained in this study help better evaluate the social and economic impacts of any policy change, particularly the policies aiming to reduce poverty and inequality by describing the linkages between the paid and unpaid work sphere of the economy in Turkey. More importantly, these linkages will be important guides in evaluating the impacts of social reforms that aim at gender equality. The vulnerability and work burden of women depend highly on how and if women can split their time freely between paid work, unpaid work and leisure. Any social reform that gives women more opportunities in the labour market will either have no effect or will increase their total work burden if they cannot be flexible with their unpaid work time.

Inequalities in Paid and Unpaid Work and Implications for Policy

One explanation for gender-based differences in work employs rational choice theory, according to which, specialisation in time allocation due to differences in comparative advantages of women and men leads to efficient outcomes when combined with maximising behaviour (Becker 1981). Accordingly, given that men earn higher wages than women in the market, increased traditional specialisation between spouses benefit both of them with a higher level of household income and at the same time a high level of household production. However, despite what rational choice theory predicts as beneficial, we observe increases in women's participation in paid work across the world. In addition, It's been observed that despite increases in women's time in the labour market, employed women still continue to specialise in unpaid work both in advanced countries as well as in the developing world (e.g. Bittman 1999; Addabbo 2003; Baxter 2002; Antonopoulos and Hirway 2010).

Investigations in time-use survey data show that while in most developed countries women presently spend 6 hours per day for unpaid work activities, men spend only about half this time, and average gender gap increases up to five hours of unpaid work per day in some developing countries (Antonopoulos 2007 and 2008; Gauthier et al 2004). When the analysis is narrowed to employed people, women still spend greater amounts of time on unpaid work as presented by the arguments of the second shift or dual work (Hochschild and Machung 1989; Schor 1991). These findings have pointed to a reverse causality between the unequal outcomes in the market and gender inequalities in the household division of labour. Inequality in the household feeds back to the former inequality in the market, a phenomenon called housework penalty (Hersch and Stratton 1997; Bryan and Sevilla-Sanz 2010). It has also been argued that the rational choice approach, at most, can describe the vicious cycle in which women find themselves.

Persistent gender inequalities, particularly in mean duration of unpaid work, whether considered an efficient outcome or not, have motivated many researchers to look for different explanations other than those the rational choice approach provides. An alternative explores and analyses hierarchical institutions and power relations to understand the sources of unequal division of labour first at home and then in the market. A prominent explanation for the unequal gender division of labour is 'patriarchy', which affects gender division both independently and directly, benefiting men by controlling women's labour (Hartmann 1979; Jaggar 1988). Women's employment as described within the 'dependent labour model' is found to be highly associated with patriarchal relations. As a result, women's participation in the labour market cumulates demands on themselves rather than increasing men's unpaid work time (Meissner et al. 1975). Another explanation focuses on relative resources, according to which the individual who has more resources, i.e. earnings, prestige, skill and education, uses these resources to negotiate his/her way out of unpaid work (Brines 1993). Yet, another line of research provides an integrative approach arguing that all individual decisions are embedded in society's social, economic, and institutional structure including social norms, regulations, laws, and also policies (Bittman et al. 2003; Hook 2010, 2006; Fuwa 2004; Geist 2005). Accordingly, any change in national context is considered to have a direct impact on decisions, while indirectly influencing the normative context in which the decision is embedded (Hook 2010).

Specifically in developing countries, given the lack of availability of time use data and existing difficulties in testing empirically to what degree rational choice or structural factors help understand gender-based inequalities in unpaid work, scholars have focused mainly on the analysis of outcomes revealed in the labour market, i.e. differences in paid work patterns and changes in observed patterns of participation in paid work over time. Evidence about transformations in female labour market participation has increased since the 1960s, particularly in developed countries, which supports the well-known U-shaped feminisation curve. Built upon Boserup's early work in the 1970s, the U-curve establishes that the participation of women in paid work declines first when a society shifts from a pre-industrial phase into an industry based economy,[4] and then increases with the advancement of industrialisation. However, while the U-curve provides a good explanation for some countries, it fails to explain why some other countries including Turkey stay at the lower stage, despite similar economic development.

In Turkey, to explain women's low participation in the labour market, many studies focus on the supply side factors, i.e. gender disparities in terms of their educational attainment, skill and training attributes (see Gündüz-Hoşgör and Smith (2008) and Kizilirmak (2008) for a review of some of these studies). Studies that analyse the demand side factors also exist, though are less in number, which brings attention particularly to sectoral and occupational differences in employment. The main focus in these studies has been on employment elasticity of different patterns of economic growth with different sectoral composition. Demand-based studies have also explored whether the underlying reason behind the low participation can be differences among developing countries with respect to the features of industrialisation and differences in export-led strategies which then lead to different outcomes.

Although similar to other developing countries, urbanisation and transition of resources to manufacturing from agriculture have led to a decline in women's participation in Turkey as well; unlike in others, employing an export-led strategy did not have an increasing impact. This is described as the 'Turkish puzzle' in a recent report by the State Planning Organisation and the World Bank (2009). One reason behind this description is the implicit assumption that decisions on participation in paid work includes only the combinations of market work and leisure time. Time spent on unpaid work activities is invisible in this scenario. Even though, in the report women's roles as homemakers is mentioned as a critical factor, the degree of the binding nature of unpaid work time for women's labour has not been explored in Turkey. In fact, studies on other developing countries have shown that unpaid work plays a very critical role in setting the standards of living for the majority of the world population, and that time requirements of unpaid work are restrictive. In addition to gaining access to goods and services from the government and the market, in developing countries especially among poor households, meeting a certain standard of living is only possible through long hours of unpaid work, particularly due to deficits in infrastructure, and meeting those time requirements has been critical (Antonopoulos and Memis 2010). However, as invisible as it is, inequalities with respect to time needs have also been left out of policy discussions, including policies to reduce poverty as well as to promote gender equality.

The importance of the sphere of unpaid work in the economy and how it might affect the outcomes of policies can be found in the research on the effects of economic crisis and of the structural adjustment programs (SAPs), which led to significant cuts in public expenditures, undertaken during the neoliberal era in many developing countries since the 1980s by the World Bank and the IMF and have led to significant cuts in public expenditures. Research has shown that women are the most important bearers of SAPs subsidising governments in many developing countries around the world by being the primary care takers of children, sick and elderly when public provision for services and security is lacking.

There are many studies confirming that the dependence of productive activities on unpaid work has multiplied in many ways[5] due to neoliberal policies. As put by Elson (1993) "the hidden '*equilibrating factor*' has been women's ability to absorb the shocks of stabilisation programs, through more work and 'making do' on limited incomes" (p. 241). As Beneria (1995) emphasises, SAP studies have made clear the extent to which economic policies focuses on the market and the sphere of paid production while ignoring unpaid economic activities and the sphere of reproduction (p. 1845).

One objective of the current study is to provide a stage to evaluate impacts of economic and social policies on the patterns of paid and unpaid work. For this purpose, in this study which uses the first available time use data at the national level, we aim to explore and identify the nature of gender-based inequalities both in paid work time and unpaid work time, which will be useful in understanding the sources of existing inequalities. We limit our discussion here on the identification of the patterns of time use and show how these patterns change through different critical phases in the course of life.

Data and Analysis

The data we use in this study comes from the first and the single national time use survey in Turkey conducted by TurkStat. The survey was carried out in 2006 and provides time use data from 10,893 individuals aged 15 or older, living in 4,345 households.[6] The data was collected from interviews and daily diaries. Time use information is provided for all household members 15 years of age and over. Respondents were asked to record their activities in ten minute intervals for 24 hours for two days of the week, one a weekday and the other a weekend day. Although the differentiation of weekend and weekdays is a good attempt to differentiate working days and days off, this survey does not allow for this kind of analysis as there are individuals who do paid work on weekends. Thus we use whole week averages in this study. The data also provides information on rural and urban areas. In what follows, we report the results for the whole sample. The results for the urban areas are usually similar with the results obtained for the whole sample. Obtained differences in results will be indicated where relevant.[7]

The descriptive statistics of the data by sex are provided in Table 6.1.[8] The average age of both women and men is 37 years, calculated according to median level age ranges.[9] More than 63 per cent of households live in urban areas and average 3.4 children all less than 16 years old. Table 1 indicates that there are major differences in the average characteristics of women and men. The labour market indicators show striking disparities: 24 per cent of women and 70 per cent of men are employed in the market, while 2 per cent of women and 5 per cent of men are unemployed. Taken together, these figures show very low levels for women's labour market participation in Turkey. The table also shows that the majority (59 per cent) of women report their status as a 'homemaker', whereas the percentage of men who report themselves as homemakers is zero. Figures support the traditional gender division of work between men and women, where women take care of the home and the children, and men are the breadwinners.

Table 6.1: Descriptive statistics of the data

	Men	Women
Number of Observations	5,154	5,739
Age	2.83	2.83
HOUSEHOLD		
Urban (%)	63	63
Number of children aged less than 16 years	3.41	3.41
LABOUR MARKET STATUS (%)		
Employed	70	24
Unemployed	5	2
Homemaker	0	59
Student	8	6
Retired	11	3
Economically inactive (elderly/unable to work)	3	5
Other	3	2
SECTOR (%)		
Agriculture	15	13
Manufacturing	16	4
Services	42	9
TYPES OF EMPLOYMENT (%)		
Employed (regular)	35	10
Employed (irregular)	9	2
Unpaid family worker	5	11
Employee	5	0
Self employed	19	3

Sectoral distribution and type of employment show that the labour market is highly segregated by gender. While employed women are still overrepresented in agriculture, the majority of men are employed in the services sector. The highest percentage of employed women work as contributing unpaid family workers (11 per cent), which is followed by the regular employed sub-group (10 per cent), whereas the majority of employed men have regular jobs with the highest percentage at 35 per cent followed by the self employed sub-group (19 per cent).

In order to analyze and describe the gendered pattern of the division of work between women and men, we first limit our sample to single adult and couple households with/without children aged less than 16 years old. We exclude here extended families, families with children over age 15 or dependent adults and families with working children. The results we obtained showed that some young children and even dependent elderly adults spend time doing paid work, housework and/or care work, which can certainly change the characteristic of the division of labour between female and male adult members. These exclusions, therefore, let us discard from our analysis the households within which work burden can be shared with other household members. This reduced our sample size to 11,798 adults (6,160 women and 5,638 men) living in 3,249 households.

We grouped the daily activities based on the following categories:[10]
- Paid work (employment:[11] work and work related activities)
- Unpaid work (housework and maintenance - food preparation, dish washing, cleaning, laundry, ironing, gardening, repairing, shopping etc.- and caring of household members -including childcare, caring for a dependent adult household member etc)
- Other activities: other unpaid work (voluntary work and meetings), personal care (eating, washing and dressing etc), sleep, study-educational activities, leisure (social life and entertainment, sports and outdoor activities, hobbies and computing and mass media), travel (travel and unspecified time use)

1- Paid and unpaid work by employment status and household composition
In the following, we first examine time use patterns by gender, first according to employment status and then by taking into account differences in household composition, i.e. marital status (single, married), the number of income-earning adult members (no-earner, single-earner, dual-earner) and the presence of children in the household (with/without children aged less than 16 years old). Then, we move to household differences, controlling for the selected household characteristics.

Table 6.2 reports mean duration of time devoted to unpaid and paid work activities by women and men. Figures clearly mark major differences in existing time use patterns. First, women who spend on average more than 7 hours for paid and unpaid work in total have a higher burden of work than men who spend less than 6 hours. The percentage distribution of time spent on total work shows differences more clearly, i.e. women spend 87 per cent of their total work time on unpaid work activities while their male counterparts spend 84 per cent of total work time on paid work. Even for the employed women, the unpaid work still comprises more than half of their total work. This ratio is very high when compared to employed men who on average spend only 12 per cent of their working time on unpaid work activities.

Table 6.2: Mean time spent on unpaid and paid work ✓

	Men		Women	
	Employed	Total	Employed	Total
Unpaid Work	0.8	1.0	4.7	6.2
Paid Work	6.1	5.0	3.9	0.9
Total Work	6.9	5.9	8.6	7.1
Unpaid Work (%)	12	16	55	87
Paid Work (%)	88	84	45	13

Note: The figures denote average daily number of hours unless indicated otherwise.

Table 6.3 and Table 6.4 below summarize mean duration of time devoted to different work activities by married couples with and without children respectively. Evidence obtained supports the picture provided by the figures in Table 6.2. In total, women work longer than men and the differences observed are higher when broken down by different household compositions. Figures in Table 6.3 state that, regardless of the number of income earner adult members, the total work burden is not shared equally between women and men. Even in dual-earner families, women spend two and a half more hours working than men: women spend 9.1 hours and men spend 6.8 hours on total work. The gap mainly reflects the difference in duration of unpaid work time. As can be seen in Table 6.3, in dual earner households where both female and male adult members spend quite a high amount of time in paid work (5.3 hours for women and 6.1 hours for men), women spend 3.8 hours on unpaid work, while their male counterparts spend only 0.7 hours. The findings are similar for single-earner and non-earner households except for a slight discrepancy. Note that the difference between women and men in total work time is much higher in non-earner households where neither women nor men do any paid work.

When we look at single-earner households, we see that it is usually the men who work in the market and women are the homemakers. This can be observed from the figures in Table 6.3, as the mean time for unpaid work is higher for women and lower for men compared to no-earner households. However, since the gap between women's and men's mean duration of paid work time is not as high as the gap in their mean duration of unpaid work time, the total work time women spend is still higher than those of men in these families too.

Table 6.3: Mean time spent on unpaid and paid work - married couples without children

		No earner	Single- earner	Dual- earner
Unpaid Work	Men	1.4	0.8	0.7
	Women	5.7	6.2	3.8
Paid Work	Men	0.0	5.5	6.1
	Women	0.0	0.2	5.3
Total Work	Men	1.4	6.3	6.8
	Women	5.7	6.4	9.1

Note: The figures denote average daily number of hours. Data of 151 families with no earner, 183 families with single-earner, and 111 families with dual-earner adult members are used.

Table 6.4: Mean time spent on unpaid and paid work - married couples with children

		No earner	Single- earner	Dual- earner
Unpaid Work	Men	1.5	0.9	1.0
	Women	8.0	7.8	4.9
Paid Work	Men	0.7	6,5	6.6
	Women	0.0	0.0	4.9
Total Work	Men	2.2	7.4	7.6
	Women	8	7.8	9.8

Note: The figures denote average daily number of hours. Data of 63 families with no earner, 813 families with single-earner, and 193 families with dual-earners are used.

It is also interesting to observe that there is only half an hour difference in men's unpaid work time between no-earner and single-earner households; when men become income-earners employed in the market; their unpaid work time declines by half an hour. However, being employed in the mar-

ket marks a significant change in women's time use: women in dual
er households spend three hours less time on unpaid work when compared
to no-earner as well as single-earner households. If there is a time substitution among different activities for men when employed in the market, it
occurs between paid work time and leisure and not unpaid work time.
However, for women, unpaid work time is substituted by paid work time
to a high degree. All these results are very similar to those in Table 6.4.

In summation, the burden of unpaid work falls disproportionately on
women, regardless of employment status or household type. As a natural
result, women on average spent more time on activities described as work
across types of households compared to men. The only exception to this is
single-earner households without children, the majority of which are characterized by a working husband and homemaker wife. This result proves
to be strong evidence for why women are less active in the labour market
and for the role of women undertake at home as providers of welfare for
their families and communities.

2- Paid and unpaid work over the life course phases

In order to examine differences in the time use patterns by marital status
and to bring out more clearly the effects of having children on division of
time between unpaid and paid work, we employ a life course analysis
based on the household labour supply and consumption literature.[12]
However, in contrast with the conventional model, we also consider
unpaid labour, as substitutes for paid work along with leisure.[13] For our
purposes, we define three critical stages in the lifetime of a household, (a)
singlehood, (b) marriage/cohabitation without children, and finally (c)
cohabitation with children, thereby splitting the sample into three mutually exclusive phases.[14]

Here, we limit our sample to individuals who are employed in the market in order to isolate results from the effect of employment status. The
singlehood phase contains singles who have no children and who are
employed in the market. The marriage-without-children phase represents
dual earner families without dependent children. The marriage-with-chil-
dren phase households include dual-earner families having at least one
child aged less than 16 years old living in the household.

Table 6.5 gives information on the mean duration of work time of
women and men within the three life course phases. The information
demonstrates that single women on average, like married ones, spend significantly more time on unpaid work compared to their male counterparts
(2.5 and 1.1 hours respectively).[15] This may reflect traditional values in

which women are responsible for doing the housework and are raised with these values from childhood. Thus, women tend more to do housework than men even when they live alone. Another reason though, for the higher unpaid work time of single women compared to single men might be due to a gender wage gap in the labour market that does not allow women to hire outside help (see Dayıoğlu and Başlevent in this volume). When women earn less in the labour market, they spend less on market substitutes that replace their unpaid work activities like house cleaning etc.

Table 6.5: Comparison of work burden of women and men

Households in:	Men (a)	Women (b)	Difference (a-b)
1.Singlehood Phase			
Paid Work	6.6	5.3	
Unpaid Work	1.1	2.5	***
Total Work	7.6	7.8	
2.Married-without-children Phase			
Paid Work	6.1	5.3	***
Unpaid Work	0.7	3.8	***
Total Work	6.7	9.1	***
3.Married-with-children Phase			
Paid Work	6.6	4.9	***
Unpaid Work	1.0	4.9	***
Total Work	7.7	9.8	***

Note: Data of 46 singlehood phase families, 111 married- without–children phase families, and 193 married- with-children phase are used.
The figures in columns a and b denote average daily number of hours.
*, ** and *** denote statistical significance at the 10 per cent, 5 per cent and 1 per cent level respectively according to the Mann-Whitney test for singles and the paired sample t test for couples.

The pattern of paid work time and total work time is similar for the singlehood phase households and married-without-children phase households: women on average do less paid work and more total work than men. However, while these differences are not statistically significant for singles, they are significant for married people. These results imply that employed single women's total work time is not much different than men's; however, although employed married women work less than their spouses in paid work, they have a higher burden of total work than their spouses have. Unlike the findings of several earlier studies[16] that indicate that men increase their unpaid work time when their wives increase their time in paid work, here we find a negative association.

The comparative effect of marital status and presence of children over the life course is presented in Table 6.6 Figures represent the percentage changes in mean duration time spent on paid and unpaid work observed when households move from one life course phase to the next. The comparison of households in the first and second phases illustrates how marriage affects the time use of women and men. Women spend longer time on unpaid work when they get married while spending almost the same amount of time on paid work as when they are single. The increase in time devoted to unpaid work is 49 per cent. On the contrary, the time devoted both to paid and unpaid work by men declines, even though their spouses are employed in the market. The change is -8 per cent in paid work and -38 per cent in unpaid work time, thus 12 per cent in total work time. The Mann-Whitney tests indicate that the changes in paid work are not significant, while those in unpaid work are significant at the level of 1 per cent for both women and men. The changes in total work time are significant at only 10 per cent for both women and men.

Table 6.6: Comparison of singles, couples without children, and couples with children (% change)

Households in:	Men	Women
Married-without-children Phase versus Singlehood Phase		
Paid Work	-8	0
Unpaid Work	-38***	49***
Total Work	-12*	16*
Married-with-children Phase versus Married-without-children Phase		
Paid Work	9*	9*
Unpaid Work	59***	59***
Total Work	14***	14***

Note: Data of 46 singlehood phase families, 111 married- without–children phase families, and 193 married- with-children phase are used.

*, ** and *** denote statistical significance at 10 per cent, 5 per cent and 1 per cent level respectively according to Mann-Whitney tests

When we compare households in the married-with-children phase with those in the second phase, we again see an increase in the unequal division of unpaid work. Women in the third phase of their life course devote 31 per cent more time on unpaid work than those in the married-without-children phase. For men, this increase is higher at 59 per cent. In total, while women's total work time increases by 8 per cent, men's mean duration of total work time increases by 14 per cent. This analysis indicates that men agree to share the work at home only when a child comes into the picture.[17]

The increase in men's unpaid work time is a phenomenon observed mostly in the comparison of families without children and families with only one young child. As Table 6.7 illustrates, men stop sharing the burden at home when the number of children increases: the increase does not affect men's time use significantly. Women on the other hand are affected significantly by the increase in number of children: their paid work time decreases and unpaid work time increases when the number of children increases from one to two. When the number of children increases from two to three or more, women's total work time rises significantly.

Table 6.7: Married-with-children phase households over the life course by the number of children (% change)

	Men	Women
1. Couples with 2 children versus with 1 child		
Paid Work	-3	-21**
Unpaid Work	-5	24***
Total Work	-3	-1
2. Couples with 3 or more children versus with 2 children		
Paid Work	10	0
Unpaid Work	-15	10
Total Work	6	5***

Note: Data of married couples in a double-earner family with children under age 16 (79 couples with 1 child, 80 couples with 2 children and 34 couples with 3 or more children) are compared.
*, ** and *** denote statistical significance at 10 per cent, 5 per cent and 1 per cent level respectively according to Mann-Whitney tests

In a nutshell, for employed women, every step in the artificially projected life course is distinguished by a significant increase in both their unpaid and total work burden. In transition from singlehood to cohabitation without children, women on average afford the increased burden by giving up time spent on "other activities" such as leisure, voluntary work and sleep, but not from paid work time. Having children, on the other hand seems to decrease both paid work time and other activities for women. For employed men, cohabitation means less paid, unpaid and total work, while having children reverses this trend. Interestingly, this V shaped pattern results in no significant changes on average in terms of work burden when the beginning (singlehood) and end (parenthood) phases of men's life course are compared.

Conclusions

This study aims to understand the gender differences in allocation of time between paid and unpaid work, teasing out the impact of number of income earners in the household, marital status and having children on gender-based time use inequalities. Evidence found reveals that a traditional gender division of labour still prevails in Turkey: women spend most of their total work time on unpaid work activities while their male counterparts spend most of total work time on paid work. This result is valid for a large range of family types. For example, single women on average, like married ones, spend significantly more time on unpaid work compared to men with similar marital status. We also observe that in married couples, even in dual-earner ones where both female and male adult members spend quite a high amount of time in paid work, women spend a lot more time than their spouses on unpaid work. A general observation is that employed women on average still spend more than half of their total work time on unpaid work.

Another significant result we obtained shows that women on average have a higher burden of total work then men. This is true for all women, singles and married living with or without children, and ones in dual-earner, single-earner and no-earner families. The amount of difference ranges from 12 minutes (for singles) to 4.4 hours (in no-earner families) per day. This is the clear indicator of women's welfare provider role in the family, the main safety net for all individuals in Turkey where the family takes up the role of providing for all where the welfare state is relatively weak and limited in reach.

When examining how being employed in the market affects time spent on unpaid work, results differ significantly by degree between women and men. When men become an income-earner employed in the market, their unpaid work time declines by around half an hour. However, being employed in the market decreases women's time on unpaid by 2 or 3 hours. Although unpaid work time is substituted by paid work time at a high degree for women, this substitution is not enough to decrease their total work time. Two observations confirm that employed women do double-shift in Turkey. One is that married employed women still have a higher burden of total work than their spouses. The second is that employed women's total work is significantly higher than that of housewives. Marriage has an asymmetric impact on time use patterns of women and men in Turkey. We observe that women spend greater time on unpaid work when they get married while the time devoted to unpaid work by men decreases even when they get married to a woman employed in the market.

Having children appears to be a critical transition in the life course which equalizes unpaid work time spent by employed women and men in Turkey. We observe that male spouses help more with the unpaid work at home if there are children living in the household. However, this observation is limited to the one child case. Male spouses stop sharing the burden at home when the number of children increases. Women, on the other hand, are affected significantly by the increase in number of children: their paid work time decreases and unpaid work time increases when the number of children increases from one to two. When the number of children increases from two to three or more, women's total work time rises significantly.

Our analysis of how women and men use their work time in Turkey reveals large gender based disparities: women work longer hours than men, particularly because housework is not shared equally. Moreover, getting married and having children is an important barrier to women's employment in the market as this increases women's unpaid work time. Thus, married women who have an opportunity to work in the market seem to be choosing between either working for very long hours for paid and unpaid work in total or not working in the labour market. This result has very important consequences for social reform programs aiming at gender equality, especially in the labour market: any policy reform that increases paid work opportunities for women without offering social services, like care services for children, will most likely be ineffective.

DOMESTIC LABOUR AND WELL-BEING: A CASE STUDY OF THE EVLATLIK INSTITUTION IN TURKEY

Hande Toğrul[1]

This chapter examines a particular form of domestic labour – unpaid, live-in labour carried out by non-family members – embodied in the Evlatlık institution in Turkey. Evlatlıks, literally child-alikes, are mostly orphan and/or poor peasant girls, who are brought into upper and middle class households under conditions of 'quasi–adoption.'[2] Practices similar to the Evlatlık institution are prevalent around the world.[3] In this book Rittersberger-Tılıç and Kalaycıoğlu explore domestic labour relationships in paid live-out form. They explore similar pseudo-family relationships in the labour process while investigating any possible changes over a decade.

Historically, the Evlatlık practice was very common. While the arrangement emerges under the pretext of charity toward and protection of the poor, an Evlatlık is brought into their new home to perform unpaid domestic labour starting at the age of five or six and continuing until marriage. Part of the charity is associated with an implicit class bargain that the girls will achieve, at the very least, a primary school education and have 'better opportunities' for their future. One such 'better opportunity' would be establishing a future life in an urban area assuming that this environment offers greater opportunities than those found in rural areas. This implicit bargain often is not achieved. In fact, the internalization of social roles for girls from rural areas is perpetuated. Women and girls from impoverished backgrounds have always been perceived as a reserve army of paid and/or unpaid domestic labour. Historically, lack of equal opportunities for women and their families, lack of understanding of women's human rights, and above all, a lack of political will to achieve human well-being instead of focusing on material accumulation perpetuated situations where domestic labour was another under-appreciated, unpaid, underpaid labour form.

The objective of this study was to assess the process and consequences of the Evlatlık institution based on interviews conducted with 22 former Evlatlıks (referred to in this chapter as P1-22) between 2004 and 2006, mostly in the Mediterranean region. Snowball sampling was used as a technique for developing the research. Initially, recruiting started from my own household and community where I was raised. I would have found more participants from other regions if I had had funding to conduct fieldwork in different parts of the country. Interviews gave me a better understanding of the level and/or lack of well-being from the point of view of the oppressed party in the Evlatlık institution. Up until now, there has been only one study[4] which sought to explore this form of labour in Turkey during the Ottoman Period. The current study explores the Evlatlık institution in the modern Turkish Republic where gender and class relations have not significantly transformed. Even though modernization has brought new patterns of economic relations and women from privileged classes have found new opportunities in different levels of the production system, underprivileged women with lack of access to opportunities have remained outside the formal production system. Therefore the Evlatlık institution remains intact, and continued production relations have kept the institution alive under the notion of charity.

The capabilities approach (CA), targets potential beings and doings of people instead of targeting people's contribution to the system of production in an isolated manner, thereby initiating a broader focus on women and the welfare regime of Turkey. Developing a more gender sensitive analysis requires us to capture information about all women, not only women in the labour market. There is a substantial percentage of women in Turkey who perform unpaid and paid domestic labour. The implications of the domestic labour process need to be understood and linked to policy-making and welfare discussions. The CA can provide a deeper understanding of resource and service creation which will inform the discussions and unpack some of the implications in a more simplified way.

The CA concentrates on service and resource creation and is used as an evaluative tool to analyze the stories of Evlatlıks. The CA categories assist in performing discourse analysis. The CA approach, as an open-ended approach, introduces multiple and evolving variables so as to understand well-being. It does not impose a fixed and/or predetermined content. In discourse analysis these characteristics are crucial. The analysis also aims to raise awareness about the Evlatlık institution and its relationships. Through the study, three stages are identified in the lives of

Evlatlıks: stage 1) the biological household; stage 2) the pseudo-household; stage 3) own household upon marriage. The primary focus of the study is the Evlatlıks' lives in pseudo-households where they performed their unpaid domestic labour. Studying such an intimate form of labour relation creates a deep understanding of socialization, internalization, and actualization of oppression in the general sense, or how an individual's personhood and own labour can be stripped off of his/her self for the benefit of others.

The Capabilities Approach

The CA prioritizes people and expansion of their capabilities, rather than solely concentrating on the expansion of material things because the CA explores what individuals can 'be' and 'do' potentially and actually. One can ask what Evlatlıks have become and done in their life cycle given their circumstances. Sen (1985, 1992, 1999) differentiates between capabilities and functionings: capabilities are potential 'doing' and 'beings', endless possibilities that an individual may achieve. Functionings however are 'doing' and 'beings' that an individual has achieved with the resources s/he possesses (Robeyns 2005). 'The capability approach not only advocates for an evaluation of people's capability sets, but insists also that we need to scrutinize the context in which economic production and social interactions take place, and whether the circumstances in which people choose from their opportunity sets are enabling and just' (Robeyns 2005: 99). For instance, satisfying basic needs is considered a functioning. An ability to engage in economic exchange, participate in educational activities or political activities is also a functioning. For example, a farmer may have the ability to cultivate land (equals functionings) but with no land with which to sow his crops, he and his family may end up hungry because the functioning does not extend into a larger capability. In the case of Evlatlıks, most of them were sent to literacy courses to learn basic reading and writing skills but they could not really use this functioning effectively to expand their capability set. Pseudo-families did not pay attention to whether Evlatlıks use their particular functionings, i.e. reading and writing, in a constructive way. Some participants reported that later in life they faced hard experiences due to not turning some functionings into a useful capability set. Pseudo-families were proud of providing basic needs which turns into a major poverty reduction at the international level. Some of the functionings cannot be transformed into capabilities due to behavioral obstacles such as absence of positive feeling, lack of self-esteem and optimism, lack of competence, lack of vitality, lack of autonomy and trust.

Although income-based measurement[5] is still influential in policy making (Aisbeitt 2004), income and resources are a necessary but not sufficient aspect of poverty and well-being analysis. They are not contradictory but complimentary. Income is needed for people to achieve doings and beings, to achieve a combination of capabilities. Different doings and beings bring people fulfillment and satisfaction. People flourish more as they figure out and achieve missing dimensions. Well-being is more than material gain.

> ...neither opulence (income, commodity command) nor utility (happiness, desire fulfillment) constitute or adequately represent human well-being and deprivation. Instead, what is required is a more direct approach that focuses on human function(ing)s and the capabilities to achieve valuable function(ing)s (Clark 2005, p. 4)

The CA framework is not about happiness, pleasure or utility but ordinary day-to-day life. This approach shifts us away from utilitarianism and towards practical ethics founded on personal and social activities (Jackson 2005). According to Alkire (2005, emphasis added):

> *functionings* are various things a person may value doing or being. *Achieved functionings* is the particular beings or doings a person enjoys at a given point in time. Achieved functionings are important because they can sometimes be measured. *Capability* refers to the various combinations of functionings (beings and doings) that the person can achieve.

The tools and the framework of the CA approach help us to gain deeper understanding while deconstructing gender and class relations. Over the years, complex interactions between gender interests and needs as well as class interests have been investigated by several researchers (Molyneux 1979; Young 1981; Aslop 1993; Moser 1989). Do people pursue functionings which they value, and why? Why can some people not obtain good education while others can? Why do some people have jobs that they enjoy while others do not? Diverse experiences in similar contexts, given a similar income-commodity nexus, reveal how the process of acquiring certain "doings" and "beings" is complex. It is not the same for each individual or group. Therefore, the achievement of some functionings may be a story of well-being while some are not. In both cases, times of well-being and ill-being can be found in one's life cycle. The Evlatlıks' stories reveal the complexity of achieving or failing to achieve different functionings. Some participants in the study explained that they had to endure oppression and deprivation of some functionings to form their capabilities set. Almost all of the participants endured disturbing treatment including psychical and emotional violence. In order to finish their primary education or literacy courses they had to endure negative emotions in everyday life. Multiple participants mentioned that getting a primary education certificate was not supported by the pseudo-families although it was an implicit bargain with the biological families. Throughout schooling, day in day out, they were told that schooling would not create any opportunities ("okuyup da ne olacaksın"[6]) for them. In the mean time, Evlatlıks observed the amount of support and encouragement for the biological children's schooling. Most of the participants explained that they had intuitively known the importance of reading and writing, therefore, they finished primary school despite the adversity. For the most part, love, affection, warmth, kindness were withheld from the girls when they were five, six, seven, or, whatever the age of arrival in the pseudo-household. They were prevented from communicating with their biological parents. The biological parents were referred to as inferior. The girls could neither identify with their biological parents nor pseudo-parents. Evlatlıks experienced loss of personhood. Loss of courage and being unable to stand up for one's self are other outcomes that impact their long term well-being. They were not able to develop a strong emotional well-being. In some cases anger and hatred developed, or they became deeply introverted and could not build or experience positive human relations.

The two main objectives of using the CA as the evaluative framework in this study are: 1) the CA analyzes diverse dimensions of well-being instead of only one, such as income and 2) the CA converts factors such as income and commodities into functionings in people, and ultimately the formation of the capabilities set (Robeyns 2008). The processes and the consequences of the Evlatlık experiences as described by the participants reveals diverse dimensions of well-being, particularly how each person's experiences, with similar access to income and commodities, led to different functionings and capabilities sets.

In this study a combination of Martha Nussbaum's and Ingrid Robeyns' list of 'doings and being' is used. Nussbaum (2000)[7] describes basic capabilities as follows: life, bodily health, bodily integrity, senses-imagination and thought, emotions, practical reason, affiliation and empathy, being able to live with other species, play, control over one's political and material environment. According to Jackson (2005), Sen prefers a broad concept of capability in the form of overall life chances rather than specific skills and abilities. Sen talks about social and structural influences on capability, however, his work in this regard is marginal and under-theorized. Jackson (2005) also argues that it is necessary to explore social structure and its interdependence with human agency. How did Evlatlıks achieve different capabilities sets, and eventually different levels of well-being? Why did some participants achieve a certain combination of 'being' and 'doing', i.e. functionings, while others did not? How did some achieve certain functionings, but some were not able to expand their capabilities. What were the obstacles? The framework in this chapter enables us to identify the obstacles, both at the individual and societal level. Some of the Evlatlıks inability to achieve certain capabilities may be explained by different life cycle phases. This approach offers great advances towards measuring the individual's and group's well-being. As with most new concepts, Nussbaum's work has inspired heated debate as to whether her work constitutes a 'real' scientific approach. In most cases, a solution for poverty or other socio-economic problems is sought by way of scientific knowledge. An important dimension, however, that has always been lost is to genuinely listen to the experiences of the participants rather than fighting to solve poverty issues, especially as an 'expert' on poverty. Dimensions such as social and personal well-being in general, and in particular self-esteem, control, dignity, autonomy, lack of time, lack of power, absence of positive feelings, lack of trust and belonging, lack of competence, and lack of prolonged social support are deep rooted issues awaiting greater emphasis. This study, while sifting through the life cycles of Evlatlıks, aims to bring that emphasis into the gender and welfare discussions.

The Evlatlık Institution in Turkey

The Evlatlık institution is an intermingling of three phenomena: child labour, migration and the informality of domestic labour relations. The emergence of the Evlatlık institution, its causes and subtleties within the process, are useful in understanding social relations as power relations. Gender and class power relations are central social categories in this study. Gender relations can be identified narrowly as women's subordination to men and women's subordination to women. Class relations can be identified narrowly as subordination between different types of households given their socioeconomic levels. Although hard to validate with formal statistics, the Evlatlık practice still exists in Turkey as well as in a variety of different forms of domestic labour where gender and class relations intermingle. Current data[8] shows that substantial numbers of working age women in Turkey engage in unpaid domestic labour as housewives or female members of the household (sisters, aunts, nieces, brides, grandmothers, cousins and distant female relatives/kin). A Majority of women are involved in unpaid domestic labour as their primary activity. Similar practices occur worldwide hidden within different types of households. Without probing different forms and relations, domestic labour may be a unifying labour form for women around the world. However, the needs and interests of women from different classes create serious conflicts for women in domestic labour relations. The Evlatlık practice highlights many of these conflicts.

Just as poor households have their strategies for alleviating poverty and improving well-being, middle and upper class households have strategies for improving and reproducing overall well-being. The Evlatlık institution is a result of the interaction between the strategies of the rural poor, and/or vulnerable urban households', to alleviate poverty and urban middle and upper-middle class households' strategies to reproduce themselves through the use of unpaid domestic labour and fulfill their class identity by engaging in what appears, at first sight, to be charity and 'giving'. The push and pull forces of gender and class relations in Turkish society created this institution. On the one hand, middle and upper middle class households needed help for household labour. On the other hand, poor and/or vulnerable rural or urban households with multiple children needed better living conditions for their children which they found in the households of those who were 'better-off'. Their intention was to have, at least, one less mouth to feed (bir ağız eksiltmek).

In this study, a little more than 50% of the participants' households were concerned about reproducing themselves. Sending off one of several children was a coping strategy in response to stress in the household. It was, in fact, a historical approach to livelihood. Özbay's (1999) 'Evlatlık Institution in Turkey; Slave or Child' reveals the same practice ocurring in the Ottoman Empire in 1885-1907. The Ottomans maintained an imperial power that stretched around the Mediterranean including Anatolia, North Africa, the Middle East, and South-East Europe from 1299 to 1922. The Turkish Republic emerged in Anatolia as the Ottoman Empire dissolved. Özbay's work traces different forms of domestic labour and illuminates the transformation of the Evlatlık institution in Turkish society; especially at the cultural level. According to her sources there were 1.5 million servants in the country in 1885. Since slavery was the norm, there were 52,000 domestic slaves and less than 40,000 free slaves known to exist in Istanbul. 'It was the privilege of Ottoman Muslims households to use both black and white slaves in domestic work, whereas non-Muslims could only use free servants. Successive attempts to ban the slave[9] trade were effective in reducing the number of slaves by the end of the 19th century. Orphan and/or poor peasant girls who were taken into middle class households in the name of 'protection' and 'goodwill' gradually replaced the former domestic slaves.' (Özbay 1999, p. 16).

After the establishment of the Turkish Republic, similar traditions, norms, beliefs, and values persisted; human relations do not change over night. Evlatlıks were brought into pseudo-households at very early ages, when girls were 5 or 6 years old. This intentional separation from the biological family which provided some basic needs repressed Evlatlıks as young children. Despite the fact that they had "improved" access to basic needs, some of the participants problematized this so called "improved" access to basic needs. They argued that they would have chosen to stay in their biological families if they had known the degree of mistreatment they would experience in the pseudo-households. Most participants presented us with experiences in which one kind of deprivation was chosen, intentionally or unintentionally, in order to satisfy other needs. In other words, they gave up some of their interests in order to achieve certain needs. For a majority of Evlatlıks, it was always a lose-lose situation considering the significantly bad treatment. In most cases, provision of basic needs justifies lack of many emotional needs which becomes detrimental for human well-being.

The push and pull effects are hidden in the monetary and non-monetary relations between groups and people, i.e. between the individual (in this case the Evlatlık) and the groups (different types of households). Several participants emphasized the power of society, complexities of social relations and lack of self-determination. Whether the participant had a fulfilling life or not depended on specific relationships and personalities involved in each case. The Evlatlıks' personalities, the personas of the members in each household, and the relations among all were key in understanding outcomes and processes. It is crucial to lay out the life-cycles of the participants to really weigh the 'net effect', if at all possible.

The Evlatlık practice can be described as a rosy model of social relations; a model of a socioeconomic security that depended on the goodwill of better-off households helping worse-off ones. This may be presented as a 'philanthropic act' that provided basic needs for underprivileged girls while opening a space between hard to dismantle large structures and individual lives. However, reality is much more nuanced. Nuances are always hidden in the life stories of marginalized groups as well as people with power. In this case, the Evlatlıks describe their perspective. The lives of Evlatlıks are shaped by context specific push and pull effects. The push and pull emerges from the reproduction needs of poor rural households as well as the reproduction needs of the well-off urban households. On one hand, too many children in the rural households resulted in a lack of provision for their needs. On the other hand, the rise of modernization created a need for domestic labourers to do the chores while housewives managed the well-off urban households. To fill this need, young girls were transported from rural to urban households under the auspices of good deeds. Motivation for rural parents and the justification for urban families was based on the potential increase in the well-being of the Evlatlıks in the long term. In the assessment of the Evlatlıks' well-being, material gain plays a role; participants talk about achieving 'better' material conditions. Nevertheless, each participant ardently disputed how her background automatically put her in a socially inferior position and how lack of emotional growth hampered many aspects of her life. Physical weakness, sickness, vulnerability, physical and social isolation, powerlessness, humiliation, lack of self-determination, lack of autonomy, lack of dignity and empowerment dominated her definition of well-being. Most participants talked about their lives in terms of the importance of health and education, and lack of access to both while they lived in pseudo-households, as well as a loss of personhood and dignity due to the kind of treatment they received. However, because participants have different backgrounds, it becomes very complicated to understand peoples/groups relations to each other and to resources.

Participants went through three different phases. First they were daughters in their *biological households*. Next they were unpaid domestic labourers (pseudo daughters/sisters) in *pseudo households*. Finally they were wives in their *own households* after marriage. In each phase there were different reasons why some capability sets could not be achieved. The three phases represent the changing roles of Evlatlıks in different households. One role that does not change for Evlatlıks is the responsibility for unpaid domestic labour. It is not possible for an individual to achieve certain functionings if that person's major economic activity takes place in the household as domestic labour. During the three phases through which relations changed in the Evlatlıks' lives, they were responsible for domestic labour. Intra- as well as inter-household relations between biological, pseudo and own households were shaped and were reshaped by this responsibility. In the following section, the three phases of the Evlatlıks' life cycles are structured and analyzed according to the CA list (Box 7.1).

Evlatlıks and Well-Being

Some characteristics and patterns emerged from the in-depth interviews, participant observation and the author's own life experiences. These patterns can be broadly divided into four categories:

a) Supply of female youth labour from biological families. Rural families send their daughters (i.e giving up daughters) to pseudo-families for several reasons such as: mother and/or father deceased; high expectations for better future; better education and marriage; poor, vulnerable rural communities without subsidies from the government to raise children.

b) Demand from pseudo-families. These households cite the following reasons for "bringing" a girl into the household: charity; tradition; status; the modernization of the housewife such that dirty chores should not be done by a modern housewife (perception of Evlatlıks), so housewives from well-off households recruit girls from poor families to do such chores.

c) Process in the pseudo-household. Hard life/work in pseudo-households characterized by low material gain with high emotional loss (with few exceptions); better nutrition, adequate clothing, better shelter, sanitation provided by pseudo-household; tough and inferior sleeping arrangements; inferior eating arrangements; emotional scars due to intentional isolation from biological families; bad treatment: mental and physical abuse; similar reasons for stopping access to education.

d) Role as housewives in own family. Conflict with husbands due to "Evlatlık" history; children of Evlatlıks upwardly mobile (with exceptions) and consequent benefit from networks of pseudo-families.

All participants originated from rural areas. All, except one who declared her ethnicity as Kurdish, presented themselves as Turkish. Their current ages (as of 2004) ranged from 32 to 69 with an arithmetic average of 51 years. Seventeen out of 22 arrived at the pseudo-family house between the ages 5-7.

Only 5 out of 22 finished 5 years of primary education which was mandatory and free at the time when the Evlatlıks were school age children. Now the mandatory number of years is eight. The remaining participants had no schooling or literacy courses. For 13 out of the 22 participants, either the mother, father, or both parents had died before the girls left their biological households. Ten of them lost mothers only, two fathers only, one both. The average number of sibling was 5.5. Most siblings stayed in the rural village. Girls mostly married in the village. Boys went to nearby cities to find employment. Most siblings are subsistence farmers. Only three participants are the youngest of all their siblings. Twelve out of the 22 participants were the middle child or youngest in the family. There were only four participants whose siblings were also Evlatlıks. There was only one participant who lived less than 10 years in a pseudo-family household. Most participants lived for 15-25 years in a pseudo-family. It is not a stretch to infer from 17 (prospective partici- pants) Evlatlıks who declined being interviewed that the practice created high levels of suffering.

Interviews with participants took minimum 3-4 hours and maximum 3-4 days. It was necessary to build relationships with some of the partici- pants in order to conduct interviews. During interviews, all participants talked about the poor material conditions in their biological households. There was not enough to eat and most housing conditions were poor. A clear lack of material well–being was described without concrete income indicators. Participants were not able to remember the household income in their biological household since they left home as 5, 6, and 7 year-old girls. Plus, most of the households were those of subsistence farmers. In the biological household, some of the participants' lives were reduced to finding food for the next meal and fixing the house constantly so that it did not leak when it rained or snowed. Life was not worth living. After such material hardship when the girls lived as Evlatlıks under better mate- rial conditions, they realized again that their lives were so undermined that they were not worth living. This time suffering was not material but mental through degrading living arrangements, continued mistreatment and humiliation, assault on personhood as inferiors, everyday oppression by any means possible. Three out of the 22 participants reported having considered suicide while they lived in pseudo-households. Although all participants became Evlatlıks due to lack of basic needs in their biological households, not all siblings became Evlatlıks.

The main finding of this study is that the majority of participants did not experience an increase in their well-being: only three participants out of 22 described an increased overall well-being in their experiences as Evlatlıks. Most of the other participants' stories offered mixed results and/or their well-being decreased. The majority of the Evlatlıks' lives in pseudo-households caused them significant loss of self-esteem and dig- nity, absence of positive feelings, lack of autonomy, lack of trust and belonging, lack of competence, and lack of prolonged social support. There is, however, some intergenerational expansion in capabilities.

Although the children of the Evlatlıks were not part of the study, almost all the participants talked about their children. Some of the Evlatlıks reported very positive developments in their children's lives due to very targetted support from the pseudo-families. Overall the results propose that charity and good intentions cannot provide sustained progress for well-being, unless these intentions focus on people's functioning and capabilities.

After analyzing each participant's experiences from biological to own household using the CA list, Table 7.1 displays the life cycle audit of the Evlatlıks, that is each Evlatlık's experiences as a little girl in her *biological household*, as an unpaid domestic labourer in a *pseudo-household*, and as a wife in her *own household*. During the interviews participants expressed their level of satisfaction regarding her doings and being in each household. NOT SATISFIED means, the majority of participants were not able to be and/or do the capabilities in question. SATISFIED means, the majority of participants were able to be and do, and expand capabilities even if it was with some *negative* consequences. HIGHLY SATISFIED means, the majority of participants were able to be and do the capability. While telling their stories about the pseudo-household, participants frequently compared themselves with the sibling they had left at their villages and/or other Evlatlıks with whom they socialize. In many cases, they do not recall details about the quality of life in their biological households since they left at such early ages, 5-7 years old. That is why there are several Not Applicable (NA) signs under the biological HH column in Table 1. The pseudo HH Column shows that Evlatlıks in general had low levels of capability development. When they move into their own households after marriage, ability to be and do increased somewhat for the entire group.

There were three participants who were fully satisfied in phase II and highly satisfied in phase III. Nineteen out of the 22 participants were not satisfied in phase II and somewhat satisfied in phase III. Those 3 participants praised their pseudo-mothers and fathers substantially. Dominant themes in their stories were gaining self-esteem and dignity, experiencing more positive feelings than negative ones. They felt a level of autonomy, trust and belonging. They built competence. From the early years of joining the pseudo-households they got social support from the family and its network. The rest of the 19 participants did not have supportive relationships with any pseudo-family members. They accumulated negative emotional well-being that still impacts their lives today.

Table 7.1: The CA framework: Summary of the capabilities through life cycle

The CAs	PHASE I Biological HH	PHASE II Pseudo HH	PHASE III Own HH
Life and psychical health	NOT SATISFIED	SATISFIED	SATISFIED
Reproductive health	NOT SATISFIED	NOT SATISFIED	SATISFIED
Education and knowledge	NOT SATISFIED	NOT SATISFIED	NOT SATISFIED
Mental well-being	SATISFIED	NOT SATISFIED	SATISFIED
Bodily integrity and safety	SATISFIED	NOT SATISFIED	SATISFIED
Mobility	NOT SATISFIED	NOT SATISFIED	SATISFIED
Emotions	HIGHLY SATISFIED	NOT SATISFIED	SATISFIED
Social relations and respect	N.A.	NOT SATISFIED	NOT SATISFIED
Practical reason	N.A.	NOT SATISFIED	SATISFIED
Political involvement	N.A.	NOT SATISFIED	SATISFIED
Other species	N.A.	N.A.	N.A.
Leisure activities	NOT SATISFIED	NOT SATISFIED	HIGHLY SATISFIED
Time autonomy	NOT SATISFIED	NOT SATISFIED	NOT SATISFIED
Control over one's material being	SATISFIED	NOT SATISFIED	HIGHLY SATISFIED
Religion	N.A.	N.A.	N.A.

Phase I: Biological Household

Throughout the interviews, the majority of the time, participants talked about their experiences in the pseudo-households while linking to the events in their biological as well as their own households. Thirteen out of 22 participants described that attaining capability for life and physical health in the biological household was questionable.

After my father died, we did not earn much from growing citrus or banana. My brothers and uncles took over. We lived very comfortably before his death. But I was in Alanya (pseudo-household) when these changes happened in the village. I was not able to be healthy and enjoy a normal life anymore in my village; therefore, I stayed in the pseudo-household. (P12)

We were so poor. I remember that we did not have enough to eat for each meal, so we ate less in every meal to have something to eat in the next meal. Food was something we constantly thought about, where to find ingredients for the next meal. (P18)

Nevertheless, several Evlatlıks who had deep emotional scars argue that their sisters and brothers were much better off even with limited access to basic needs.

I have not forgiven my mother to this day. I could have eaten a piece of bread with them. I could have drank water for some meals. Why did she give me away? Why? My siblings who remained in my biological households were happily married and in a better material and especially a better emotional state than me. (P5)

If biological parents could control their material being, may be Evlatlıks would not have to suffer what they have suffered in pseudo-households.

I could never understand why we were so poor. Why did my father or mother not work? There was not much work in the village but we also did not have land to cultivate, maybe a few chickens to look after. It was not enough. We did not have a cow or a goat. If we had a little piece of land, everything would be different. (P18)

According to participants, it was simple logic. If their parents had some kind of livelihood, they could have provided them with necessary life and health support. This situation creates justification for pseudo-families. They argue that their goodwill act had a solid foundation.

I was very convinced about the fact that these kids needed me. When I went down to the village, P11 and her sister were sitting in front of a cave-like, mud house. They were with their grandmother... I brought her home, cleaned the fleas of her, cut her hair, and dressed her up. She looked like a human being. (P11's pseudo-mother.)

Phase II: Pseudo Household

Phase 2 elabourates on the experiences of the Evlatlıks within the pseudo-household. Given the stories of 22 participants, they were deprived of mental well-being, emotions, social relations, respect, and practical reason. They did not have control over their own time, mobility, even bodily integrity and safety in a significant number of cases.

> We were not stupid; we know where we came from. But we needed some level of respect. Respect as a human being. That did not exist. Otherwise, why not. We had better conditions, better shelter. We did not worry about the next meal. (P13)

> I feel like puking when I remember those days. We were fed like dogs. The grandmother of the house soaked dried out bread into the left over meals and set it aside for a while... I see these days, animals are actually treated much better than how we were treated. (P1)

> The families started to accept us at their dinner table after the boys grew up. We believe that the boys influenced their parents. Since we raised them we were emotionally attached. (one Evlatlık made this statement and other two agreed) (P8, P16, and P17)

> I just cannot understand why they didn't send us to school. It was even a challenge to go to the literacy courses. They had it at the local primary school from 5-7pm three times a week. I never had time to do homework or go to the classes on time. How could I finish work at 5pm...When I went to change my name on the national identification card last year, you know, I did not have my real name on it forever! When the Judge asked me about by situation, I could not talk. I would cry if I did. He asked me about the pseudo-family who did not send me to primary school. He said that it was a crime. I said "they are good people". (P1)

Issues about Evlatlıks formal education, health, autonomy, dignity, self-respect, access to assets and income, mental health, and access to community relations manifest themselves in this phase.

> It is almost like time did not exist in our lives. Every single minute

belonged to them. I could not fall a sleep, I had to get permission to go to bed. Sleeping arrangements actually made it this way. For a long time, I had a make-shift bed. I had to set it up in the living room after everyone else went to sleep. (P1)

The stories are complicated due to existing power relations within the pseudo-households. The Evlatlıks complained about pseudo-mothers more than pseudo-fathers. In fact the above mentioned participants continued.

Abi (pseudo-father) was much more understanding, He was ready to give me a hand all the time. I remember abla (pseudo-mother) whispered "let her do it by herself, what other things does she have to do... that is her job". (P1)

P8 talked about the same issue in the pseudo-household. She mentioned that the pseudo-father was very soft spoken and protective towards her. The pseudo-mother always talked down to her but he tried to argue against it. Most stories around emotional scars, dignity, autonomy, and control were told in the context of the Evlatlıks not being treated like human beings.

She was a queen in the house and wanted to use me like a dirty rag. (P8)

We were treated so badly. I knew other Evlatlıks. Okay, we come from misery and destitution but they did not have to insult us this way. They thought we were mindless. They thought we did not have brains. It is very harsh to be treated like stupid children. It is very degrading. Everyday was misery, real misery! Not what I came from. From when we woke up until late at night. I sometimes asked myself how long I could take this. Why am I doing it? Why did I not escape and go back to my village. (P20)

Abla was always negative. Especially when the children and I were having a good time, she was ready to find something to ruin the moment... Abi and her mother were good people. They supported me. They knew that abla had some problems. (P8)

One pseudo-mother (to P9) told me knowing that I had lived in a household with multiple Evlatlıks: You would know it so well, it is the hardest thing to adjust. What do you want to do with this studying? It is simple, honey. It is poverty. When people are poor, they need everything. Of course, we were not very rich to provide everything but food, shelter and some support. The poor cannot easily access. You should also talk to us. It is not so easy to raise them. It is a lot of work. A lot of patience is need to deal with them. (P8's pseudo mother)

Phase III: Own Household
The third phase questions the Evlatlıks' relations within their own nuclear households after marriage. Twelve out of 22 participants reported that they built stronger relations with their biological families after building their own households. Five of the 22 participants were able to contact their biological family during their life with the pseudo-families. Those five built the best bargaining power within their own households strengthened both by their biological and pseudo-household relations.

I was at least treated like a person. I had to make my own decisions, raise my kids according my own rules. Even though the pseudo-mother was able to make comments about me, I was able to go to my home and shut the door. It was a very liberating point in my life. (P1)

Sometimes, husbands can be as hard as the pseudo-parents. However, one can talk back and yell at the husband. I know my fellow Evlatlık was beaten up by her husband but it is different than being beaten up by the pseudo-mother. I know this is not normal to say but... (P5)

Conclusion
This study motivates a new type of analysis and sheds light on a practice that is otherwise invisible. The invisibly comes from the way in which the welfare of a country and societies at large are assessed. Certain sectors, parameters and indicators are considered in the assessments of gender and welfare, however, many aspects are left out. Even though the importance of the details of gender relations are acknowledged in gender and welfare studies, a deeper understanding of these relations is yet to be captured and brought light to the invisible. Above all, a higher level of awareness has to be achieved among women from all class levels. Understanding human relations is central to understanding how the personhood of a woman (or

man for that matter) can be removed. In this study we see such removal achieved through emotional means and justified through the provision of 'material' needs. There were 3 participants who were fully satisfied in phase II and highly satisfied in phase III. As they tell their stories, they indicate the importance of the fair and just human relations they experienced. The rest of the participants carry deep emotional scars which have hampered their overall well-being. If welfare reform is meant to assist all women and girls from diverse backgrounds, then the process and outcomes of a welfare state have to target the personal and social well-beings which relate to the emotional well-being of individual people and society.

In this study, we did not expect to find three fully satisfied participants. Their experiences in the pseudo-households and the details of their relationships can give some hope for the betterment of gender and class conflicts. In other words, self-esteem, dignity, the absence of negative feelings, the presence of positive feelings, autonomy, trust and belonging, competence, and prolonged social support are pivotal for overall well-being. The next stage of this study suggests that the pseudo families[10] should be involved in the study as participants, especially, those who created positive processes and outcomes for the Evlatlıks. As mentioned at the beginning, similar relationships to those that are described in this study exist within paid domestic work relations in Chapter 12. Domestic labour processes and outcomes will continue to impact women in Turkey and around the world as part of the fabric and understanding of well-being at the personal and social level.

Box 7.1: List of Capabilities

1- **Life and physical health:** being able to be physically healthy and enjoy a life of normal length, not dying prematurely, or before one's life is so reduced as to be not worth living. Adequately nourished; to have adequate shelter.

2- **Reproductive Health:** being able to gain knowledge about sexual and reproductive health; having opportunities for sexual satisfaction and for choice in matters of reproduction.

3- **Education and knowledge:** being able to be educated and to use and produce knowledge.

4- **Mental well-being:** being able to be mentally healthy. Being able to use the senses, to imagine, think, and reason and to do these things in a "truly human" way, a way informed and cultivated by an adequate education, including, but by no means limited to, literacy and basic mathematical and scientific training. Being able to use imagination and thought in connection with experiencing and producing works and events of one's own choice, religious, literary, musical, and so forth. Being able to use one's mind in ways protected by guarantees of freedom of expression with respect to both political and artistic speech, and freedom of religious exercise. Being able to have pleasurable experiences and to avoid non-beneficial pain.

5- **Bodily integrity and safety:** being able to be protected from violence of any sort. Protected from sexual assault and domestic violence.

6- **Mobility:** being able to be mobile.

7- **Emotions:** Being able to have attachments to things and people outside ourselves; to love those who love and care for us, to grieve at their absence; in general, to love, to grieve, to experience longing, gratitude, and justified anger. Not having one's emotional development blighted by fear and anxiety.

8- **Social relations and Respect:** being able to be part of social networks and to give and receive social support. Having the social bases of self-respect and non-humiliation; being able to be treated as a dignified being whose worth is equal to that of others; being able to be respected and treated with dignity; feeling sense of family.

9- **Practical Reason:** Being able to form a conception of the good and to engage in critical reflection about the planning of one's life. (This entails protection for the liberty of conscience and religious observance.)

10- **Political empowerment:** being able to participate in and have a fair share of influence on political decision-making. Being able to participate effectively in political choices that govern one's life; having the right of political participation, protections of free speech and association.

11- **Other Species:** Being able to live with concern for and in relation to animals, plants, and the world of nature.

12- **Leisure activities:** being able to engage in leisure activities; being able to laugh, to play, and to enjoy non-work hours.

13- **Time-autonomy:** being able to exercise autonomy in allocating one's time.

14- **Control over one's Material being:** Being able to hold property (both land and movable goods), and having property rights on an equal basis with others; having the right to seek employment on an equal basis with others.

15- **Religion:** being able to choose to live or not to live according to a religion.

PART TWO

THE EFFECTS OF THE WELFARE REFORMS ON WOMEN'S STATUS IN THE EU ACCESSION PROCESS

8

GENDER EQUALITY POLICIES AND FEMALE EMPLOYMENT: THE REFORMS IN THE EU ACCESSION PROCESS

Saniye Dedeoglu

Turkey officially became a candidate country to the EU in 1999 and began its EU accession negotiations in 2005. Seen as an 'awkward candidate',[1] Turkey's trajectory for candidacy has created an unprecedented impetus in state action for legal reform in the area of gender equality. The landmark policy and mentality shifts in relation to general gender equality policies in Turkey are reflected in four aspects of legal reform: the Constitutional amendments since 2001, especially the 2004 amendment; the adoption of the new Civil Code (2001); the new Labour Law (2003); and the new Penal Code (2005). The adoption of equality policies has also been supported through policy reforms in the existing social insurance schemes and the healthcare system. The outstanding result of these reforms is the changing perception of women in the society, where the shift in perception saw women move from being dependent citizens to independent participants in society (Kılıç 2008).

While a great deal of the necessary legislation is now in place, it is still difficult to argue that they are fully implemented especially because of dominating patriarchal values and the lack of support mechanisms for implementation. These reforms seem to be only one more tick on the to-do list of the government's EU accession agenda. In reality, there is no political willingness or commitment to promote gender equality and to challenge traditional gender norms and relations, such as setting employment quotas for women and increasing public child and elderly care provisions. This is because the structure of the Turkish welfare state is based on the role women play in society as homemakers and this perception has as yet not changed.

Although many reforms have been brought into force, gender inequality still remains one of the main concerns in Turkey. Despite some remaining problems in the area of parental leave, Labour Law operates in parallel with the gender equality directives of the EU.[2] The adoption of the new Law was an important attempt to ensure the equality of women and men in working life and to eliminate discrimination of women entering the work force. However, gender inequality is still the most distinct in employment, where by women's workforce participation is among the lowest in OECD countries, at 25 per cent. There is a strong gender divide in the labour market partly coinciding with the urban/rural divide depicted by a high concentration of low educated, working women in agriculture, unpaid employment and informal activities. The historically low economic activity rate of women helps to maintain a limited welfare state wherein the largest portion of welfare provisions are offered by the housewifery roles of those women staying outside the labour market.

This article is an attempt to assess the potential of recent gender equality policies to promote female employment and women's position in the labour market in Turkey. While focusing on the area of employment, the chapter questions whether a number of these changes are to increase the vulnerability of the majority of women or contribute to strengthen their position as independent participants in society. The adoption of gender policies in some cases worked against women during recruitment or the existing national laws over-protected those staying as homemakers rather than entering the workforce. The impact of gender policies on female employment is highly related to the interplay of the gendered nature of the welfare state, the current situation of female employment and unpaid care arrangements in Turkey. These three areas are elaborated on in this article. In the following pages, I will first explain the theoretical question of the article, then outline the ongoing gender equality reforms, and Turkey's modernisation process which extends into the EU accession period. I later focus on how far these policies have potential to affect women's paid work as well as to reduce their care responsibilities at home.

The European Union and Gender Equality

The historical debate summarized as 'equality vs. difference' stands at the centre of the formation of gender equality policies. The recognition of the male worker as the ideal citizen in the realm of social rights has produced women's historical exclusion. The remedy for this exclusion was either to include women on the same terms as men (gender-neutral citizenship) or to support the difference of women and their inclusion through differential treatment (gender-differentiated citizenship) (Lister 2003; Longo 2001). In social policy, three main approaches are distinguished to the conceptualisation of gender equality: equal treatment based on assumptions of the ultimate sameness of women and men; equal valuation of different contributions by women and men; and the transformation of gender relations (Rees 1998; Verloo 2005; Walby 2005). Booth and Bennett (2002) interpret the trilogy of models of 'equal treatment perspective', the 'women's perspective' and the 'gender perspective' as strategies rather than as end visions. They argue that the three approaches are complementary rather than mutually exclusive, suggesting that they are better conceptualised as components of a 'three-legged stool', in that they are interconnected and that each needs the other.

The European Union's gender policy dates back to The Treaty of Rome in 1957. At the time, all Member States signed Article 119, which granted women equality with men. It meant that working women had to be treated the same as working men (Young 2000: 84). In this regard, gender equality was defined more in terms of labour market participation at the EU level and it was assumed that women as well as men would be citizen workers (Lewis 2002). Therefore, the prime aim of the EU policy has been to get more women in employment. However, the EU's emphasis on the sameness of women and men later shifted to developing strategies of 'reconciliation of working and family life' in the 1990s and more recently to 'gender mainstreaming'. Although granting the equal treatment of women remained at the centre of the EU's gender policy, in recent years there have been measures focusing on the articulation of care work, often via the regulation of time rather than payment, such as care leaves (Walby 2004: 19). Lewis et al. (2008) commented that the EU's encouragement of childcare services, in the 2002 Barcelona Council, rather than care leaves was again an emphasis of the target of increasing the rate of female employment.

Later in the 1990s, equality policies eventually became a policy tool of active labour market policies of the larger paradigm of the neo-liberal project. Feminist writers heavily criticised them for being instrumental in following a neoliberal agenda rather than a social one and not having a firmer target of transforming unequal gender relations (Lewis 2006:429). In the policy scene, the aim of changing the behaviour of men has slipped out of the picture and the policy focus has narrowed substantially to the provision of childcare services, which is more likely to promote female labour market participation than measures of home-care leaves that provide time for care. Bacchi (1999:140-141) also expresses, in a European

Commission White Paper on social and economic policy, that reconciliation of family and work life policies were to facilitate the full integration of women into the labour market. She shows that childcare policies are the result of economic necessity to draw women into the labour force as a way of reducing the welfare burden or a way of moving reserve labour into employment during economic boom times. Regarding the equal treatment directives on social security, Young asserts that they were subsequently used to justify levelling down pension rights rather than addressing the issue of gender equality (Young 2000: 85). In the hands of national governments, equality policies became convenient legal instruments to reduce social expenditures. The Netherlands and the UK have already shown that the equal treatment reform can be implemented against a background of severe cost-reducing in the social security system (Young 2000: 85-86).

The aim of this chapter is to seize the potential of gender equality policies to affect the current state of female employment in Turkey. Thus, not only an evaluation of the nature of these policies but also their potential of generating a change in the state of women's paid work is necessary. In this regard, Walby's framework assesses the effects of the EU gender policies on gender regimes in which gender regime transformation can take a different route from domestic to public form (2004). She offers three main typologies in the context of the EU and North America, which are market-led, welfare state-led and regulatory policy-led. The welfare state-led is presented in the social democratic public service route followed by the Nordic countries. In this system, the development of public services provided women with the capacity to increase their paid employment. The market-led route is followed by the United States, where provision of the service necessary to support women in employment takes place through market mechanism. The regulatory policy-led route is developed by the EU, through which women's access to employment is facilitated by the removal of discrimination in the regulation of working time so that women can have time for child and elder care. These different routes produce different outcomes in gender transformations that also depend upon the degree of gender inequality and the form of gender regime (Walby 2004: 10-11)

The Turkish case presents a mixture of the market and policy-led routes through which gender equality policies are well placed in legislation but institutional developments in labour market regulation and care provisions are left solely to the market. However, consequent to these realities, the outcome of the EU gender policies for female employment in

Turkey is an interaction between the current position of women in the labour market, the gendered nature of the welfare state and the unpaid-care regime in Turkey. The welfare state regime is highly dependent upon women's being mothers and wives who hold a strong family unit together. On the labour market front, there is an unfavourable economic environment in which the informal sector and high unemployment emerged as the main characteristics in the 1990s and have created a relatively low level demand for women workers. In addition, public provisions for care remain highly insufficient and give little institutional support in increasing women's move into the labour market. Thus, gender equality polices alone are not sufficient to promote female employment, and even in some cases work against women. So, they are destined to remain as legal texts or reach only a small fraction of women if the laws are not supported by sufficient policy measures to improve women's position in society.

Welfare State and Gender in Turkey

Since the early years of the Turkish Republic, gender has been the main yardstick of the Turkish modernization project. Coined as 'symbolic pawns' (Kandiyoti 1989), women have been the defenders of the Kemalist reform, which promoted the sameness of women and men and provided suffrage rights for women. However, the beneficiaries of these reforms have been mostly the urban bourgeoisie women. Kandiyoti (1987), while appreciating the legal, political, and cultural reforms of the Republic, describes Turkish women as 'emancipated but unliberated' because these reforms mostly failed to address the inequalities brought through the internalised patriarchal system. The result is that domestic violence, sexual harassment, honour crimes and gender inequality in the labour market and parliament remain consistent problems in Turkish women's lives.

The main focus of the women's movement gained momentum in the 1980s was on the short falls of the Kemalist reform and maintained gender inequalities. This overlapped with the increasing international attention paid to women's issues at the time by the UNDP, World Bank and the ratification of the Convention on the Elimination of All Forms of Discrimination against Women (CEDAW) in 1986. These developments resulted in the foundation of national gender machinery in 1990, General Directorate for the Status of Women. Even though it helped gender equality issues become institutionalised and formalised, the main approach to gender policy remained unchanged, following the Republican legacy of considering all forms of inequality a private matter or a problem of modernisation. While the reform process reached only a small group of women pro-

CEDAW - 1986

ducing class specific results, few attempts were made to address those social circumstances that weaken women's position in the labour market. Turkish governments did not follow a systematic policy supporting women's entrance into the labour market, but rather there was strong support to keep women within the confines of the domestic sphere as part of a family union. In general, the nature of the welfare state is rather rudimentary and in recent years this has been influenced by Turkey's attempts to become an EU member. Some argue that the welfare state in Turkey resembles those states in southern Europe and can be classified as a Latin Rim country (Manning 2007). The welfare regime provides a patchy coverage for citizens and is organised in a highly hierarchal way in which access to health services and the pension system is designed for those who are in the formal labour market and for their families (Buğra and Keyder 2003). In this form of welfare state where informal work, self-employment and unpaid family workers outnumber the formal workers, social service and social security systems are far from providing protection for the vast majority of the population (Buğra and Keyder 2006: 212).

In the absence of formal social protection mechanisms, family and personal networks become vital for the survival of the masses. Kinship and family networks and systems of reciprocity and mutual support for protection and income maintenance are central in many people's lives. In a society where households are the main providers of security and social provisioning, women's roles as mothers and wives are central for the maintenance of that family structure. When women are confined to the domestic sphere, society can reproduce the family unit which is the most important security providing institution in that society. Women not only do domestic chores and care for children and the elderly, but also maintain communal ties that keep the network of solidarity and reciprocity going. This social fabric results in the low female labour force participation rate and most of those women who are in the labour market do informal and home-based forms of work. This in turn results in women's low involvement in formal social provisions and women remain out of the formal health and social security systems as independent citizens.

The legal system used to support this traditional structure in gender relations stigmatised women as vulnerable and dependants of male citizens until the current reform process began in the late 1990s and early 2000s. Gender equality came to the governments' agenda as a major component of EU accession negotiations which gave unprecedented impetus to state action for legal reforms. Despite the gender equality principal in the Turkish Constitutions and numerous ratified international documents, civil, penal and labour laws in Turkey continued to include various discriminatory provisions and was characterised by an overarching patriarchal perspective. In the early 2000s, the situation changed dramatically. The legal changes followed one another, the four pieces of legal reforms, the Constitutional amendments, the adoption of the new Civil Law (2001), the new Labour Law (2003) and the new Penal Law (2005), which together represent a new approach in gender equality policies. This approach is based on improving women's individual freedom and protecting their position in the private sphere by granting them individual rights rather than those based on motherhood or wifehood.

The attempts to improve gender equality records fuelled legal reforms to eliminate fundamental discriminatory provisions against women. For example, the new Civil Law abolished the 'head of the family' concept by equalising the status of husband and wife before the Law. It also brought into force a new matrimonial property regime whereby property acquired during marriage is equally divided between spouses upon divorce. These legal reforms – amendments in the Civil and Penal Laws and the Constitution – addressed the place of women not only in the public but also in the private spheres and rested on the principle of women's rights as individuals rather than as community and family members. In some cases, the equal treatment may adversely affect women's situation as in the case of healthcare (see the chapter by Ağartan in this volume). The current reform of the healthcare system indicates a further step in the gender-neutralisation of welfare benefits, ending the former entitlement of dependent daughters of the insured persons to lifelong health insurance (Kılıç 2008: 493). Although this reform replaced the former paternalistic framework, it made women more vulnerable as they have not yet achieved the conditions necessary for independent status in the labour market or in the home.

The adoption of EU Directives and the ratification of other international standards were put into effect under the power of the AKP (Justice and Development Party) which has Islamic roots. Although the AKP does not seem to promote traditional roles sanctioned by religious reading, the infiltration of religious cadres into state bureaucracy and education institutions does propagate these values (Arat 2009: 14). Feminists argue that the AKP government discouraged female employment through its initiative of Social Security and General Health Insurance as it retracted women's rights in the labour market by increasing the retirement age for women. While women's rights were raised to be equal to men in the labour market, the Prime Minister, Recep Tayyip Erdogan, advocated that women have at least three children while at the same time offering no political commitment to increase public childcare facilities. In this light, Arat argues that:

> This conservative mind set resonated with orthodox interpretations of the religious texts that encourage maternal roles for women and restrict substantive opportunities for them. Independent of the party program that cited CEDAW as the politically correct means of approaching EU, the party cadres held restrictive views on women's roles in line with religious teachings. (2009: 15)

It is difficult to foresee the AKP government acting following support of affirmative action programmes for women who start the race with different and/or unequal abilities and offer political commitment to improve women's position in the labour market. Without a political willingness to design remedies that address women's strategic needs, gender equality in the labour markets is destined to be a utopia for most in Turkey. In fact, only granting gender equality in the legal text without affirmative programmes is not sufficient to bring gender equality in an economy in which only a small fraction of women already in formal sector jobs or civil servants can enjoy the improvements.

The following is an evaluation of both the potential of gender equality policies to change the women's secondary role in paid work and to lighten women's role in care work by shifting childcare from the private to public sphere.

Women's Paid Work and Gender Equality Policies

The reform process witnessed an increasing visibility of employment issues and gender equality in the labour market. So, in 2003, a new Labour Law which aimed at meeting the changing demands of business was introduced to adapt the EU Directives into national legislation. It also promised greater gender equality in the labour market. As the new Law, despite some remaining problems, operates parallel with the gender equality directives of the EU it has been welcomed by women's groups and legal experts. The new Labour Law includes the principle of equal pay for work of equal value; equal treatment as regards employment; protection of pregnant and breastfeeding women, and women who recently gave birth; the reversal of burden of proof to the employer in cases of sex-based discrimination at the workplace, and non-discrimination against part-time workers. It brought for the first time provisions against recognition of sexual harassment at the workplace.

Another important development in equality policy discussions occurred in February 2006, when the Confederation of Employers' Associations of Turkey (TİSK) had a Women's Employment Summit and published its concluding comments (TİSK 2006a). These remarks were mostly designed to increase women's employment through neo-liberal policies, supporting private employment agencies, flexible employment strategies and tax reductions to support employers employing women workers. After the publishing of these remarks feminist women's groups came together in order to make a declaration against the TİSK Summit's concluding comments. The focus of this reaction was more on the elimination of gender-based discrimination and provision of equal opportunities through employment quotas and public childcare provisions for women in the public and private spheres[3] (KEIG 2006).

The withdrawal from the labour force and the resultant low activity are the main characteristics of female employment in Turkey. Female employment was 32 per cent in 1989 and dropped to 21 in 2008 (TurkStat 2008). This is seen as a result of the joint effect of the rural-urban migration and the limited employment creation capacity of the Turkish economy. Women, unpaid family labourers dropping out of agricultural activities, became inactive in cities. High female inactivity rates coupled with unregistered informal work is another feature of women's activity in Turkey. Around 30 per cent of those women in non-agricultural employment are working unregistered without any social security coverage or protection. In agricultural areas, women are recorded as unpaid family workers whose rate has declined from 70 per cent of all female employment in 1988 to 34 per cent in 2008. However, they still represent an important share of total female employment. What remains outside these categories is a small fraction of women working in formal sector employment and enjoying social security protection and rights.

The recent legislative changes, aiming to promote gender equality in employment and in workplaces, are still insufficient in improving women's labour market position. For example, Article 5 of the New Turkish Labour Law 2003 grants equal treatment and equal pay to men and women and prohibits discrimination on the basis of sex in work relations. Supported by the equality principle in the Constitution, the Article is compatible with universal equality values and complies with the EU gender equality Directives. However, experts warn against the weaknesses of the Article, not including the exact definition of discrimination and the access to all types and to all levels of vocational training and practical work experience. Not only is the content of the Article seen as short of providing equality for women but the current position of women in employment is far from equal.

The traditional social security system was established around a normative model of family in which men are the principal breadwinners and women are kept by male heads of families, either fathers or husbands (Kılıç 2008: 492). So women receive benefits like healthcare on the basis of the labour market status of 'their men'. The assumption of this model has been most obvious with regard to the tax-benefit system of Turkey, which has treated women and men differently for a long-time and has conventionally included protective provisions for women. It can be argued that the unequal treatment of male and female dependants reflects the existing traditional gender roles and ideology and supports women's dependence on men (Kılıç 2008: 493). These policies encourage women's reluctance to join the workforce, support their exit from the labour market earlier than men, both leading to lower retirement pensions for women. For example, Labour Law Article 14 regulating severance pay, outlines that if a woman leaves her job within a year of marrying, she is entitled to severance pay but men are not entitled to such payment. Again in Social Security Law, there is a distinctive difference between women's and men's entitlement to survivor's benefits.[4] A different treatment of the female children regarding survivor's benefits is an encouragement for women to stay out of productive activities and focus on domestic roles, which thereby strengthens traditional gendered roles in Turkish society.

A gender equality approach based on sameness, pursued at the expense of certain practical interests, would bring an end to provisions formerly enjoyed by women. This makes women more vulnerable in the face of present risks before introducing structural changes to women's status in the labour market. In this regard, the gender difference in retirement age did not comply with the Council Directive 86/378/EEC of 24 July 1986 and the new Social Security and General Health Insurance Law introduced in 2006 aimed at an equal treatment of women and men in terms of retirement rules. According to the Law, the current gendered policy would be maintained until the year 2035 and then a gradual equalisation would be realised in retirement ages until 2048, when the minimum retirement age for both sexes would rise to 65. The ground for equal and later retirement is based on higher life expectancy rates, which are even higher for women than men (Kılıç 2008: 496). However, such a high minimum retirement age for women seems unrealistic in the Turkish context. If women are to be treated on equal terms with men, then domestic responsibilities and women's labour market position must be taken into account as women stay shorter in the labour market and their work is relatively more interrupted due to maternal and domestic responsibilities. In such an environment, the labour market policy supporting women's specific needs such as childcare provisions and parental leave schemes gains more importance.

Attempts are also made to improve Turkey's gender equality records by adopting a new perspective in public sector recruitment strategies. In 2004, as a response to discriminatory practices, the Turkish Prime Ministry published the Circular on Observing Gender Equality Principles during Recruitment to combat gender-biases in recruitment practices. It included a recommendation to develop a gender-sensitive approach in recruitment at State institutions, with measures to improve the gender equality at work, and the redistribution of tasks between women and men. However, even having such a Circular did not stop discriminatory recruitment in public and private institutions. In many instances, the jobs advertised by public institutions called for specific sex recruits. The 2005 CEDAW shadow report by Flying Broom[5] stated that gender-based discrimination is widespread in the areas of male-dominated jobs such as engineering, construction, and mining, and that even for civil service jobs men are preferred to women. In addition, it is reported that female candidates were being asked about their intentions of marriage and childbearing during job interviews in the overwhelmingly feminised banking sector.

The current state of female employment is a reflection of traditional gender-based divisions carried into the labour market. While most women remain out of the labour market, those working overcrowd informal and insecure jobs. Women's position in the labour market and employment policies, however, does not seem promising for gender equality yet. In the Turkish context, informal, especially home-based, work may serve some women's practical interests and thus provide reconciliation between work and family life, but in an affirmative way (Kılıç 2008). Such work provides the flexible working time women need to perform their domestic duties and facilitates the consent of their husbands or fathers to allow them to work, either at home or in female-dominated environments like those in the garment industry, resulting in no social security benefits at all. These gender-differentiated approaches, coupled with the realities of domestic life and the labour market, have suggested a second-class citizenship for women.

Female inactivity is still the norm in Turkey. Although some attempts, such as active labour market programmes and programmes to give support to women entrepreneurs, are made to increase the rate of women's employment, these policies remain patchy without strong support from a national employment strategy. In addition, little is actually done to encourage women to move into the labour market. In fact, some policies such as childcare provisions at workplaces and maternity leave seem to end up discriminating against women and pushing them further out of the labour market as these policies make female labour more expensive for employers.

Women's Care Work and Gender Equality Policies

Gender arrangements in a society affect the way in which care is provided and how care work is rewarded. These also have an impact on gender inequality. Care is usually done at home without any pay. For example, parents care for their children and adults care for their elderly, disabled or ill relatives. Paid care is demanded when women move into the labour market and some of these women offer their labour to provide paid care. In both cases, women's work is devaluated either as unpaid homemakers or under-paid care workers (England 2005). In Turkey, care work is almost always done at home by women. Children are cared for at home until they reach school age, seven. This means that unpaid care and homebound women are the form of gender arrangement in Turkey, and there is almost no public support either in the form of services or financial help for pre-school childcare.

Women's position in the labour market can effectively be improved by reducing the burden of care work in the domestic sphere through increasing public provisions of care, especially childcare facilities. In an environment where no systematic policy initiative pushing women into the labour market or economic need requiring women's labour force participation exist, it is no surprise to see little state support in child care and very limited public childcare facilities for those pre-school children. In 2007, only 16 per cent of all children between 3 and 7 years old are attending nurseries and pre-school classrooms. Public sector provision covers 90 per cent of all these children whereas only 7 per cent is in private sector care. The Ministry of National Education opens nurseries and pre-school classrooms for children between 4 and 6 years old. The mentioned 16 per cent of those children cared for in nurseries and pre-school classrooms is over 3 years old, whereas no study can be found for the care of children under 3 years old (The Ministry of Labour and Social Security 2007). However, we can easily claim that those children under 3 years old are mostly cared for at home by women and only a small number of private nurseries provide care for this age group, servicing only middle-or-upper middle class families. The absence of public support for childcare is a reflection of the state vision of women's primary role in society.

Whereas a very limited number of children benefit from public childcare provision, an existing piece of legislation regulates working women's childcare. *The Regulation on Working Conditions of Pregnant and Nursing Women* issued in 2004, obliged establishments employing more than 100 women workers to have nursery rooms for nursing mothers, and those employing more than 150 women workers to have pre-school facilities for children between 36-72 months. The employer was under obligation to recruit personnel considered to be necessary for the proper functioning of these institutions. Although no reliable data exist, the enforcement of the Regulation has assumingly remained very limited. Ineffectiveness of the existing regulation is being criticised for its bias against women workers taking only the number of women employees into account as a precondition for having a nursery at the workplace. This is the result of the assumption that mothers are primarily responsible for childcare. In this regard, the Coalition of Women's Groups for Women's Work and Labour (KEIG) argues that the regulation has negative effects on women's employment that discourages employers to hire an increasing number of women in that it would lead to the additional expense of opening and operating a nursery. Therefore, it may cause a strong unwillingness to hire women.

Flexible, part-time work has emerged as a formula for women to combine work and childcare duties. In the Turkish context, the introduction of the new Labour Law, securing the rights of flexible workers, is expected to increase women's labour force participation. Bringing many economically inactive women into the labour market through flexible working arrangements would also remedy childcare issues as women are expected to juggle work and care. However, part-time work is not a prevalent type of employment in Turkey, and most of women's flexible and part-time work takes place in the informal sector. Therefore, as the law does not rest on social reality but rather on prediction of future rises in women's part-time and flexible work, it lacks the capacity to offer any improvement. This argument is validated by the fact that since the new Labour Law was enacted in 2003 the rate of female part-time employment did not show any noticeable change (Tunalı 2005). These provisions were introduced in a parcel of legal reform mainly demanded by EU accession requirements and were not motivated by a real concern over the reconciliation of family and work life for working women and men in the specific context of Turkey.

In the European context, parental leave is seen as transforming the traditional gender relations and a potentially challenging the conventional understanding of parenthood in which women are naturally responsible for raising children. By giving men time off work, some of the care duties are delegated to men. In Turkey, parental leave was brought to the political agenda as a policy measure to combat the low rate of female employment at the General Assembly of İş-Kur (Turkish Employment Organisations). A draft law on parental leave was prepared in 2005 but it was pushed out of the agenda of the Parliament when it was extensively discussed in different commissions at the Parliament and could not find support from the employers' organizations (Şenol et al. 2005). The draft [6] proposes to give six months of unpaid parental leave for each spouse upon their request. The leave could be taken after the paid statutory maternity leave of sixteen weeks and the leave is not transferable.

Despite the existing support for parental leave legislation,[7] TİSK the leading employers' association in the country, expresses its opposition to this legislation with the argument that granting fathers parental leave may not lead to their greater involvement in the care of children. They argue that the Council Directive on parental leave is in response to the problems of an aging population and declining birth rates, which are mainly irrelevant for Turkey where there is an abundance of inactive women.[8] Therefore, in the debate on parental leave, the employers' discourse does not have any reference to gender equality but to economic parameters like efficiency. Women's NGOs have supported the draft law and pressed for the urgency of passing the parental leave law with the argument that it would eventually affect and challenge the existing conception of gender roles in which childcare is seen as the sole responsibility of mothers.

While focusing on gender-based differences and providing services for gender specific needs we cannot argue an improvement in women's labour market access supported through this line of policy tools. Even a cursory look at child care facilities shows that state provisions are very limited, and it is clear that children until school age, 6 years old, are cared for at home by their relatives, namely their mothers. Lack of state policies addressing women's practical needs in Turkey is an indication that women are seen as mothers and wives in the existing welfare regime. In this regard, policies encouraging women to join the labour market are almost non-existent and the effect of gender equality policies is very limited.

Conclusion

This chapter discussed the potential of gender equality policies, lately implemented as the partial requirement in Turkey's EU accession process, to promote female employment. Until now, the Turkish welfare state has rested on the idea of women's main role in society being mothers and wives. This manifested itself in low female labour force participation and other structural inequalities between women and men in Turkish society. Depending on their conceptualisation, equality policies can bring the ultimate sameness of women and men, the equal valuation of different contributions, or the transformation of gender relations. In the EU level practice, equality policies are instrumental in channelling women's labour into employment rather than transforming traditional gender divisions. In Turkey, where the welfare state conceptualises women as homemakers, this chapter showed that gender equality polices are not alone sufficient to promote female employment, and even in some cases work against women. So, they are destined to remain legal texts or reach only a small fraction of women if laws are not supported by sufficient policy measures to improve women's position in society.

While Turkey's legal reforms, as a part of her strategy for European Union accession, have helped to eliminate fundamental discriminatory provisions against women there is still need to put the provisions of the new laws and amendments into practice. Inconsistent policies on gender equality and a weak commitment to implement recent changes are traceable in every policy document as well as observable in the actions of social partners engaged in policy making. In the absence of a strong feminist defence of gender equality in the area of employment, the most influential social actors have been employers' organisations as they found the opportunity of introducing flexible work conditions into the Labour Law. Yet, as their motivation is neither feminist nor women's-rights-determined, when an issue such as paternity leave is raised, they oppose the legislation. Feminist women's groups' recent attempt to form an NGO specifically operating in the area of women's work and employment is, in this sense, a very new development.

The main concern is, nonetheless, in regard to how many women are under the protection of this law and how effectively the new law is implemented in a context where high inactivity and informal work are the dominant features of the labour market. This is a common concern expressed by state authorities, trade unions, business associations and women's organisations. Therefore, in the Turkish context, it is possible to argue that gender policy has been predominantly involved in the creation of equal opportunities and is mainly on effective implementation of legal provisions. As part of gender equality policies, the issue of equal pay is secured in the Constitution and the new Labour Law. In the long run, these provisions may have a positive impact on women's activities in the labour market. However, this legislation lacks the support of a positive discrimination/quota policy for women and is insufficient in tackling the implementation of equality during recruitment, training etc. Similarly, there is no provision in the legislation and ensuring labour policies to address the gender pay gap with a view to eliminate it. Obviously, future impact of the legal reform rests on how effectively these problems are handled.

9

THE SOCIAL SECURITY REFORM AND WOMEN IN TURKEY

Mustafa Şahin[1]

The economic crisis of February 2001 led to massive social deterioration in Turkey. In the aftermath of the major crisis of 2001, the Justice and Development Party's (AKP) move into power was the result of deep crisis. The AKP government strictly followed the neoliberal macroeconomic program which was designed by the former government. This meant that the party took even more radical steps in favor of capital and further deepened the liberalisation of the economy. When the AKP came into power, the period also became characterized by high international liquidity and large volume inflows of external funds which then reduced interest rates and the exchange rate. Also, the increase in domestic consumption resulted from credit expansion and increases in private fixed capital formation which then led to high growth rates (Boratav 2009). Thus, the high economic growth and intensive privatizations gave the AKP the ability to manoeuvre within the expanding limits of the national budget. The AKP managed to put into effect a set of partial regulations and implementations in social security – especially in the health services – from 2002 to 2007, which will have a serious redistribution effect in the medium- and long-term. On the other hand, the government aimed to improve the rights and freedom of historically oppressed social groups (women, Kurds, etc.), initiated through pressure from the European Union accession process.

The Social Insurance and General Health Insurance Law, in effect as of 2008,[2] is a typical neoliberal structural reform program which dispossesses the improvements in civil rights and freedoms from the social right base. The two main purposes of the reform are quite explicit. One is to cut social security deficits which began to accelerate in the mid-1990s. The other is to promote the private pension system (see Şahin and Elveren in this volume) and to privatize the public health services (see Ağartan in this volume) altogether. There is no doubt that the level of social welfare severely crippled by the frequent economic crisis will be further reduced as a result of these policy preferences.

Furthermore, the Reform may lead to adverse results in the near future which will reverse the improvements achieved concerning the rights and freedoms of women both in the national (Civil Law, Penal Law etc.) and international (CEDAW, UN Conferences etc.) context. In other words, the steps taken to provide women with the civil and political rights to ascend to equal citizen status have been negatively affected and their social rights deteriorated. For all women, the right to have social security plays a key role in the practice of civil and political rights. It is rather difficult to expect women to enjoy their civil and political rights in a society in which they are considered dependants to men as wife, daughter or mother to obtain basic necessities rather than being considered an equal citizen. This structure limits the scope of the supply of these necessities or leaves them unobtained.

The aim of this chapter is to examine the effects of the Social Security Reform on women in Turkey. After a brief discussion on the welfare regime in Turkey, the Reform will be examined with respect to compulsory coverage, social benefits, and entitlement conditions, as well as the effects of changes on women.

The Welfare Regime and Gender in Turkey

It can be argued that the welfare regime in Turkey has a hybrid structure (Lewis 1997; Orloff 1993; O'Connor 1993; Korpi 2000). The contributor – non contributor distinction that is based on the gendered division of labour within the family and nationalist-solidarist citizenship construction both can be seen in a particular way through conservative-corporatist regimes. It is similar to the Southern European Model with its clientalist-particularist social aid distribution, weak social protection for those who do not have a chance to be employed formally and low capacity of public services (Gough 1996; Buğra and Keyder 2003). Especially social security mechanisms that are gradually being marketed and commercialized based on purchasing power bear the stamp of liberal regimes by highlighting the income-need based programs.

(i) The fundamental feature of the welfare regime in Turkey is a necessity for formal/registered employment and occupational status as a condition to be included in the formal security system. This results in a much lower provision of insurance for women since female employment has been historically low and women are mainly expected to perform unpaid family work in rural areas. The female employment in Turkey fell behind the world's rising employment trends in the services and manufacturing sectors (Toksöz 2009). Only 5.9 million of the women out of 26 million who are working age are employed today, as opposed to 15.3 million men out of the same number of men at the working age.[3]

(ii) The social insurance system is based on the norm of a strong familial ideology in Turkey. The entitlement of dependants (spouse, children, etc.) and survivors (widow, orphan, etc.) are determined according to their relations with the insurance holder. The existence of a strict sexist division of labour (husband-earner, wife-carer) in the family between the actively-insured and the dependants can be considered the first sign of the hegemony of the male breadwinner in Turkey. This is quantified by the high number of housewives and 61.9% of women who are not participating in the work force who remain housewives (TurkStat 2010).

(iii) The inequalities that women face in working life in Turkey results in a lower range of social benefits according to their insurance holder status. The low level of social protection for women results mainly from the low level of premiums due to gender wage gaps. Similarly, the number of years of contributions paid is another actual variable that determines the level of social protection. The rate of unemployment is much higher for the majority of women as a result of their lack of opportunities to work. Also, opportunities for promotion are much lower as compared to men both in the public and the private sector; the insurance holder status for women is again a subordinated status. On the other hand, it is observed that the scope of being involved in informal working relations is much broader for women. In February 2010, 56.1% of women were involved in the informal sector as compared to 36.2% of men (TurkStat 2010). While on the one hand, women are left out of the coverage of the social security system as a result of working in the informal sector, quite a number of the features of the existing social security system can push women to work in the informal sector.

(iv) The non-contributory regime (i.e. social assistance) is the weakest area of the welfare state in Turkey. Not only are the public resources allocated for the non–contributory regime within the general administration too low, but the institutional administration is ineffective. Social aid is distributed on the basis of means testing either as cash or in kind. The Social Assistance and Solidarity Encouragement Foundations, a positive development in the local decision making, are disabled by the extent of subjective, even clientelistic, partisan relationships in the distribution of social aids. Another non–contributory regime application is the Green Card which provides access to health services and medical expenses. The fourth category is the aid for disabled individuals. This benefit is provided to the family member who is performing the care, usually a woman. In this situation, poor families are determined with respect to their income level.[4] In general, the family is provided with several options by the state and the state pays the value of services purchased from the private sector. Likewise, services might be provided through a public agency. Still one other important option is to pay the family a certain amount for care service in case they prefer to provide care themselves. In most cases, families choose the last option. This can be considered a positive development in the recognition of women's unpaid services. On the other hand, some others argue that women have to stay at home for the care service under the control of the state.

(v) The accumulation regime of the economy is an important aspect of the Turkish welfare regime. Especially after the liberalisation of capital flows in 1989, the capital accumulation process and growth performance have become dependent on the external inflows (hot money inflows, foreign direct investment, external debt, etc.) in Turkey.[5] The structural adjustment policies and the stability programs of the 1980s and 1990s have been replaced by the strategies for improving the investment climate and the governance models in 2000s. The vast majority of the population has been still exposed to the negative impacts of the neoliberal model (Boratav 2010). The gender inequality has increased as a result of a set of policy applications such as decline in wages, a real decline in peasant incomes, a contraction in public services, privatisation and the rise in the proportion of indirect taxes in public revenue (Çağatay and Elson 2000; Çağatay 2003). Another important feature of the Turkish economy in the 2000s is its inability to generate employment in line with the global employment trends despite a relatively high growth rate.

(vi) The question of how the relationship between citizenship and gender is built is very important in the classification of the welfare regimes. This relationship in Turkey, grounded on the public-private duality (Pateman 1989), is similar to other nation-state models (Lister 1997). However, it involves some different –even specific– properties concerning role expectations (the role of mothers as the bearer of ideology, virginity, denial of sexuality, etc.) based on a secular, nationalist ideology (Özar and Şahin 2009; Kadıoğlu 1999; Sirman 2002). The gender-citizenship relations in society have a more hybrid quality with the inclusion of ideological inputs resulting from the conservative-Islamist or intrinsic social belonging (Kurdish, Alevi, Non-Muslim minorities, etc.). It is observed that there are two fundamental discussions for women in Turkey even though these two can be scaled with respect to variables such as class, ethnicity and religion/sect. The first is the high discrepancy between the constitutional/legal framework of civil, political and social rights of women and their de facto utilization level as compared to men. The second is that the interactions among the civil, political, social rights of women are much more powerful than men's. It is observed that inequalities which are seen historically in the utilization of rights and freedoms are gradually increasing depending on the multi-dimensional relations among people.

Turkey is not avoiding adherence to the accepted agreements in the field of women's rights and freedoms in the international arena. CEDAW is the most significant development in this field recently. However, it is still a mystery as to how much CEDAW will help to transform the hegemonic codes in the gender and citizenship relation in Turkey. Elson (2006) underlines that gender budget analysis can help in monitoring compliance with CEDAW. The greatest deficiency in the recognition of gender equality recently in Turkey emerges in the lack of synchronization between favourable distribution/redistribution preferences.

(vii) The relation between women's collective political struggle level and the gender inequality is also covered in the literature. It is emphasized that if the struggle increases then gender inequality has the potential to decrease (Huber et. al. 2004). In this context, the activism of the feminist movement in Turkey is increasing. It can be said that, an expansion of the feminist agenda covering issues such as sexual violence (honour killings, rape, harassment, etc.) and domestic inequality in terms of social policy and even economic policies is emerging. The fundamental demands of the reformist feminist opposition included the right to retirement without being dependent on father or husband, depreciation allowance based on gender, early retirement with low premiums, etc. The bundle of these demands was based on compensation for unpaid domestic labour without confining women to a housewife identity (Acar-Savran 2010). The feminist movement is diversifying gradually and forming allegiances and coalitions. In addition to this, there is a positive transformation in the communication among feminist organizations, and the number of female parliamentarians is rising (around 10%). From this point, the Committee on Equal Opportunities for Women and Men in the GNAT (Grand National Assembly of Turkey) founded in 2009 will constitute a significant political-institutional ground.[6]

Compulsory Coverage

With the reform, the social security system which had a five-pronged institutional structure (workers, public servants, self-employed/employer, agricultural workers and self-employed in agriculture) was abolished and replaced by a singular system.[7] As in the former, the new system, too, adopts a model which is based on forms of employment and occupational status, with the exception of general health insurance. The types of insurance holders associated with forms of employment were reduced from five to three. Agricultural workers and those self-employed in agriculture (i.e. small farmers) were integrated into the categories of workers and self-employed/employer, respectively. Compared to the former system, there are now larger working groups remaining outside compulsory coverage. Especially, most of these groups are composed of the working poor who are in precarious forms of employment and women are particularly over-represented.

Discrepancies between social security norms applicable to three employment statuses (workers, public servants and self-employed/employers) were reduced. Even a series of norms were made applicable to all three statuses. Naturally, the positions of dependants (wife/husband, children) and their survivors (widowed, orphaned) were accordingly redefined. The priorities of the reform (except for general health insurance) can be summarized as follows: (i) abolishment of social security schemes specific to agricultural workers and small farmers, (ii) expanding working groups not covered by the scheme, and (iii) bringing rights and obligation associated with three statuses (worker, public servants and self-employed/employer) closer to each other.

(i) Abolition of social insurance systems specific to agricultural workers and small farmers

One of the social insurance systems now abolished (Law no. 2925) was introduced in October 1983 to cover those temporarily employed in agriculture on the basis of service contracts. It proved ineffective since inclusion in the system was voluntary. Given this and also considering that employer-employee relations in agriculture are not covered by the Labour Code (Law no. 4857), it becomes clear that agricultural workers (particularly migrant workers and their families in seasonal employment) face extremely hard working and living conditions (Yıldırak et al. 2003).[8] While the reform was expected to introduce an institutional structure to cover these long excluded groups, results were contrary to initial expectations.

The other social insurance system (Law no. 2926) abolished with the reform was introduced together with the former and targeted small farmers in agriculture. Based on compulsory coverage, this scheme yielded relatively more satisfactory outcomes than Law no. 2925. As of 2007, there were 1,092,000 insurance holders in this scheme. Of this total, 95 per cent were men and only 5 per cent were women. Of 190,000 persons receiving old age pensions, 98 per cent were men and 2 per cent were women. While there were 96,000 persons receiving survivors' benefits (widowed, orphaned, parents), 8 per cent were men and 92 per cent were women. An important reason for this striking imbalance is a provision which determines insurance holder status in the system and which was in effect until 2003. According to this provision, males over age 22 and female household heads over age 22 are the compulsory insurance holder. In other words, the system is in a way consciously built on gender inequality. While women in the status of unpaid family labourers had the option of voluntary coverage in the same system, in practice it was observed that this option remained largely unused.

In the most recent years, shrinking budget support for agriculture and particularly excessive pressure on farmers' labour exerted by on-contract farming and market dynamics have further galvanized the importance of social security in this sector. Striving to introduce uniform norms and standards for industry, services and agriculture will in fact make it more difficult for farmers to have access to social security. In the process of agricultural production where household and farming activities intermix, such policy priorities will inevitably depreciate the wellbeing of rural women and further aggravate already existing gender inequalities.

(ii) Expansion of working groups left out of compulsory coverage
In both old and new systems, workers engaged in different forms of employment as well as those self-employed are excluded from social security coverage. Most of the unpaid family workers and domestic workers left out of the social insurance system are women (KEIG 2006). Note that women employed in these ways exceed one-third of total female employment.[9] However, working groups excluded from the new system are not confined to those mentioned above. Small farmers, temporary and migrant agricultural workers and small urban shopkeepers/artisans and producers who are exempt from income tax can voluntarily remain out of the system if they declare incomes lower than the minimum wage. Considering this provision together with the heavy contribution obligations (33.5-39 per cent of gross minimum wage) there is a large group remaining without coverage (Mülkiyeliler Birliği 2005). Further, the pro-

portion of those working in agriculture without any social security increased from 83.9 per cent to 85.6 per cent over the same period in 2009 (TurkStat 2010).

Leaving such work out of social security coverage suggests that informal employment is legally recognized at least in this respect. In the Household Labour Survey, the question geared to obtaining data on informal employment is: "Are you registered with any social security institution as a result of your working?" On the other hand, the relevant legislation itself prescribes work and working relations not considered for social security coverage; thus, informal employment is not, at least in the context of this type of working relations, a violation, but a legal norm of the system (Eren et. al. 2010). Note that the phenomenon of informal employment is not limited to those mentioned work practices. There is a considerably large population in which women outnumber men, employed informally, explicitly in violation of the existing legislation.[10]

Besides the high number of women in informal employment, women's exist in the social security system as dependants. For instance, as of 2007 (SGK 2007) there are 8.5 million insurance holders within the compulsory social security system and of this total 1.9 million are women. In the same system, on the other hand, the number of persons entitled to survivors' benefits is 1.27 million. Of 798,000 entitled to survivors' benefits for their spousal status, 783,000 are women. In the same context, of 462,000 children, 357,000 are girls, and of 10,000 parents, 9,000 are mothers.

The shrinking coverage of social insurance can be counter-balanced to a certain extent by such measures as widening the scope of non-contributory regime, enrichment of what it offers so as to bring it closer to the contributory regime and its gender sensitive sharing in terms of social risks and needs. However, there is no country where a non-contributory regime has turned out to be as effective as a contributory regime. Leaving this aside, the non-contributory regime in Turkey is far behind that of countries at similar levels of development in terms of both coverage and the level of protection provided as well as the amount of public resources mobilized (Buğra 2008).

In this section, we tried to address the priorities of the reform in relation to agricultural workers, small farmers and excluded working groups. The relative proportion of women is higher than men in these working relations. At the same time, the dependent position of women in the old system involves a risk that can narrow the compulsory coverage. Of course, when the issue is considered within the framework of the life experience of women and the multi-dimensional nature of the welfare regime in Turkey, it is possible to reach much more explanatory outcomes and a range of new questions can emerge. In other words, thinking on how the reform may affect the pattern of stratification and inequality within and among gender will create further clarity in this process (Orloff 1993).

(iii) Social Benefits

Social benefits can be assessed in the framework of the short and long term social insurance programs. The short term social insurance programs cover job accident/occupational disease, sickness and maternity insurance branches. All social benefits paid in cash are the main forms of daily temporary incapacity allowance, permanent incapacity income, etc. Furthermore, health-care services are given to the insurance holder and his/her dependants so as to regain health in case of sickness, job accident, and occupational disease, maternity.

First, the reform is to treat insurance holders equally on some aspects. This has both positive and negative effects among insurance holders: it broadens the temporary incapacity allowance that self employed/employer can take. Before the reform, there were no social benefits paid in cash in case of sickness, job accident, and occupational disease, or maternity for the self-employed/employer. While the same social benefit given to public servants as replacement rate was 1:1, this proportion was reduced to 2:3. However this regulation will not be enforced for existing public servants. It will be valid for new public servants after this provision takes effect.

There are inequalities between the insurance holder and his/her dependants in both the old and new system. Especially dependants facing social risks do not have income security (economic assistances) in short term social insurance programs. In other words, daily temporary incapacity allowance or permanent incapacity income are given only to the insurance holder facing social risks. With respect to women, the impacts of this regulation has led to big inequalities on gender relations. The social insurance system does not take into account the welfare effects of women's unpaid labour and household production in society.

The long term social insurance programs consist of invalidity, old-age and survivors insurance branches. By focusing on the financing side of the insurance process, the reform shows serious deterioration in the case of long term schemes. These pensions that constitute one of the largest expenses in the system have decreased in real terms by changing actuarial variables such as replacement rate and updated coefficient. The old system's replacement rates have changed to 2 per cent with the reform. The other is due to the change in the definition of updated coefficient from "inflation + economic growth" to "inflation + 30 per cent* economic growth" with the reform.

In addition, there are two new regulations that cause disadvantage for women directly. The reform eliminates the social right of the daughter of a deceased father to benefit from health services from her father's survivor insurance. The old system made it possible for daughters to use this social right (health security) as long as they were not employed and not married. Another regulation detrimental to women is that the widows, when they start working, lose their entitlement to receive survivor pensions from their deceased husbands' survivor insurance by a factor of one-third. This is discouraging women from participating in the labour market, at least in the formal one.

As is underlined in the literature, the social insurance systems that are based on insurance schemes accentuate the various inequalities in income and earnings (and hence the premiums set according to these criteria) with respect to gender and class. Especially for the case of insurance holders, lower premium payments result in lower social protection. However, the link between the premium amount paid and the social protection level, such as old-age pension, were weaker in the old system. This situation favoured insurance holders with low social rights where the majority were women. Strengthening the linkage via the reform lowers the income substitution rate and widens the gap between the social protection levels among different social and economic groups.

Entitlement Conditions

As in the former Social Security System, the entitlement conditions in the new system are also classified according to six social protection functions: job accident/occupational diseases, sickness, maternity, invalidity, old age, survivors. Each social protection function has separate entitlement conditions (i.e. age, number of contributions paid, etc.). The basic conditions for entitlement to the job accident/occupational insurance and maternity insurance have mostly remained unchanged. Only sickness insurance within short term insurance branches has been completely restructured. The minimum number of contributions that must be paid in order to benefit from sickness insurance has decreased for self employed/employer and workers insurance holders and their dependants. In the old system, these individuals were obligated to make contributions for at least 8 months in order to benefit from sickness/health care insurance. The reduced period of responsibility is now one month with the reform.

The conditions for entitlement have made it harder to qualify for old age insurance. Some of these changes have even been called the "Retirement Coffin" by the public in 1999. Namely, the 1999 reform changes amended the social insurance laws relating to old age insurance in number of day of premium payment and age level. For public servants and self employed/employer, there is a contribution period of 25 years (9000 days) and women age 58 and men 60. There are simultaneously two basic conditions to obtain a full pension. For workers, age level is the same, but the contribution period is 7000 days. With the reform, the retirement age for women and men will gradually increasing by 2048 to 65. The number of days of premium payment and age level for old age insurance is unrealistic in terms of working conditions.

The other retirement form in old age insurance is especially for flexible workers. Entitlement conditions are made difficult by setting the retirement age as 61 for women and 63 for men, with the period for premium payment set to 5400 work days. Furthermore, the conditions are made stricter for the disabled (according to the degree of disability) in terms of premium payment period.

Moreover, the raises that were set according to a person's active working period each year, 90 days, for the occupations performed largely by women such as hostesses, and printing and publishing jobs have been eliminated. This change contributed further to the general increase in the amount of contributions paid and the age limit for these jobs. The raises according to active working period for jobs related to defence and protection that are mostly performed by men have been preserved (KEIG 2006).

There has been a reduction in premium payments under the old age insurance schemes for women who have disabled children. According to this new regulation, for these women workers, the amount of contribution paid would be multiplied by 0.25 and the result would be deducted from the age limit. This last change benefits women in this respect; however, it also makes it obvious that the responsibility for men/society/the state has been placed on the shoulders of women according to this gendered division of labour.

Another branch of long term insurance is survivor insurance. The contribution eligibility requirements paid have been shortened. However, the requirement for the widow for not marrying again in order to receive the death pension under the old system has preserved under the new reform package. This reinforces the male breadwinner perspective. The daughters of the deceased in turn need to be single and not employed in order to receive the death pension. In general, the sexist policies are most visible under the social protection schemes concerning wives, widows, orphans and motherhood.

The group for which the premium rate has increased mostly is housewives who choose to become the voluntary insurance holder. Under the old system, the housewives, when they chose to become the voluntary insurance holder, needed to pay a premium of 20 per cent of minimum wage in order to be protected against long term risks (old-age, death and invalidity). With the reform, housewives who choose to get insured lose their entitlement health service benefits as dependants of their husbands. Therefore, in addition to the aforementioned 20 per cent of gross minimum wage, they need to pay 12 per cent of the premium base set for the General Health Insurance Scheme. In addition to this increase rate for housewives, the premium rates for self-employed agricultural workers (small producers) and those returning back to employment in their retirement periods have increased as well. However, the new legislation decreases the premium rates for those that are insured by the private insurance schemes as well as the public ones, and hence those that are more privileged. Specifically, the reform allows them to deduct 30 per cent of private insurance premiums from their premium base. The same rate was specified as 5 per cent under the old system. This change can be seen as in favour of the both private insurance companies and high income group with private insurance. Furthermore, the health insurance premium rate for self-employed has been reduced from 20 per cent to 12.5 per cent.

Conclusion

The IMF, World Bank, EU and business organizations in Turkey hailed this reform. These international organizations and the capitalist sector argue that the policy will maintain the fiscal discipline which was absent in the period of social system running deficits. The intended results are larger working groups remaining out of the compulsory coverage, lower social protection, and more challenging conditions for entitlement. Nonetheless the reform's emphasis on private pension and health insurance schemes and the privatisation of health services creates new niches from which to extract profits by capital. In this respect, the reform is a perfect example of an integration process of the periphery into the world economic system.

Traditional masculine codes (norms) are implicitly strengthened in this social insurance context. Women's vulnerability to social risk is affected by the gender norms constructed in these economic, legal, political, and cultural contexts (social expectations for appropriate behaviour in the gender roles). Likewise, unless women accept and adapt to the norms, they face more risks. The reform creates a vicious cycle and has ignored the varieties of new social risks for women. Hegemonic male powers reaffirm a strong position against improvements towards the recognition of gender identities in Turkey.

It is widely accepted that the definition and classification of social risks from a gender perspective take into account women's experiences (Kabeer and Sabates-Wheeler 2003; Lutrell and Moser 2004). In the most recent period, there have been two main changes in terms of inter-related constraints and opportunities facing women as agents.

Firstly, the transformation in the state's role and industrial relations has created new potential social risks for women. The high rates of unemployment, large informal economy, job insecurity, the decrease in real wages and agricultural producer prices, the privatisation and restructuring of public services, the cessation of public subsidies, and the increases in indirect taxes are the main mechanisms that restrain household welfare. This period also witnessed both changing consumption patterns and a transformation in the ideological role of consumption.

This chapter emphasized the disadvantages of the reform for women. Furthermore, these disadvantages put immense pressure on women's unpaid and paid labour, making it difficult for women to satisfy even their basic needs. This in turn, imposes a downward limit on social welfare expectations (Elson 1998, 2002, 2006).[11] It is argued that this type of reform and introduction of user charges will increase the effectiveness of the social security system without sacrificing the social dimension by making poor people immune to these additional fees. In practice, due to poverty, most of the poor people and especially women and girls cannot benefit from these services (Barnett and Grown 2004). This increased pressure on women's unpaid labour can be seen as a disguised tax increase (Antonopoulos 2008) or from women to the men/capital class/state a resource transfer.

Despite deepening structural inequalities, all these social risks and needs cannot be attributed only to changes in redistribution. Elsewhere in society, growing social tensions center on struggles for recognition of difference according to gender, ethnicity, religion, and sexuality. There has been a war ongoing for nearly 30 years in the Eastern and South-Eastern parts of Turkey within the Kurdish problem context. The war has mostly disadvantaged women (Çağlayan 2008). The rising Islamic movement has revealed a polarisation within Turkish politics and society that has emerged in the recent period. The placing of women with headscarves at the center of the tension has come under vigorous attack (İlyasoğlu 2000; Göle 2008). With the rise of gender awareness, women started to fight against various harassment issues, including sexual harassment. The pressure on the recognition of homosexual identities has gone hand in hand with widespread homophobic attacks (Dünşen 2010).[12] These issues should also be taken into account by the social security policies.

There is no doubt that, empirical research as well as conceptual studies should be carried out to better understand and address the gender issues in the reform.

10

GENDER AND HEALTH SECTOR REFORM: POLICIES, ACTIONS AND EFFECTS

Tuba İ. Ağartan

This chapter examines the implementation of gender approaches in the wider context of new health policies and institutional restructuring that has been taking place since the mid-1990s in Turkey. Focusing on recent changes introduced in the health care system as part of the Health Transformation Program (HTP), and parallel but separate gender mainstreaming policies, it aims to contribute to the discussions in this book on the effects of welfare reforms on women within the context of Turkey's neoliberal transformation and its accession to the EU.

In the Gender Empowerment Measure,[1] Turkey ranks 101st out of 109 countries, while it is 79th in the Human Development Index among 83 countries at very high and high development levels (HDR 2009: 187). Despite important steps taken since the mid-1990s to improve gender equality through changes in the Constitution, the Penal Code, the Civil Code and the Labour Act, and growing attention to gender mainstreaming, the implementation of these policy steps and achievement of gender equality are still considered major challenges for the country. As the Millennium Development Goals (MDG) Turkey 2010 Report notes, women's participation in politics is still very low, with a representation of 9.1 per cent of women in the Parliament; the female literacy rate is increasing but not at a desired pace; violence against women and high acceptance levels of violence against women remain crucial issues to address (MDG-Turkey 2010: 29-32). In addition, as some of the articles in this volume highlight, the extremely low levels of participation of women in the paid labour market is another important issue.

Following a review of the recently introduced policies aimed at improving women's health and incorporating a gender perspective to health policies, this chapter will explore the gender implications of the Health Transformation Program (HTP) which was introduced in 2003 by the incumbent Justice and Development Party (AKP). Despite a growing literature on Health Sector Reforms (HSRs) comprising comparative as well as individual case studies of advanced industrial and developing countries, gender has not received much attention until recently (Kuhlmann and Annandale 2010; Standing 2010). In Turkey, too, except for some reports published by women's organizations (KEIG 2008), there has not been much discussion about the lack of a gender perspective in the HTP. This chapter aims to initiate a debate on the gender dimension of health care reform by exploring the following three questions: 1) Is the HTP gender-sensitive? 2) To what extent has the implementation of the HTP improved women's access to health care? 3) Has the HTP promoted gender equality?

An interesting feature of the Turkish experience with health reform has been the extent to which progressive initiatives in gender mainstreaming were disconnected from the reform process. Following the lead of international organizations like the WHO, the UN and the Council of Europe, Turkey has recognized the need to adopt gender mainstreaming policies, and the process gained new momentum with Turkey's accession to the EU. Yet, the reform program itself can hardly be described as 'gender-sensitive' both in terms of the policymaking process and its implementation. A discussion of both gender mainstreaming policies and details of health reform can serve as the first step in identifying ways to bridge this gap.

The chapter will begin with a survey of the literature on health sector reforms and gender mainstreaming which will discuss policy steps taken especially in relation to health care. It continues with a review of the policies introduced by Turkish policymakers since the mid-1990s with the purpose of addressing women's health needs and incorporating a gender perspective into health policy. Focus then shifts to the HTP, analyzing the implications of the reform in terms of access, affordability and availability of health services for women. The chapter concludes with a discussion of how to incorporate a gender perspective into main dimensions of the reform, emphasizing the role of women's movements in the process.

Gender and Health Care: Reviewing the Literature

Gender relations of power have long been recognized as an important social determinant of health. Gender interacts with class, economic or racial inequalities to determine the health status of women and men, their differing needs, their vulnerability to ill-health, their help-seeking behavior, and the delivery of health care services. Women also carry an unequal burden as caregivers to sick or disabled family members. Despite this, gender has been a relatively low priority issue in both health policy research and the reform agendas of governments. One reason that explains the insensitivity of political institutions and actors in health policy has been the prevalence of gender biases and inequalities in terms of influencing resource allocation, policy-making and implementation. Societies have different assumptions and norms about women's positions as dependants, as equal partners and earners in households or as 'mothers and daughters' of male breadwinners. These assumptions are then reflected in the policy decisions about organizing the financing and delivery of health care services.

Since the late 1980s and early 1990s, governments in advanced industrialized countries as well as in the developing world have carried out reforms which involved a profound transformation of the division of labour among the state, market, family and the community in their health care systems. Major justification for these reforms was provided by the so-called 'health care crisis' which was defined in general terms as the inability of governments to meet rising needs and growing costs in an environment of fiscal crisis and global economic pressures. It has been argued that health care systems have reached the limits of what was economically possible and therefore substantial reforms were needed to deal with growing pressures (Defever 1995; Gonzales Block 1997).

Although, in the context of developing countries, there were additional and somewhat different pressures that influenced the perception of the so-called 'crisis' – such as frequent economic crises, political factors and social dislocations, demographic and epidemiological factors and additional socioeconomic factors such as massive migration to urban centers and regional inequalities – the reform agendas presented important similarities with the those in advanced industrial countries. Markets were seen as a panacea to many problems, framed mostly in terms of efficiency or costs, whereas the public sector was denigrated as corrupt and inefficient. The 'global' health reform blueprint that emerged included elements such as the institutional separation of provision and financing functions, the introduction of new financing mechanisms like user-fees, enhanced participation of non-state entities, increased reliance on market mechanisms, the introduction of cost-control measures, improvement of management systems and decentralization (Green 1999; Standing 1999; Cassels 2006). The earlier attempts during the 1990s, as Standing points out, consisted of "technical and managerial reforms to improve the functions of government bureaucracies", rather than measure "the impact on and outcomes of service delivery" (Standing 2010: 58). In this context, the health needs of women or the implications of reforms on women's access to health care services were largely neglected in health policy discussions.

This is not to say that gender issues were totally invisible. Indeed, at the international level, there were some important initiatives to bring gender equality to the center of health policy. In 1994, promotion of gender equality and empowerment of women was mentioned as one of the objectives of the Cairo Conference on Population and Development (Cairo Conference). The Fourth World Congress on Women held in Beijing (Beijing Platform) led to increased efforts to 'mainstream' gender in all sectors including health care. The WHO defines the concept of 'gender mainstreaming' as:

> the process of assessing the implications for women and men of any planned action, including legislation, policies or programs, in any area and at all levels. It is a strategy for making women's as well as men's concerns and experiences an integral dimension in the design, implementation, monitoring and evaluation of policies and programs in all political, economic and social spheres, such that inequality between men and women is not perpetuated. The ultimate goal is to achieve gender equality (WHO 2010).

Adapting this definition to the field of healthcare, a major purpose of gender mainstreaming is to achieve gender equality by identifying and addressing "inequalities in health status and unequal access to and inadequate health care services between women and men" (Beijing Declaration 1995: 38). At the same time, it is "a technical and a political process which requires shifts in organizational cultures and ways of thinking, as well as in the goals, structures and resource allocations" (WHO 2010). Governments and other social actors are expected to identify and address the effects of policy decisions for women and men before they are made while simultaneously creating mechanisms for equal participation of women and men (Theobald et. al. 2002). Such 'enabling' of policy environments should be viewed broadly in terms of combating the male-bias embedded in healthcare services and reform strategies, what Sen et al. call the 'organizational plaque' (2007: xvii). Gender mainstreaming policies ran the risk of being ignored or diluted at the implementation stage as they challenge long-standing, male dominated power structures within organizations, and force people to learn new ways of doing things and/or unlearn old habits (Sen et al. 2007: xvii).

Given these obstacles to successful implementation, progress has been uneven mostly due to insufficient resources, weak organizational mechanisms and poor political commitment (Sen et al. 2007). Serious gaps between political rhetoric on gender and actual practice still exist in many countries, yet gender mainstreaming remains popular on the agenda of national governments as well as international institutions as the MDGs demonstrate. Gender equality is a prominent commitment in the MDGs: while MDG3 calls for the promotion of gender equality and the empowerment of women, MDG5 focuses on maternal health and aims to reduce maternal mortality (Target 1) and achieve universal access to reproductive health services (Target 2). Gender mainstreaming is also a major policy priority for UN agencies like the UNDP in shaping the activities of country offices as well as national governments.

Overall, when we consider health sector reforms, recent literature identifies a nuanced approach to reforming health care systems in the developing world, placing more emphasis on the link between health and development (Langer and Catino 2006) as well as health sector reforms and anti-poverty strategies (Standing 2010). Especially during the 2000s, as part of this expansion of focus from improving efficiency and controlling the costs, the involvement of civil society actors and patients were actively encouraged in reform processes and in delivery of the health services. Signs of such an approach were also noticeable in the MDGs. Yet, despite this nuanced approach and other important policy steps towards mainstreaming gender in health care, it is hard to argue that health sector reforms have taken gender equality issues into consideration. In hindsight, the reformers have been rather slow to integrate a gender perspective and to encourage the active participation of women in the making and implementation of reform policies.[2]

Turning our attention to the Turkish case, it must be noted that important policy steps have been taken since the mid-1990s in the direction of addressing women's health needs and improving their access to health services. What remains to be achieved, as Standing (2010) rightly observes in most health sector reform initiatives, is the coordination of these positive steps with reform initiatives. In addition, efforts on addressing women's health needs should not simply focus on maternal health but should expand to include other issues such as addressing growing pressures on women as providers of care in both the private and professional spheres or identifying gender biases in the treatment and diagnosis of health problems such as coronary heart disease. The next section aims to provide background to this discussion, presenting an overview of the policies that were introduced in the direction of gender mainstreaming and those proposed and implemented within the context of the HTP.

Gender and Health Care in Turkey
Gender and Turkish Health Policy

'Achievement of Gender Equality' and addressing women's health needs, though usually limited to reproductive health, were identified as among the major priorities of Turkish governments since the mid-1990s. The international organizations and their initiatives in the health sector have clearly influenced these policy goals and priorities. Turkey adopted its Program of Action after attending the Cairo Conference in 1994, which was followed by the development of the 'Gender Equality National Action Plan' (1996) prepared in line with the Action Plan of the Beijing Platform. Although it was important in terms of identifying major targets, such as increasing women's access to high quality health services or launching gender sensitive initiatives on reproductive health, the plan could not be implemented effectively due to important gaps in the identification of responsible actors and definition of proper mechanisms of evaluation and monitoring (KSGM 2008: 22).

The new century heralded new initiatives in women's health as MDGs were developed within the framework of the UN, and the EU emerged as an important donor in the Turkish health sector. Closer relations with the EU have led to the development of sector wide programs with the Euro Mediterranean Partnership (MEDA) in 1995. When the AKP government took office in 2002, it repeated previous governments' commitments to reduce maternal mortality and announced 'making pregnancy and child birth safer' as among its major priorities (Akdağ 2007). The 'National Strategic Action Plan on Sexual Health and Reproductive Health for the Health Sector (2005-2015)', as updated in 2005, defined reducing maternal mortality, preventing unwanted pregnancies, improving the health of the youth, preventing sexually transmitted infections, and decreasing inequalities between regions in the field of health as its major priorities. The 'Reproductive Health Program' (RHP) was one of the sector-wide projects receiving MEDA funds in Turkey aimed at reaching these objectives.

The RHP, implemented in 2003-2007, represents one of the cornerstones of gender mainstreaming strategy in Turkey. On the one hand, in terms of resource allocation, it provided grants to improve access to reproductive health services, increase their scope, coverage and quality and t. to address regional disparities. On the other hand, in terms of creating an 'enabling policy environment', the program aimed to increase knowledge and develop a better understanding of rights and preferences concerning sexual health and reproductive health among the members of parliament, policy makers and decision makers. Furthermore, within the framework of this program, studies have been conducted to provide data on mortality rates (National Maternal Mortality Study 2005), women's access to reproductive health services and their health seeking behaviors (Health Seeking Behavior Study 2007). Given the lack of gender-sensitive data, these studies constitute initial steps to fill an important void.

'Addressing regional disparities', perceived as among the most important barriers in accessing health services, has been a major policy priority for Turkish governments. As National Maternal Mortality Study demonstrates, the maternal mortality ratio is the highest in Northeast Anatolia and East Black Sea with a ratio of 68.3 for both regions compared to a national average of 28.5 per 100,000 live births (2005:6). Difficulties in reaching a health facility (due to factors such as road and weather conditions, limited means of transportation or high transportation expenses), shortage of health personnel and equipment are listed as important factors limiting access to health services.

To deal with this major problem, the Ministry of Health has recently begun experimenting with an innovative project, the 'Winter Guest House Project', within the framework of the RHP. Like many other projects, it was designed and implemented with no participation of women's non-governmental organizations. As part of this project, guest houses were established in cities like Ağrı and Iğdır[3] where pregnant women living in rural areas would come and stay during the last four weeks before delivery, and get necessary care during and after the delivery, all free of charge (MoH 2008). In 2008 the project was expanded to other cities which experience harsh winter conditions.

Another initiative to improve access to health care services and reduce maternal mortality is the 'Conditional Cash Transfer Health Assistance' which has been implemented throughout the country by the General Directorate of Social Assistance and Solidarity since 2003. The program makes regular cash transfers to families on the condition that they take their children to health check-ups and to pregnant women on the condition that they receive regular antenatal care. In this way, it aims to ensure that children (0-6 years of age) and expecting mothers in the poorest segments of society can benefit from basic health care services in a timely manner. The number of mothers and children benefiting from the Conditional Cash Transfer Health Assistance in 2007 was 29,636 and 991,143, respectively (KSGM 2008: 25).

While these projects were crucial in identifying and addressing women's health needs, especially in maternal and reproductive health, they were not concerned with the systematic integration of a gender perspective in the broader sense. A major step, however, was taken with the National Action Plan on Gender Equality (2008-2013) that saw women's health issues from a wider lens and aimed to develop a gender mainstreaming strategy in the health sector. This plan, developed within the framework of the EU's 'Pre-Accession Financial Program for Turkey' (2005), included clear targets and strategies to promote gender equality in health care. The policy document, 'Women and Health in Turkey' (KSGM 2008), prepared in accordance to this plan, summarized the steps taken and laid out the objectives for future initiatives as follows: 1) improving women's access to health services as well as the quality of these services; 2) developing gender sensitive behavior and attitude in relation to health issues; and 3) disseminating research, scientific studies and data on women's health. The plan was also important in terms of strengthening the General Directorate on the Status of Women (KSGM) as the main agency responsible for improving gender equality with the cooperation of ministries and other national agencies.

In sum, the concept of gender mainstreaming has clearly entered into the discussions on women's health since the mid-1990s; new programs were created by the AKP government to improve women's access to maternal services; and, studies were conducted to collect gender-sensitive data.

 However, major gaps remain in the design and implementation of these policies. First, although, sexually transmitted diseases (a surveillance study on sexually transmitted infections was conducted as part of the RHP) and gender violence (the National Action Plan for Combating Domestic Violence Against Women was prepared in 2007) figure as important components of gender mainstreaming policies, implementation largely remained focused on reproductive health issues. Yet, efforts to address women's health problems should tackle the cost and affordability barriers not simply to maternal health services but to 'comprehensive' care, and address their needs not only as users of care but also as care providers.

Second, changes proposed to create an 'enabling' policy environment still remain on the rhetorical level. Clear strategies have not been identified to produce the much-needed changes in the organizational culture concerning the way policies are made and implemented. Long-term strategies must be developed that incorporate the non-governmental organizations, including women's organizations, as major partners. Last but not least, these mainstreaming policies that require significant changes in the organisation and delivery of health care services are hardly linked to the major reform initiative, HTP, which similarly envisions a major reorganization in the health care system. The next section will discuss the main dimensions of this reform, followed by an analysis of its gender implications.

Health Transformation Program

In December 2003, the AKP government announced its reform program, the 'Health Transformation Program' (HTP). In many ways, HTP is very much in line with the waves of reforms that have been carried out all around the globe with the purpose of 'restructuring' the public sector. Sharing the dominant view that markets are a panacea to many problems that are framed mostly in terms of inefficiencies or costs, HTP promised to bring about a major overhaul of the old inegalitarian-corporatist system.

In the financing dimension, with two new laws (Law 5502: Law on Administrative Unification of the Social Security System in 2006 and Law 5510: Law on Social Security and Universal Health Insurance in 2008) a single-payer system is created by uniting all public funds under the Social Security Institution (SGK). This single-payer system represented a major move away from the previous inegalitarian and hierarchical system in which major differences existed among the three groups of formally insured – workers who were members of Social Insurance Institution (SSK), the retired state employees of the Retirement Fund (ES), and the self-employed who were covered by the Social Insurance Institution for the Craftsmen and Artisans and Other Self Employers (Bag-Kur) – in terms of the level of contributions, types of health care facilities accessed and quality of services received.

Under the previous model of financing, the health needs of the poor were financed through the Green Card Scheme if the latter could prove that they were under the poverty line and owned no property. HTP kept this means-tested scheme, though it was brought under the umbrella of the single insurer (SGK) and the cardholders were allowed to have access to the same benefits package and same health facilities as the rest of the insured.

In terms of provision, HTP envisioned a major transformation in the organisation of primary and secondary care alongside the changes in the relationships among major actors in the health care system: payers, providers and patients. First, a purchaser-provider split was introduced whereby the single payer (SGK) contracted with public and private providers competing freely to provide the 'highest quality services at the lowest cost'. A major step in this direction was the transfer of the health facilities owned and operated by insurance funds and municipalities to the Ministry of Health in 2005, thus introducing a strict separation of the insurance organisation from the providers. Second, family practitioners or family doctors were introduced in primary care as the first point of contact for the patients and as the 'gatekeepers' of the system. The family doctors are expected to provide curative and preventive services to individuals and their families, visit their patients in their homes, provide mobile services to individuals who cannot come to health facilities and keep records of personal health. Acting as gatekeepers, they would coordinate care for the patients in the complex health care system while also controlling costs by ensuring appropriate use of health care services. The pilot implementation that began in 2005 was extended to the whole country by the end of 2010, representing a major overhaul of the primary care system in Turkey. It also constitutes a significant step in reaching three of the key purposes of the reform initiative: improving access, increasing efficiency and controlling costs.

As this summary of the reform initiative demonstrates, the Turkish health care system has undergone a major transformation with the implementation of HTP. Substantial changes were introduced in the health care system which aimed to improve equity while introducing market elements: on the one hand, major differences among the social insurance funds were dismantled with the creation of the single payer system, representing an important step towards improving equity in access to health services. On the other hand, market incentives were introduced at different levels in the health care system, private provision of services was encouraged and public investment in health care was reduced (Soyer 2006: 257) leading some critics to argue that the main purpose of the HTP reforms was gradual privatisation and commercialisation of the system (Hamzaoğlu 2004; Önder 2006; Soyer 2006). The next section will discuss the implications of these changes from a gender perspective.

Gender Impacts of the HTP
Financing Mechanisms introduced by the HTP and Women's Access to Health Services
Changes introduced in the financing dimension with the HTP may influence women's access to services in two ways: 1) defining coverage – i.e.

who is included and excluded – and range of services covered under lic insurance; 2) setting levels of contributions and user fees, and thus determining affordability. Therefore, this section discusses both the implications of the decision of Turkish reformers to finance the health system through contributions (Social Health Insurance – SHI model) and the level of out-of-pocket expenditure which is an indication of the level of financial protection provided by the newly-established system.

First, the choice of financing health care through contributions places women at a disadvantage because entitlements are based on direct participation in the labour market or dependence on a worker. In this type of social protection system, women who are outside of formal employment are usually included as 'wives' or 'daughters' of male breadwinners. While such 'dependent' status, in the Turkish context, is rightly criticized by some women's organizations for deepening gender inequality by reinforcing women's economic dependence on men (KEIG 2008: 7), the generous benefits provided insurance coverage to many women. First, daughters were considered dependants of insured persons, regardless of age, as long as they were not married or formally employed. Second, reflecting a "mentality of paternalist protectionism", in case of the death of the male breadwinner the state guaranteed health insurance coverage to the wife and daughter through survivor pensions until they started to work or until they (re)married (Kılıç 2008: 493). Coverage is also guaranteed in case of divorce and unemployment when survivor wives and daughters are re-entitled to the benefits. Men, on the other hand, did not enjoy these benefits. Male widowers were subjected to means-testing since they were assumed to be the breadwinner, whereas survivor sons were entitled to benefits only until a certain age in parallel to their educational status.

Changes in the legal system since the mid-1980s, however, brought about somewhat of an 'equalization' of benefits. Conditions were equalized for male and female widowers during the 1980s and the recent reform law (5510) extended the marriage allowances to male survivors. However, Law 5510 went further by limiting the entitlement to benefits to 25 years of age for both daughters and sons who after 25 were expected to pay premiums. In addition, daughters lose their 'dependent' status permanently when they get married or find a job in the formal sector. Given the low rates of female employment, health reform, as Kılıç nicely puts it, "treats women as independent earners before they have been integrated into the labour force" and therefore increases their vulnerability (2008: 494).

Especially in countries like Turkey where there is a large population engaged in informal economic practices, adoption of a SHI model is also criticized for excluding these segments of population from the social protection system. In practice this means that those individuals who fail to find a job in the formal sector or pay their contributions out-of-pocket are not entitled to use health care services. In the Turkish case, there are some programs available for these 'excluded' groups: if they succeed in proving that they are poor enough, they qualify for a Green Card and access health services nearly free of charge, except for the recently introduced co-payments that will be discussed below. As discussed in the preceding sections, some women also benefit from conditional cash transfers that require pregnant women to get regular antenatal care, or for women with young children to take them to primary care providers for routine controls. However, these benefits are by definition 'conditional': they are either means-tested or conditional upon meeting a criterion and thus those women who do not meet the conditions, regardless of their needs, are not allowed to access health care services. Nor can every woman be aware of these benefits or know how to get them. Considering high rates of illiteracy among women, especially in some rural regions of Turkey, the paperwork required to benefit from these programs may constitute a serious barrier.

Additional problems emerge for those women who work in the informal sector. Some of these women are domestic workers who work in other people's houses to do housework and/or provide care for children, the elderly or disabled (see Rittersberger-Tılıç and Kalaycıoğlu in this volume for a discussion on this type of domestic labour). Others are home-based workers who sell some products (such as homemade pasta, knitted goods, etc.) they make at their own homes. Some others work on a temporary basis on other people's land (seasonal workers) or informally in small workshops, especially in textiles. According to Social Security Law 5510, these women could be covered as 'voluntarily insured' if they paid 32 per cent of their declared income as contributions, which has been criticized for being 'too high' as they are usually poorly paid and have irregular income (KEIG, 2008: 8).

In response to the criticism that the social security system systematically excludes large segments of female workers, the SGK has taken some important steps to expand coverage to some of these groups. First, in 2008 with Law 5754, domestic workers who are salaried and continuously employed are included as insured workers. Second, in 2009 SGK announced that home-based workers could be formally insured if they pay TL140 as contributions (which correspond to 16 days of work per month in 2009) to the SGK.

Implications of these policy steps remain unclear at this point. Although, according to the Turkish Statistical Institute's data, in September 2010 coverage of health insurance has increased to 96 per cent of the population (SGK 2010)[4] compared to 67.2 per cent in 2002, there is no recent study shedding light on to the number of formerly excluded women who have begun to receive coverage in the new social security system. Furthermore, even if they are 'categorically included', it remains unclear whether these women can afford to pay their share of the contributions to access health care services. Last but not the least, some categories of women such as seasonal agricultural workers or those employed informally remain excluded from the system. In view of these factors, it is hard to argue that the HTP has drastically increased coverage for women, despite all of the recent efforts.

In addition to the percentage of women included in the system, it is necessary to examine the services covered by social insurance and other health services provided to some groups free of charge. As discussed in the previous sections, HTP has improved equity by introducing the same benefits package for all groups of insured, including the Green Card holders. Second, maternal services are covered until after the delivery (8 weeks for single pregnancy, 10 weeks for multiple pregnancies) under public insurance and these services are offered free of charge to the previously uninsured women. For the pregnant women to benefit from this scheme, they are expected to consult a health care provider who will then submit the request for general health insurance coverage to the SGK.

While these represent very important steps towards extending services provided to women, there seems to be a discrepancy between laws and their implementation. A recent study, the Health Seeking Behavior Study (HSBS), carried out in selected regions of Turkey with widespread problems in accessing prenatal and maternal health care, clearly demonstrated that 'lack of health insurance' and 'financial problems' constitute the most prevalent barrier to accessing antenatal care (2007: 70). Many of the uninsured women and those who could not afford to pay hospital expenses out-of-pocket also admitted that they gave birth at home, given that no major health problems were experienced during the current and/or previous pregnancies (HSBS 2007: 65). Furthermore, according to the same study, health centers which were expected to provide 'free' reproductive services were not really an option for these uninsured or poor women who reported that antenatal care was almost never provided, except for very basic services like pregnancy tests or vaccines like tetanus (HSBS 2007: 63).

In sum, especially in the underdeveloped regions of Turkey, significant inequalities in terms of accessing maternal care exist: the better-off women who participated in the above-mentioned study said they often preferred private facilities or private offices of physicians who also worked in public hospitals and/or made informal payments to hospital workers during delivery to get 'good' care (HSBS 2007: 61). There were significant problems in terms of the 'content' and 'quality' of 'free' or 'covered' services received in public facilities in primary or secondary care. Thus, despite commitments to improve maternal health, to answer question 2, the HTP has done little in terms of improving the access of women to much needed health services. Neither did it address gender inequalities or take steps to reduce social and economic inequalities among the Turkish women.

Second, out-of-pocket payments – including formally charged user fees and informal payments – are widely discussed in the health reform literature in terms of their impact on affordability and hence access to health services. Introduction of user-fees for publicly-provided services is a common strategy adopted in many HSRs to control demand for health services. Interestingly, the AKP government did not adopt this policy in the early stages of the implementation of the reform program. It was only in 2008 that user fees in the form of co-payments were introduced for all curative and rehabilitative services provided by private and public facilities, with the exception of primary care services. Recent changes announced by the government such as increases in the levels of co-payments suggest that user-fees will remain a favored mechanism to control demand for health care services.[5]

Considering that, especially in developing countries like Turkey, women and children are the largest users of primary care services which include basic preventive and curative services for maternal and child health, the introduction of user charges have a disproportionately adverse impact on these groups. For instance, in Zimbabwe, Kutzin (1995) found that increased user fees implemented during the 1990s were associated with a decline of 30 per cent in the use of maternal and child health services. In the Turkish reform experience, we do not yet have the data to see similar adverse effects on women's access to health services.

At this point, it is important to differentiate between reproductive health services and all other health services women receive. In the case of reproductive services, adverse effects of user fees may be quite small as, according to Turkish Ministry of Health, antenatal care is provided free of charge (no user fees or other forms of payments), of course if the pregnant women were able to find a public facility which adequately provides it. For health services not related to reproductive health, the adverse effects can be much more noticeable since there are no exemptions in place to protect the poor who pay a greater share of their incomes out-of-pocket for health care than those that are better-off. Citizens with a Green Card still have to pay the same user fees, suggesting increased difficulties in seeking care for poor women who already struggle to obtain cash for personal expenses, including medical ones. When women are struggling to make ends meet, as the Health Seeking Behavior Study highlights, they may forego seeking health care in order to purchase food or fuel (HSBS 2007: 86).

In sum, gaps in coverage and recent policies implemented within the framework of the HTP such as making provision of (non-emergency) health services conditional on the payment of premiums or introducing user fees place women at a more disadvantageous position as they use health services more often.

Changes in Provision of Care and Women's Access to Health Care Services
The HTP brings about important changes in the way primary care services are provided and paid. The reform program assigns a significant role to primary care, which would be provided by individual primary care physicians called 'family doctors', which is expected to improve the population's access to essential clinical and preventive care and ease the pressure on secondary and tertiary levels. Currently, family doctors sign contracts with the Ministry of Health, but there is no change in their employment status or benefits. What is 'new' in this model of family medicine is the method of payment which assigns the responsibility of operating family health centers to the doctors: family doctors are not paid by salary but on the basis of their value scores that take into account the number and types of patients they see (children, pregnant women, prisoners, elderly, etc.) and whether they are family medicine specialists or not. There are additional payments for providing mobile health services; for the expenses of family health centers and a fee calculated on the basis of the socioeconomic status of the cities they serve. Some performance criteria are included in this payment method such as additional payments for points beyond 1000, provision of mobile services and for better conditions at family health centers. More interestingly, a percentage of their income is deduced depending on how far they fall below the predetermined levels of preventive services (Ministry of Health 2010).

At these early stages of implementation, all citizens are entitled to free primary care services, even if they are uninsured and family doctors are not expected to enforce strict gate-keeping. Therefore, the market incentives embedded in these new payment mechanisms do not yet have any influence on access to services. However, if and when access to family physicians is made conditional to the payment of the insurance premiums, the family doctors may avoid providing services to the uninsured groups. Given the constraints to provide all the listed services to their insured patients, these doctors would hardly find the time and resources to provide essential care (including antenatal care to pregnant women, family planning services or any other medical or preventive services) to uninsured women. Naturally, this would represent a major barrier to reaching the major purposes identified in the reform documents: making pregnancy and childbirth safer, improving children's health and addressing women's health needs.

It must be noted that other components of the reform program relating to the provision dimension, such as the purchaser-provider split and autonomization of public hospitals, may create additional barriers to access to good quality care for women especially if they lead to the closing of public hospitals. Public hospitals have been the major providers of uncompensated care for poor and/or uninsured women all around the country. Therefore, consequences of the reforms must be analyzed carefully in terms of access and equity: full privatisation of provision will exacerbate regional inequalities, increase inequities among the poor and the rich, and limit access of vulnerable populations, including women, to health care services. Private corporations cannot be expected to invest in health facilities in remote and poor regions of the country where maternal mortality rates remain much above the country's average. In addition, private, especially for-profit, health facilities will not provide uncompensated care for the uninsured women who cannot afford to pay for their care. For these reasons, public facilities need to be kept operational in order to implement many of the initiatives like Winter Guesthouses for pregnant women, to improve women's and children's access to essential services and address the problem of regional inequalities.

To summarize, reforms introduced in the provision dimension as part of the HTP to increase efficiency, improve access and control costs may in fact end up limiting the access of uninsured women and increase inequalities among the rich and the poor as well as among the developed and underdeveloped regions. Policymakers should ensure that public hospitals remain viable, high quality alternatives to private facilities and family doctors provide most needed primary care services to uninsured women, just like the health centers and health posts have done since the 1960s.

Conclusion: The Way Forward

The health care system in Turkey has been undergoing a major transformation since the election of the first Justice and Development government in 2002. Turkish policymakers acknowledged the need to improve and equalize opportunities and establish gender policies on the one hand, and to modernize the healthcare system in order to achieve greater effectiveness of services and quality and safety for patients (HTP reforms), on the other.

The two strands of this broader process of transformation lack systematic policy coordination: the HTP is not gender-sensitive in the sense of assessing the implications of new policies for women at the decision-making stage or making women's concerns and experiences an integral part of implementation. Gender biases are clearly prevalent in the program and at later stages of implementation: women, who are not formally employed, are viewed as 'dependants', and do not receive benefits as a matter of citizenship rights but on the basis of the market status of their parents or husbands. Possible consequences of policies such as user fees or new payment mechanisms in primary care in terms of limiting the access of women to health services are not taken into consideration. Regarding our second question, there is no evidence that recent initiatives to expand coverage to previously excluded women were successful. It remains unclear whether these 'categorically included' women will be able to afford the premiums required to access care.

Nor has the HTP been proven to reduce the inequalities among Turkish women. Inequalities among rich and poor women may actually be increasing, especially in terms of accessing high-quality health care services. Better-off women access antenatal care and deliver their babies at private facilities or get better care at public facilities with the help of informal payments, whereas poor, uninsured women either get very limited services from public facilities or go without care in order to purchase food or fuel. In addition, access to essential services is guaranteed for the insured women who, with the new primary care reforms, will be receiving care from their family physicians. In the aftermath of health care reform, the uninsured women who fail means-testing are thus faced with additional barriers to access essential and comprehensive care.

In short, despite political commitment that is evident especially in gender mainstreaming policies and additional resources coming from international organizations like the WHO or the EU, there is a major gap between the political rhetoric on gender and actual practice in the Turkish context. In many ways, the HTP does not tackle the cost and affordability barriers to health services and implementation of the reform program will potentially deepen the problems of access. To bridge this gap, long-term strategies are necessary to change the attitudes of policymakers towards gender issues. The top-down approach to policy-making has to be abandoned and new mechanisms that encourage the participation of non-governmental organizations, and especially women's organizations, should be developed. The General Directorate on the Status of Women (KSGM) can also play a significant role, in this regard, as the government agency responsible for integrating a gender perspective in all national policies and programs and for coordinating policies across different policy areas. In health care, such coordination would also help expand the policy focus of gender mainstreaming beyond reproductive health issues.

It is true that since the mid-1990s, parallel to the international initiatives, Turkey has taken important steps towards the promotion of gender equality. In health care, governments have made some progress in the long run to achieve the MDG5 on maternal health, but there is much to be done to achieve the MDG3 which calls for the promotion of gender equality and empowerment of women. Many challenges lay ahead such as addressing growing pressures on women as providers of care in both the private and professional spheres, improving the evidence base for policies by collecting data disaggregated by gender, and identifying gender biases in the treatment and diagnosis of health problems such as coronary heart disease.

11

GENDER GAPS IN THE INDIVIDUAL PENSION SYSTEM IN TURKEY

Şule Şahin and Adem Y. Elveren

Since the 1980s, pension systems in many countries have been reformed in line with neoliberal principles, and the traditional pay-as-you-go (PAYG) systems began to be replaced by private pension systems. Due to increasing costs of traditional systems resulting from aging populations, an expanding informal economy, low pension coverage, and inefficiency in the administrative and political management of funds, privatisation was declared as the reason for the liberalisation of pension systems. Therefore, private pension systems either replaced the PAYG systems entirely or became a significant part of the whole social security system.

Turkey was (is) not beyond the reach of this neoliberal wave. The Individual Pension System (IPS), a defined contribution (DC) scheme in which benefits are determined by the investment return of workers' total contribution to the system, was introduced in 2003. This private pension system does not just assign accrual risk to the individual worker but also widens the gender gap. As one's benefit is totally based on his/her contribution to the system, women, who are involved more in lower-paid jobs traditionally, will have lower retirement payments. This chapter aims to discuss the gendered nature of the IPS, so as to examine effects of social security reforms in Turkey on women's welfare. We aim to determine the real position of the IPS within the Turkish welfare regime, investigate its possible effects on gender inequality in terms of earnings in retirement years, and propose policy implementations to remedy the gender gaps in the system.

Gender Inequality, Social Security and Private Pensions
This section discusses the main issues that cause the greater gender gap in

private pension schemes. The gender inequality effects of the privatiza-tion[1] of a social security system may differ but still exist to a varying extent and with varying content in different countries. Since one's benefit is totally based on one's contribution to the system, the gender inequality in retirement payments is greater in private pension schemes than in tradi-tional pay-as-you-go systems. Women were better off before pension reforms because social benefits were usually more generous in the tradi-tional systems (Bertranou 2001; van Ginneken 2003; Gimenez 2005). Reforms in the 1990s have strengthened the link between pension bene-fits and life-time earnings and the redistributive aspects of pension formu-la have weakened (Steinhilber 2006). Indeed, this means women's depend-ency shifts from husband to labour market. However, due to embedded inequalities in the labour market and lower female labour force participa-tion, this dependency results in a decrease in the well-being of women. As the European Commission acknowledges, increasing labour force partici-pation is necessary but not sufficient to reduce the gender pension gap since the gap is linked to structural gender inequalities in the labour mar-ket (EC 2003). Similarly, it is crucial to acknowledge that changing incen-tives through social security regulations (i.e. treating women and men "equally") does not create equal labour market outcomes. That is, causali-ty is from labour market to social security system, not the other way around. In contrast to the policy aim of equity and equality in the EU, the recent reforms tend to increase the gender gap (Frericks et al. 2007). According to data of Central and Eastern European nations, privatisation of social security has indeed decreased the scope of social services; the old systems were very generous to women in that there was encouragement for early retirement, high replacement rate and credits for child rearing (Fultz and Steinhilber 2004). In countries that introduced private pension schemes, there is evidence of a rising gender disparity in retirement income (see Bertranou 2001; Turner 2005). For example, the gender inequality in pension systems in the USA, UK, Kazakhstan, Chile, Australia, Argentina, Poland, Sweden, Germany, Denmark, and Mexico are revealed in several studies (Even and Macpherson 2003; De Mesa and Montecinos 1999; Korczyk 2003; Hinz et al. 2005; Bardasi and Jenkins 2004; Dion 2006; James et al. 2003; Jefferson and Preston 2005; Stahlberg et al. 2004; Balcerzak-Paradowska et al. 2003; Makinen 2002; Ginn 2004).

Recent social security reforms extended to 40 years the contributory periods required to attain a full labour market-related pension for so-called life-long careers (Frericks and Maier 2007). However, the intermittent working life of women makes it harder to qualify for these conditions[2]. Informal work includes short-term contract labour, casual work, part-time work, and home-based piece work.[3] Women remain in the informal sector due to poverty, lack of skills and education, and employer preferences for informal labour. Women essentially become the "secondary earners." Undertaking a huge proportion of labour over unpaid care causes women to remain in full-time employment for less time than men (see the chapter by Memiş, Öneş and Kızılırmak in this volume). This translates into lower real earnings which in turn results in a significantly smaller pension in privatized pension schemes (Williamson and Rix 1999). This secondary position of women's wages and social entitlements, on the other hand, is favored and maintained by some family-support tax policies, where the 1.5 earner household is a basic assumption of the tax system (Sainsbury 1999, 2001). However, even the possibility of women being absent from work to provide childcare for their own children causes employers to invest in young men rather than young women, preventing women from enhancing their skills and training. This so-called 'statistical discrimination' (Esping-Andersen 2002) is detrimental for the prospective careers of women, and consequently substantially worsens the prospective pension income.

Privatisation has more harmful results for women since they tend to live longer than men. Public systems (i.e. PAYG) which treat men and women equally by using "unisex" life tables, redistribute income in favor of women.[4] Even if they have the same capital accumulation throughout their working years; since women have a higher life expectancy compared to men, their retirement income will be lower due to the distribution of the capital over a longer period of time (i.e. by adding five years early retirement and higher life expectancy of three to five years, it can be said that women have a retirement period 7-10 years longer). In addition, greater longevity means that inflation-adjusted annuities would be more expensive for women (IWPR 2000). However, women gain more with the 'wage-indexation' of annuities when compared with men (Stahlberg et. al. 2004).

Women, as investors, are more risk-averse than men. This affects them negatively. Women who prefer less risky portfolios will have smaller returns (Williamson and Rix 1999; Watson and McNaughton 2007). Some studies also conclude that it is not gender alone that determines investment decisions, but also marital status and the ability to share risks within the household (Ståhlberg et.al. 2006). However, in some cases, being more risk-averse may be relatively beneficial if retirement decisions are made when the stock market is down. Also, it is shown that women have a tendency to invest a smaller amount of their wealth in the private pension schemes (Bajtelsmit et. al. 1999; Bernasek and Shwiff 2001).

The penalty for early retirement is higher in the private pension schemes than in the traditional PAYG system. Women who must leave the workforce in order to care for their families are likely to lose more of their benefits under a privatized scheme. In general, women retire 5 years younger than men. This is due to the demand by women for compensating unpaid work (Ginn and Arber 1995) and letting couples enjoy their retirement years jointly – since most women are younger than their husbands – as a way of supporting the institution of marriage and family income (Steinhilber 2006: 6). However, the recent reforms in many countries have either shortened the retirement age difference or lifted it (ibid, p. 6). Of course, in contrast, later retirement (for instance, at 65 rather than 60) means higher contributions to the system which results in higher returns for women thereby decreasing the gender gap about 10-15 per cent, as shown in some simulations for Argentina and Chile (James et. al. 2003). Therefore, it is important to evaluate the fairness of the late retirement carefully.[5]

In sum, privatisation of pension funding systems and transition to a defined contribution scheme pose a threat to the financial sustainability of aging women, as women are forced to rely on benefits that reproduce discrimination that they have already confronted in younger years.

The Individual Pension System in Turkey
The social security system has presented an increasing deficit since the early 1990s. The report by the ILO, which was prepared for the government, predicted that the total deficit of the social security system in Turkey will reach 10.1 per cent of GDP by the year 2050 in the absence of intervention (ILO 1996). The same report projected that in the case of a proposed reform, the deficit of the system will drop to a negligible level by 2040 (i.e. 0.6% of GDP). Thus, the government realized that comprehensive social security reform was a matter of urgency in order to reduce the pressure of social security institutions on the public deficit. Following this report, the central government implemented two main reforms, one in 1999 and the other in 2006, in line with the IMF and World Bank's approaches as well as the recommendations of the EU.

With the 1999 reform, the government implemented a two-pillar system in which current social security institutions (the first pillar) were structurally overhauled but maintained, along with a private pension scheme which serves as an alternative means of retirement in the general social security system (the second pillar). That is, the idea of the Individual Pension System (IPS) was established in the 1999 social security reform, and after issues of the law and other legislation to strengthen the base of the system, the IPS began on October 27, 2003 with the contributions of six pension companies. As of this writing, there are thirteen pension companies operating in the system.

The basic feature of the IPS is that individuals can voluntarily participate in the system through which they then gain an additional income on top of their pension. By participating for at least 10 years in the system, contributors are eligible to retire at the age of 56. Pension rights are specified based on the defined contribution system, i.e. on the total amount of the contributions and their returns. Pension mutual funds are managed by specialists from portfolio management companies established within the Capital Markets Law.

Since the IPS was introduced, there has been a steep increase in the number of participants in the system. While there were about 315,000 people in the system by the end of 2004, this number had doubled by the end of 2005 reaching 666,000. The participation rate continued to increase and around 400,000 more people have become involved in the system each year since then. This number has reached over 2.4 million by March 2011.

The government officials stated that the IPS was introduced as a complement to the public pension system on the basis of voluntary participation and the DC principle to provide a supplementary income during retirement (Elveren 2003b, 2005). The architect of the system often recalled that these individual savings turning into investment also would contribute to economic development by creating long-term resources for the economy thereby increasing employment (Elveren 2003a).

However, we consider the IPS as a part of the ongoing commodification process of the welfare regime in Turkey which accelerated in the late 1990s. Turkey introduced the IPS as a retrenchment project of the welfare state and to increase the role of the private sector in the area of social security. Although it is stated that the IPS is "the complement" to the public system and that participation to the system is voluntary, the system is important for the welfare regime for two reasons. First, the system grows at a substantial rate. In its first five years the number of participants had increased to over two million, and the same growing pattern is expected to continue. The role of attractive conditions, such as participants being provided with tax incentives at the saving, investment, and retirement stages, is important. Second, some argue that the introduction of the system is an intermediate stage, a preparation process for a more radical long-term transformation where the private pension is expected to develop enough to be the main part of the social security system (Elveren and Elveren 2010). Therefore, we consider the IPS to be the hidden face of the commodification of the welfare regime.

Gender Gaps in the IPS

The traditional social security system in Turkey has rested upon the principle of securing women's roles as mothers and wives. Women have been seen as dependent. However, the traditional paternalist state, which ties women's entitlements to their "breadwinner" husbands and "protects" girls and women in the absence of a "man", has been weakened in recent reforms. After the adoption of social security reforms, equalized conditions and benefits for survivor spouses and extended invalidity coverage for married survivor girls, and change in health care benefits for dependants may be seen as signals for a move toward a "universal breadwinner" model (Kılıç 2008).

The major concern about women in the traditional social security system is the issue of dependency which comes with the very low female employment rate in the non-agricultural sector. Therefore, the fact that women are no longer entitled to health security as the dependants of their families is a double-edge sword, forcing them either into marriage, in order to benefit from the insurance of their husbands, or into accepting unfavorable working conditions in the large informal sector.

That is, although there is no discrepancy between women and men in terms of social security coverage, there is (at least should be) significant concern about the vulnerability of women in terms of access to social security. Women are dependent on their husband in terms of social security coverage. Table 11.1 shows the source of social security (i.e. health, retirement pension and survivors' pension) in Turkey for women and men, in which the higher dependency ratio presents a clear picture of the vulnerability of women. The table shows that while 92.6 per cent of men are actively covered, for women the same ratio is as low as 16 per cent. In other words, 84 per cent of women are insured as dependent on other family members, especially on husbands (i.e. 68.4 per cent).

When it comes to the private pension system, opposite to the common case, there is no remarkable gender inequality in the case of Turkey since all participants are from the same socio-economic group, and the system seems to present "equal" outcomes for men and women. However, it is also a captious picture. We argue that it is more likely that existing gender inequality in the social security system will rise as Turkey moves toward a more market-oriented social security system and thereby retrench social benefits. This section examines the gendered dimension of the IPS and proposes the minimum pension guarantee as a way of lessening the gender gaps inherently in the system.

Table 11.1: Source of social security for women and men (per cent)

	Men	Women
With Social Security coverage	66	67.8
Actively covered	92.6	16.0
Covered as the insured's dependent; of which	7.4	84.0
Covered as the insured's spouse	1.2	68.4
Covered as the insured's child	4.3	12.9
Covered as the insured's mother/father	1.9	2.7

Source: Elveren 2008, p. 46

Is there a gender gap in the IPS?

There are two studies which use actual data to analyze the existence of the gender gap in the IPS in Turkey (Bozkuş and Elveren 2008; Şahin 2008). These studies mainly focus on the amount of regular contributions rather than retirement incomes since the system has not yet yielded its first retirees. Their studies' common finding is that the overall gender gap in regular contributions is negligible. This is reasonable as entering the system is voluntary and the participants are from middle or upper classes. However, for some income categories, the discrepancy can still be explained by gender differences.

Bozkuş and Elveren (2008) analyze the IPS in Turkey by decomposing the determinants of the discrepancy in the premiums, i.e. regular contributions (RC) between men and women in a specific income category in which the amount of contributions made by women is higher than the amount of contributions made by men. They have found that different variables have various effects on the regular contributions for both sexes. For example while age affects the RC for both men and women, the education level and occupation have significant effects on men's RCs only. Number of years of contribution has a positive effect on the RC for both sexes. Bozkuş and Elveren (2008) indicate two main findings: first, even after controlling income, the amount of RC can still partly be explained by some social variables such as age, education level and human development levels of provinces. Second, the explanatory powers of the social variables on RCs differ according to the sex of the participant, although there is not much gender gap among men and women in terms of RCs.

Şahin (2008), in an updated and a more sophisticated analysis, shows that as age and education level increases the contribution rate increases; while students/unemployed contribute less, retirees, self-employed and people having income from business profits contribute more than housewives; participants living in the medium level development cities contribute slightly less than participants living in the high development cities; the RC rate of married people is less than singles, and the divorced or widowed are less than the married. Also, the RCs of single men are significantly higher than the RCs of married men. This can be explained in that males are the sole "breadwinners" in most of the families in Turkey, and when they get married they may not have enough money to contribute to extra savings. The contribution of women's incomes to household incomes is usually perceived as a kind of "pin money". Therefore, it is expected that marital status might be a significant factor affecting RCs, especially for males.

To sum up, there is no significant difference in the regular contribution rates between females and males. This no unexpected result with participants coming from middle and high income categories, and results are based on the amount of participants' regular contributions to the system in its first five years, not the retirement incomes of its first retirees. However, it is a captious conclusion since, as we discussed, introduction of the private pension schemes increases the gender gaps in retirement earnings across the world. Therefore, it is important to analyze the gendered dimension of the IPS further in order to capture the real picture of inequality. The following section aims to reach this goal by investigating the inherent gender gap in the system by means of some simulations.

Is there an inherent gender gap in the IPS?

This section examines the discrepancy between men and women in terms of pension benefits in the case that the whole working population switched to a privately managed pension scheme (i.e. in case of privatisation of the public scheme).

There are two studies examining the retirement benefits based on the private pension scheme in Turkey. In the first study, Elveren and Hsu (2007), take the shorter work life, fewer earnings, and longer life expectancy for women into account. They calculate capital accumulation, as the lifetime contribution made by the individual, and the annual annuity based on capital accumulation in several projections for various working years. They found that gaps in retirement earnings between men and women range between 55 per cent and 76 per cent due to different assumptions, and to the initial salary gap between men and women.

The second study, Elveren (2008b), reinvestigates the gender gap through an advanced model which includes more variables, such as real wage growth, administrative costs, and risk, in order to show the total effect of some disadvantages women experience in private pension schemes. These variables are important in assessing gender inequality in pension schemes for three reasons. First, due to intermittent labour participation and some other gender biases, women get fewer wage increases (i.e. promotions). For women, starting at a low pay level and receiving fewer promotions creates significant discrepancies with men in terms of wage growth. Second, since women have smaller accounts (i.e. less capital accumulation) they undertake higher administrative costs (i.e. fees charged by pension companies) in real terms compared with men. Finally, because of the direct relationship between portfolio choice and return, women preferring less risky investments have lower capital accumulation. Therefore, the addition of these three variables gives a more precise understanding of the gap between the pension funds of men and women.

Taking a male participant, who works for 30 years in a full time job (from age 26 to 56, which is the minimum retirement age in the IPS), as a basis for comparison, Elveren compares the gender gaps in retirement benefits between men and women looking at different working years and investment strategies of women. The study considers the fact that women are more likely to work in part-time jobs, have lower-paid occupations, and prefer less risky investments represented by government bonds while equities represent risky portfolios (Elveren 2008: 47-48).

The simulations show that, first, for every age and education category the gender gap is wider in rural areas than urban areas; second, both for urban and rural areas gender inequality in pension earnings increases as age increases; third, omitting the illiterate group, as education level rises the gender gap narrows; and finally, using a gender-neutral mortality table decreases the gap significantly (Elveren 2008). The study also reveals that working in part-time jobs for several years due to pregnancy and child bearing and then choosing a less risky portfolio (i.e. bond) as a result of more risk-averseness widens the gender gap in retirement earnings. Overall, the study shows that, in terms of the woman's retirement benefit as a percentage of that of a man, the gap increases up to 20 per cent in rural areas, in the elderly and for those with low education levels, whereas the smallest gap, at 79 per cent, occurs among the youngest individuals in urban areas (see Table 11.A1 in the Appendix).

These studies focussed on a pure case, in which there were no regulations in the system favoring women, in order to show the origin of the causes creating the gap, which goes back to the discrepancy in education level and its effect on the labour market. The IPS was established to create an additional income for middle and high income groups. Therefore, this scheme, along with curtailments in social benefits, deteriorates income distribution. That is, in fact, we see those conditions provided by the state and favorable for participants in the IPS as a redistribution of income other way around. Therefore, we acknowledge that this system has not had a direct effect on poorer women (i.e. housewives). It is, as in its current situation, rather a major instrument to deepen the capital markets, while involving a non-negligible threat against an already retrenching welfare state. As this scheme grows toward being a major part of the social insurance system, the current unequal income distribution will further deteriorate and the gender gap effect between middle income men and women will extend to the whole society. That is, the dependency of women on their husbands will increase significantly.

On the other hand, from the point of view of policy makers who argue that the system is necessary for deepening capital markets in a well functioning economy, there may be some implementations that could decrease the gender gap and make the system more attractive in a marketing sense. We, elsewhere, have proposed the minimum pension guarantee for the IPS. The next section discusses the minimum pension guarantee that addresses the inherent gender gaps in the system. However, this would be a partial solution, because, as we mentioned, these sorts of implementations address only the results and not the roots of the inequality.

Minimum Pension Guarantee as a Tool of Decreasing the Gender Gaps in the IPS

The minimum pension guarantee (MPG) can be thought of as a particular form of means test for individual pensions. The government can top off the pension income if it is below a certain level. Since it is mostly women who constitute a higher proportion of the poor, all social safety nets in essence favor women. The MPG, as a redistributive benefit, may be a crucial instrument in lessening the gender gap, particularly to lower the poverty among elderly women (Smeeding and Sandstrom 2005)[6]. Since women mostly shoulder the higher portion of unpaid work throughout their lives, this unpaid work can be "priced" through some income transfers from husbands to wives, and from married couples to single women by means of the MPG. It is a way to create solidarity between men and women.

Based on the discussion above, Şahin and Elveren (forthcoming) attempt to examine the MPG for Turkey by showing the cost and probability of guarantee payoffs. In the same study, we assume that the IPS is still based on voluntary participation; however, the mandatory MPG is a government requirement for all pension companies while the state itself is the final guarantor. We also consider the whole population to be participanting in the system, rather than the current over two million people in order to be able to sketch a more realistic picture of the gender gap. We argue that the final guarantor should be the state as in the case of Chile. However, the initial finance should be based on the special fund that is created by the pension companies through "taxing" the pension accounts which receive higher returns than the predetermined threshold level. This extra money should be used for topping up.

We mostly utilize the model introduced in Şahin and Elveren (2009). Similarly, we calculate the costs of guarantees as the differences between the accumulations of individual accounts. Through this application, the discrepancy in the costs and probabilities of the minimum pension guarantee between men and women is shown. The minimum guaranteed amount has been determined as the real minimum wage in Turkey.

According to the simulations, contribution period has a high impact on the cost of the guarantee. As the contribution period extends the guarantee cost decreases. Investment strategy plays an important role in the cost of the guarantee as well. Since the return of equities is higher than bonds, as the percentage of assets invested in equities increases, the cost of guarantees decreases. Further, there is a significant difference between the costs of guarantees in males and females retirement incomes due to a significant difference between the average earnings of men and women in Turkey (Şahin and Elveren forthcoming).

Another factor affecting the cost of the minimum guarantee among females and males is life expectancy. Since the simulation results are the annual retirement income, due to the longer life expectancy of women, the total amount is divided by a larger number for women and produces lower annual amounts for individual accounts. This leads to higher costs for the proposed guarantee for women.

Regardless of the investment type and contribution period, the probabilities of guarantee payoffs for women are higher than for men. On the other hand, a 10-year contribution invested in bonds, one of the main scenarios applied in the study, is not enough to have a retirement income higher than the proposed guarantee amounts. Therefore, any contributor from either sex will need some guarantee payoffs for a 10-year contribution. The higher volatility in equity returns increases the probability of having retirement accumulations below the guarantee threshold. As the contribution period increases, the probabilities decrease (see Table 11.A2 in the Appendix).

To sum up, depending on the wage discrepancy and life expectancy between women and men, and portfolio choice and length of contribution into the system to different extents, women are more likely to need topping up in order to reach a minimum level of retirement earnings. That is, existence of the MPG prevents women from having very low retirement income and shares the risk of lower returns with all participants. Obviously, this is not a solution to the existing problems of the private pension schemes (i.e. IPS in our case). Rather, it is a tool to reduce the detrimental effects of fluctuations in the stock market on retirement incomes, and a way to transfer money to women within the private pension context. On the other hand, from the view point of government officials (or pension companies that want to attract more customers) the MPG can encourage higher participation in the system.

Conclusion

The goal of this chapter was to reveal the gender gaps in the IPS, an essential part of the ongoing reforms in the social security system. Turkey introduced the IPS as complementary to the traditional PAYG system in 2003. This was a crucial part of the changing structure of the social security system. Although participation in the system is voluntary, we believe it is worth analyzing in detail due to its remarkable growth trend and its potential threat to the traditional system. This chapter endeavoured to sketch a comprehensive picture of the gendered dimension of the system by answering three main questions: Is there an actual gender gap in the system? Is there an inherent gender gap in the system? And finally, what can be done against the gender gap?

To answer the first question, we looked at the early works which analyze the actual data of the current participants. Accordingly, there is no overall significant difference in the regular contribution rates between females and males. Since the system is on a voluntary basis and the participants of the system are from middle or upper classes, their contribution rates are close to each other. So, there was no unexpected result. However, it is shown that the existent gap, although it is not much, can be explained by some social variables such as age, marital status and particularly education level.

There are two main studies which answer the second question. The first study finds that gaps in retirement earnings between men and women range between 55 per cent and 76 per cent due to various assumptions, and to the initial salary gap between men and women. The latter work reveals more detailed results using an improved model and considering more variables: First, for each age and education level category the gender gap is wider in rural areas than urban; second, both for urban and rural areas gender inequality in pension earnings increases as age increases; third, the gender gap decreases as education level increases; and finally, using a gender-neutral mortality table decreases the gap significantly. Accordingly, it is shown that the gap, represented as a woman's retirement earnings as a percentage of a man's, increases to 20 per cent in rural areas, in the elderly, and in low education levels, whereas the lowest gap, at 79 per cent, occurs among the youngest individuals in urban areas.

Finally, to answer the third question, we, elsewhere, propose a minimum pension guarantee implementation and analyzed its cost and probability in a simulation model. Our simulations show that contribution period and investment strategy have a high impact on the cost of the guarantee. As the contribution period extends, the guarantee cost decreases. Since the return of equities is higher than bonds, as the percentage of the assets invested on equities increases the cost of the guarantees decreases. Our findings show that there is a significant difference between the costs and the probabilities of the guarantees in male and female retirement incomes due to a significant difference between the average earnings and life expectancy of men and women.

To conclude, it is important to note that women are better off in traditional systems compared with private pension schemes. Turkey needs to maintain and strengthen the traditional PAYG system, which is the core component of the social security system. A further step toward privatisation of the social security system, as the chapter shows, would deepen the inequality between men and women – no need to mention further depravities on the whole of society.

Appendix

Table 11.A1: Women's yearly annuity benefit as a percentage of men's yearly annuity benefit according to education and age

| | Bond | | | |
| | Gender-Specific | | Gender-Natural | |
Age-Educa.	Urban	Rural	Urban	Rural
16-24	65	47	74	54
25-34	50	30	57	35
35-44	40	27	45	30
45-64	38	32	43	37
65+	43	29	49	34
Illiterate	59	41	67	46
Primary	36	26	41	30
Junior High	36	20	41	23
High School	42	37	48	42
Junior Colleg	48	41	54	47
University +	45	50	51	56
	Equity			
	Gender-Specific		Gender-Natural	
Age-Educa.	Urban	Rural	Urban	Rural
16-24	70	50	79	57
25-34	53	32	60	36
35-44	42	28	47	32
45-64	40	32	46	37
65+	46	30	53	35
Illiterate	61	44	70	50
Primary	39	27	45	31
Junior High	37	20	42	22
High School	42	39	48	44
Junior Colleg	48	43	55	49
University +	49	54	56	61

Source: Elveren (2008), p. 51.

Table 11.A2: Probability of guarantee payoffs

	Years of Contribution	%100 Bond	%50 Bond %50 Stock	%100 Stock
MALE	10 years	1	0.8807	0.8225
	20 years	0.7767	0.4740	0.5957
	30 years	0.5302	0.3719	0.5716
FEMALE	10 years	1	0.9704	0.9144
	20 years	0.9952	0.6886	0.7221
	30 years	0.6397	0.4027	0.5907

Source: Şahin and Elveren (forthcoming)

12

CHILD AND ELDER CARE PROVIDERS: WOMEN IN THE INFORMAL SECTOR

Helga Rittersberger-Tılıç and Sibel Kalaycıoğlu[1]

The characteristics of domestic and care work in Turkey are still reflecting inequalities in social class, status and gender which originate as forms of servitude. These inequalities are manifested in labour relations. Domestic and care work are part of a sensitive field in the labour market, a sphere where "private" and "public" intermingle in space, i.e. in both the work places/private homes and also in employer – employee relations.

Demand for this kind of work has gradually increased in parallel with how societies are aging and with changing gender relations. In general, it is still common that domestic and care work are provided by poor, uneducated women, who often have recently migrated to urban centers. Not only in Turkey but in most contemporary societies, there is a rising demand for care work, which involves mainly women who have low level skills and credentials and little chance to join the labour market elsewhere. According to the International Labour Organisation (ILO) report, the demand for care work increases due to the growing participation of women in the labour force on the one hand, but also due to the decline in state provisions for care services following privatisation and neo-liberal restructuration processes. Also demographic factors like the aging of societies and the "feminization" of international/national migration have to be seen as factors increasing the demand for care work (ILO 2010: 1-5). Due to a neo-liberal turn and the structural adjustment programs in the last two decades, Turkey has experienced important changes in her welfare regime (see Buğra's chapter in this volume) which directly altered the arrangements of care in a society where families mainly rely on women's labour.

esent study will discuss the informal nature of domestic and as articulations of different policy changes based on field research in Ankara completed at two different times approximately ten years apart. The initial research was conducted in 1995-96, using a representative sample of domestic workers mainly involved in cleaning and cooking. The second field study took place in 2009-2010; this time, however, it mainly included care workers who had found work through firms typical for the newly emerging care work market. Between these years, market opportunities for domestic work had transformed and expanded from domestic cleaning work towards care work mainly managed by private firms. The later fieldwork indicated that the informal nature of domestic and care work has transformed from a "job market based on a traditional model of patron-client relations" to a "job market controlled by private firms" as will be explained below. In discussing this research, we aim to contribute to the understanding of the changing status and forms of exploitation of women's labour in the informal labour market excluded from existing social welfare policies.

Structure and Development of Domestic Work in Turkey

Turkey faces many challenges in the labour market due to her young population, low labour market participation rates, especially of women, high rates of unemployment and unregistered work. In terms of labour market dynamics, first one should consider Turkey's population profile. According to TurkStat statistics the share of working age population (15-64 years of age) is increasing in Turkey. The proportion of the population between 15 and 64 years of age was 67 per cent in 2009 where 26 per cent fell in the 0-14 age group, and 7 per cent was 65 and over. On the other hand, the unemployment rate has been rising (11 per cent in 2008 and 14 per cent in 2009). The social structure is still characterized by migrants moving from the rural parts of Turkey to the urban centers. The incoming migrants join the informal labour market; men being able to find employment in seasonal construction jobs, tourism, street peddling and minor trade. Women frequently stay at home or find employment in clothing and textiles, sometimes in the tourism sector, but mainly in domestic work which has recently turned more into care work. The jobs found by migrants are, however, almost all in the informal sector.

In the Turkish setting, female labour force participation is very low, 23.5 per cent in January 2009 (World Bank 2009). Main factors affecting women's labour market participation and employment can be defined as follows: structural factors related to lack of equal opportunities; lack of women friendly policies, most important of which are harmonisation of work and private life policies; few part-time work opportunities; low educational attainment; cultural factors affecting women's paid work outside the house. Another barrier for women's participation to the labour market is related to the limited public provision for child care, since women have to choose between taking care of children and going out to work. Almost all formal child care is provided by the private market at high costs; almost all informal child care is provided by parents (mainly women), grandparents and/or both. In the urban areas, families who can afford it can take up formal care while others either depend on relatives or stop working and stay as housewives or become involved in home-based work or piecework from home.

In terms of women's labour force participation, although in urban areas the importance of waged labour is increasing; urban women still have only marginal opportunities to participate in the labour market and active economic life. Especially in the formal, organized sector jobs (industry and services) women have only very limited opportunities of participation (Ecevit 1990). Mainly, paid employment opportunities for migrant women in the services sector are very low in prestige and income, and include cooking, cleaning, child care, secretarial services, waitressing, counter work in banks, and customer service in supermarkets and shops. Most of these jobs occur without any social security. Jelin underlined the productive role of migrant women in the cities, especially their role in domestic services (Jelin 1977).

All in all, we can argue that the Turkish labour market has a segmented structure with high informality and low participation rates of women (see Toksöz's section in this volume). This kind of work and labour market situation is not particularly a Turkish experience. Studying Filipino migrant domestic workers in Rome, one of the Filipino communities in the economic diaspora worldwide, Lindio-McGovern explains the feminization of export labour, where the majority of Filipino migrant women are incorporated into domestic services (Gamburd in: Lindio-McGovern 2003). This movement of Filipino domestic workers is situated in a "gendered system" of "transnational capitalism" (Parrenas 2000).

Domestic work in Turkey has been a practice since Ottoman times when workers were known as "adopted daughters" among urban middle class households (Özbay 2009). Özbay explains how [o]rphan and/or poor peasant girls who were taken into urban middle-class households in the name of 'protection' and 'goodwill' gradually replaced the former domestic slaves. The young women were called *evlatlıks*, and in later years this practice became institutionalized through the illegal purchase of peasant girls among middle-class households. This practice was banned, along with a general anti-slavery law, only in 1964 (Özbay 1999: 559).

In another study of Özbay (2009: 21) she thoroughly discusses how these young women became part of the family but usually in a marginalized position. Giving reference to Neyzi (1985) Özbay states that *evlatlıklar* held an important role in the transition from slavery to paid servants (2009: 26, also see the chapter by Toğrul for further discussion on the evlatlık institution).

After the announcement of the new Turkish Republic, such practices continued especially with rural girls being adopted by urban families to provide childcare. This practice ceased around the 1980s where rural migrant women started to provide such childcare as paid employment. Especially with urbanisation and the emergence of new and better educated women in urban middle classes, educated women have begun participating more in the labour market, especially as civil servants (Öncü 1981) in large metropolitan centres. Such women in paid employment in formal sector jobs gave way to the need for domestic help for childcare and/or for the fulfilment of domestic duties which were mainly taken over by rural migrant women who looked for paid work which did not demand skills.

Since the 1980s the model for childcare in Turkey has been heavily dependent on the labour of women who have stayed out of the labour market functioning as mothers / housewives, or grandmothers. Very few families could obtain formal childcare services through, for example, crèches and nurseries. Still relatively few middle class families with double incomes tended to employ rural migrant women for childcare in their homes.

The last decade has seen major social transformations and changes; also the demographic structure of Turkey has changed. Turkey's population is still relatively young with the average age being about 29 years. The proportion of people over 65, however, is growing. The majority of these elderly are not economically active and about 44 per cent of the elderly are not entitled to retirement benefits. We are talking, therefore, about a growing old age dependency. Interestingly, about 95 per cent of the elderly do live with or close to their families. State services provided are complex, yet service provision shows great insufficiencies. Home-based care of the elderly is the government's policy objective. Institutionalised care is an exception and many relatives of the elderly as well as the elderly themselves attribute negative connotations to this practice in Turkey (Kalaycıoğlu 2003) as do policy makers and service providers (Kalaycıoğlu 2007).

Until very recently, for the reasons mentioned above, the major living and care arrangement for elderly care has been the family. Family care arrangements also took many different forms like living as elderly couples; living with one of the children (mainly with sons); living with a poor relative as the caregiver; living with an in-law, and so on (Kalaycıoğlu 2003). After 1995 state nursing homes for retired civil servants started to be established. This was quickly followed by private nursing homes after the 2000s. In this period the aged population started to increase. It rose from 5.3 per cent in 2000 to 7.5 per cent in 2008. However, ageing and elderly care is still not considered a major social responsibility of society at large, and rather is understood as a family duty. Since nursing home care is thought of as "negligence" by the children or "bad treatment of the elderly parents", home care is preferred more (Kalaycıoğlu 2003). This also creates paid employment for rural migrant women who provide home care for the elderly. In an article Da Roit discusses the transformation and commodification of elderly people's care in Southern European countries (Da Roit 2007). She stresses how the Mediterranean welfare state through the growth of commercial services, mostly provided by migrant women hired by families in the informal market, changes intergenerational solidarity within families relying on the work of unpaid women (ibid). In Turkey this market opportunity is also shared by foreign women care workers.[2] This is an important feature of globalisation. Poverty is a powerful force that makes women migrate to find work.[3]

As explained above, care work stays within informal sector practices. This type of work stays outside the formal legal regulations, without any coverage of social security or insurance. Employer-employee relations take place in the private sphere of a "home" where "trust" between the two is based on the development of "fictive kinship". All the arrangements of this kind of work are informal from finding the job to bargaining and payment as well as the determination of job requirements and job performance.

After 2000 a major shift occurred in the arrangement of domestic work. Especially with the start of the EU Accession Program after 1999 and the restructuring of the social security system (see Şahin's chapter in this volume) and the Health Transformation Program (see Ağartan's chapter in this volume), a new mechanism of employment has emerged mainly monitored by İş-Kur (Turkish Employment Organisations) under the Ministry of Labour. This development took place in line with global developments when international competition increased, resulting in important changes in national labour markets. These developments ask for a reconsideration of employment policies and new forms of employment. It is argued that the ongoing flexibilisation and growing need for services in the domestic labour market resulted among others in the increasing demand for the Private Employment Agencies (PEA) (Yüksel and Sivgin 2008: 107). If these newly set up agencies follow the rules set by İş-Kur, their licences are renewed for another three years. The international acceptance of PEAs goes back to the Congress/Convention of Private Employment Agencies organised by the ILO in 1997 and an agreement (No 181) on PEAs. In Turkey PEAs are active only in certain employment spheres; these agencies take on a mediating function between employers and employees. Together with the introduction of these PEAs, the "Association of Private Employment Agencies" was founded in 2004. The law that sets the legal frame for the control of the agencies' activities clearly states that no payment shall be taken from persons asking for a job.

PEAs emerged in Turkey as well as on a global scale in an attempt to organise informal employment processes and to fight unemployment (especially activating unskilled labour). It was thought that together with these agencies the service sector and specifically lower level services would experience improvements in employment conditions. At the end of 2009 there were 274 PEAs registered with İş-Kur in Turkey. Respectively the most populated agencies can be found in Istanbul (184), Ankara (23), Izmir (24) and Antalya (14). The sectors and specific areas of work assigned to the employees vary. These offices have particular areas of specialisation: allocating managers in leading positions, education, information/advice services, human resources and career planning (Cam, 2008). One of the most important areas they serve is domestic labour. The PEAs are considered to have potential to create organised and stable employment. In that sense, domestic labour stands out as one of the areas in need of reorganisation and stabilisation. Hence, PEAs can transfer women workers looking for domestic care work to newly established "Firms who deal with Care Work". PEAs have made agreements with such firms and control and inspect their work in accordance to the rules of the Labour Code. With this development it can be argued that domestic work has been reorganised through PEAs and İş-Kur. However, this has only a partial effect since due to the informality of the labour market there are wide opportunities for unregistered firms to emerge much greater in number but for which no information exists. These firms work in a subcontracting relation and do not have to abide by the rules of the Labour Code. They employ workers on a daily basis for one-off jobs (cleaning or care) and do not have to pay any social insurance payments for those daily workers. With the development of these firms the basis of "trust" in work relations has been transformed from "fictive kinship" as experienced in the 1990s towards "secure work" expectations from workers in the 2000s.

To conclude, we can say that although the new development of PEAs and firms are in line with global trends and are expected to reorganise, transform and integrate work life and the labour market into a more controllable system, they have either caused only partial impact for "decent work" or more significantly new forms of labour exploitation due to the dominance of informality in the market.

The Dynamics of Domestic Paid Labour in the 1990s

In different countries some innovative regulations on domestic workers have emerged. These may be integrated into a general labour code and/or separate regulatory instruments.[4] In Turkey, as well, such regulatory mechanisms began after 2000, especially with regard to the integration of domestic work into the formal labour market.

In our first study, which actually forms one of the bases for this article, we used a representative sample from the Turkish Statistical Institute's (TurkStat) database; where 5,618 households were selected. Screening these addresses we managed to find 151 women employed in domestic wage labour. We collected information about their social and family backgrounds, work histories, present work conditions, and relations with their employers, family status, self esteem criteria, and their future prospects for themselves, their children and family as a whole. We also interviewed 81 female employers to compare the evaluations of work and employer-employee relations between these two groups (Kalaycıoğlu and Rittersberger-Tılıç 2001).

A brief profile of the sample is as follows: Paid domestic women workers were found to be almost all first generation migrants from rural areas, mainly from Central Anatolia. On average they had lived for about 10-20 years in Ankara. The majority came with their husbands and families. Most of them continued their relations with their villages of origin, at least in the form of visits (weddings, funerals, religious holidays, etc.). The women employers, on the other hand, originated largely from urban backgrounds.

To understand domestic work class and gender relations are other important aspects to consider, as Bora puts it, stressing that middle class women employers through the existence of paid domestic work are able to position themselves as equal to men and construct themselves as modern individuals. They distinguish themselves from their employees, who are considered uneducated, powerless, crude, etc. Paid domestic work and daily life practices thus actively reproduce gender and class differences (Bora 2010: 185-186).

How did the domestic women workers find their jobs?

Women found their jobs through family and kin networks. This pattern of job-finding provided a guarantee for the continuation of social control, at the same time guaranteeing a workplace in which women can work while "maintaining their honour". Here "honour" is a term which specifically refers to the *women's honour*, her *family's honour*, the *sexual purity* or *untouchability of a woman*, and it should not be understood in the sense of individual prestige or pride. On the other hand, the employer too gets the guarantee of a trustworthy, honest and loyal worker. Thomson (2009: 284) in her article on household workers in Mexico comes to similar conclusions: "The employer might confide in her employee, talk about family matters, and ask her about her own family. However, the *patrona* is in a superior position: the one who gives the orders, but who is also a benefactor, giving presents to the worker of second-hand clothes or leftover food."

In looking for work, the social respectability of the workplace is a significant factor since the reserved sphere of another's home constitutes a risk factor with respect to social control mechanisms, especially those related to women. In other words, maintaining the "honour" of a woman was seen as a significant factor within the work situation. Therefore, an isolated and unknown home means social control mechanisms cannot be applied by her male family members so as to "protect" her from possible interaction with male members of the other family.

The same reasoning worked as an argument against the, at that time newly-arising, firms providing cleaning services. Most of the husbands and the women themselves were against working for such firms where control could not be applied.

What about work conditions, working hours and earnings?

Job definitions were broadly defined; also working hours often were longer than an 8 hours day. The schedule of workdays and differences in working hours make a difference in earnings and the work load. Many preferred to work on a monthly basis, either working 5 days a week in the same household; others worked one day every two weeks; or one day a week, again in the same household. Some of the women stressed the importance that working in the same households allows developing an individual work order/schedule and routines which ease the work, while working in different households was considered more demanding and exhausting (the employers asking for a "full" cleaning program in only one day). Rate of pay again was determined through informal networks, by employers as well as employees using their social networks to get an idea of standard payments.

The monthly incomes of the women actually constituted about 42 per cent of the household incomes, without doubt an important contribution. Yet, the women recurrently mentioned that their contribution to the family budget is of lesser importance than their husbands'. They actually preferred to refer to it as a "pin money", and stressed that their incomes were often paid not on a monthly basis, but on a daily or weekly basis, and therefore "easily and fastly used for daily expenditures" (Özbay 1990). This can be mainly explained through the traditional social norms and values which define the male members as main breadwinners of the family. In our findings, the husbands' attitudes were found to be quite different when asked about their views about women working as paid domestic workers. While most of the husbands were positive about women being employed outside in general terms, their positive attitudes changed when asked about their wives working as paid domestic workers. That is to say, husbands were not pleased with sending their wives to do someone else's cleaning. The women could only legitimize their active participation in the labour market, especially in low prestige and low income jobs, under the condition of severe economic deprivation of the family and when their earnings constituted a major "contribution to the family budget".

"Mutual Trust" As the Basis of Work Relations

Despite cultural variations between employers and employees in family lifestyles, religious practices, formation of social networks within the community, and the gender division of labour in the house, and with such conditions as lack of job guarantee, social security or health security, domestic workers had no other choice except to "trust" their employers. The employers on the other hand trusted in the "honesty" of their employees. This kind of a "mutual trust" relationship is a kind of "fictive-family relation" substituting for a formal contract. Working conditions, hours, salaries, and responsibilities in principal relied on verbal agreements. Payments were basically low, but other forms of material as well as immaterial support were common. Thus, employers helped find jobs for unemployed husbands, sons or daughters of their helpers; provided support in-kind in the form of clothes, food, school materials for children, help in bureaucratic affairs, or most significantly help in health issues. The findings indicate an integration of religious and traditional values with a "modern" condition like paid work. In their understanding of religion, the paid domestic workers found a place to locate themselves in paid domestic work, in spite of the "negative" connotation of these kinds of jobs in the larger society.

Revisiting the Field (2010)

More than a decade has passed, and Turkey has experienced important changes in economic and welfare conditions. Neo-liberal economic, social and political global developments have also reflected themselves in the sphere of domestic labour. Domestic labour is still dominated by a strong focus on cleaning and child care work, and the model of "family like relations" is still widespread, but important changes can be realised, too. Thus, there is a growing demand now not only for child care, but specifically for elderly and ill persons' care. This demand also causes changes in legislation and government policies.

How do these developments reflect themselves in informal/formal domestic labour? A follow up study has been made to answer this question. The follow-up study is only a partial revisiting of the fieldwork conducted a decade or more ago. The main aim of this up-date is an attempt to address changes in the sphere of paid domestic women's labour. The mainly structural changes taking place in the economic-political sphere are reflected in the personal and daily life experiences of domestic women workers. The up-date was a small-scale qualitative study, in which we specifically tried to consider the growing demand for elderly, child and health care. We used qualitative methods and conducted a number of in-depth interviews, incorporating three representatives/ owners of Personal Employment Agencies (PEAs controlled and licensed by İş-Kur), to obtain insight into new institutional developments; furthermore, we talked to one woman who found her job through a PEA; another woman taking care of the elderly/ill in a private household who found the job herself; and finally, eight women who worked in private households providing carework and/or in different workplaces working as cleaners through unregistered cleaning firms. For this last group of women these unregistered firms call them for different type of jobs on a daily basis or whenever there is demand. These women usually work in groups for cleaning jobs. For carework the firm assigns one woman to a private household during a time of illness. The up-date cannot be considered a representative study; still the data collected from these personal experiences are important in gaining a better understanding of the recent situation of paid domestic women's labour in Turkey. The second study, like the original one, was conducted in Ankara.

When the findings of the revisit are considered, at least two trends additional to the findings of the earlier study can be observed: firstly, firms and agencies gained greater importance. However, the status of the firms and the work conditions of women differ greatly between those firms who work jointly with the PEAs and those firms unregistered who call women for different jobs on a daily basis. Secondly, although the work relations are still informal, the relations of "trust" between the worker and the employer have shifted more towards the "amount of money earned and secure work" rather than the "fictive kinship" relation as in the case of the earlier study. More than a decade has passed and as the market for domestic work has gradually come to be dominated by firms, the wages and earnings of women have decreased below minimum wage. In this regard, the occurrence of women finding their own jobs through family and friend networks is still widespread and preferred because of better working conditions and higher earnings. It is the work arrangements in care taking jobs that are still more commonly following the "fictive kinship" pattern.

The New Work Conditions

Women are recruited by the unregistered firms on a daily basis to go out for cleaning jobs in private homes or offices. These firms pay an extremely low wage of 25 TL[5] for a whole day of working (often starting at 7.00 o'clock in the morning, when the bus comes to collect the women from the neighbourhood, until 23.00 o'clock at night, when they return). Usually two or three women work in one place. The job is finished only when the house/flat/office is totally cleaned, and if some members of this little group work slowly or do not perform well enough, the others have to compensate. They have no job security, no bargaining power, no health security. The women declare: if the price of cleaning a three storey villa is 750 TL, each woman (usually a group of three) is paid 25 TL plus the lunch and transport to and from the house. The firm also supplies the cleaning material or any machines needed. The rest is profit for the firm as they do not have to pay taxes or any insurance for daily based workers.

In such a work arrangement the women complain about low wages; all need to earn money, and they want to work as many days in succession and as often as possible. Others, those who have to take care of children or grandchildren, are happy to work once in a while. Interestingly, they strongly expressed the lack of solidarity among themselves. They lament, but at the same time they state that they are content, if they are offered the job and not their neighbours; they are willing to work for less; they are ready to spy on their colleagues, if these colleagues, for example, secretly take tips in the places they work, etc.

Another group of women, working for firms controlled by PEAs, work on a monthly basis, have social security, work contract and regulated working hours. Nevertheless, for women with little and often no education it becomes more and more difficult to find a job in such firms. The emergence of PEAs, which function as mediators, acting as recruiters of employees and representing the interests of employers supports such formalisation trends. The criteria required to apply for a job, are relatively high in terms of educational and vocational/occupational background and experiences. Poor women, like the ones we typically investigated when studying domestic work, cannot attain such qualifications and skills. We are referring to women, between late 40s and mid 50s, who basically migrated to the city about 25-30 years ago, or were born as the first/second generation of rural-to-urban migrants. Their daughters are not necessarily in better situations. Although most do have a school certificate, vocational skills and work experiences are still rare. Hence, we argue that even if the profile of women has changed in terms of better education due to longer years of urban experience, they still lack the major skills essential for employment in "decent domestic work".

When we asked about the specificities of firms engaged in domestic and care work, interestingly, none of the owners or partners of the firms had any previous training or experience in this sector. They stressed that there is no need for special training; anybody good in human relations is able to do the job. The first firm was founded in 2005; the two others, respectively, were established in 2008 and 2009. Although the legal frame was established in 2003, the emergence of the firms lagged by a few years. All three firms define their areas of activity as care of the ill, elderly, children, and the care/support of patients in hospitals by accompanying persons (*refakatçı*), as well as domestic labour, i.e. cleaning, cooking, and gardening. Within this list, care of the ill and elderly, as well as cleaning services, are mentioned as most important. All three firms mention, however, that there are (illegal) firms, not linked to İş-Kur, all of which have service cars which they use as "offices". In this context, they refer to the fact that these kinds of firms especially employ foreign women labour. They complain about these illegal firms which function as mediators for foreign labour and which they call "mobile firms". These firms have no office and basically exist in cyperspace as a handy number; they have no equipment; all employees are simply collected in a bus in the morning and as soon as a call comes in, the employees are dropped off at the employers' address.

In terms of personnel politics and firms' service quality, the persons applying to a PEA are allocated and employed on a demand basis; there is no stable staff. The agency managers state that honesty, experience and skill are the most important characteristics for care work. In this field nurses, pre-school teachers, pedagogy graduates, or others holding a related certificate are common. The employers prefer experience and are less concerned with professional credentials; some of the employees even insist on untrained personnel and basically ask for a "docile" worker. The determination of wages is determined by the employers and can vary according to type of work and number of hours. The firms can not ask for any kind of payment from workers. Workers take their wages directly from employers and do not take any other financial support from the firms. Unregistered firms, on the other hand, ask for commission from the worker equal to one month's wages although it is against the law.[6]

In terms of job security, the firm does not take any responsibility after they make the contract between the employer and the worker. Hence, firms only play a mediating role in introducing the two sides but then leave the worker without any support in the relationship with the employer. Interviewed women say that the most important thing for them is to feel happy in the workplace (the house). They feel relaxed and secure if there is 'mutual trust between them and the employers'. One of the women who found work through a firm said that the most important thing is 'to be able to receive a decent wage for her labour as well as to work in a non-humiliating and respectful environment'. Hence, it can be claimed that women who find work by themselves still base their security on mutual trust or fictive kinship, but those who find work through firms emphasise respect and a decent wage. From this finding we argue that over a decade the women have experienced a transformation in terms of their work experiences becoming more formalized although the transformation is still in an embryonic stage.

How do Women Find Work?

Despite the emergence of the firms in the market, finding work through references of relatives, neighbours and kin is the dominant tendency. The firms claim that this tendency is common for domestic cleaning work but that women prefer going through firms when looking for elderly and child care. They argue that such demands have increased in the last 10 years. On the other hand, the firms which work with PEAs discuss that this market still carries risk because of the increase of unregistered firms in the market which do not have to obey rules. Due to this, unequal competition prevails in this market, which they argue needs better regulation and control by the state. Also networking among these firms is lacking which leaves the ground open to such illegal firms. The state has to develop a registration mechanism.

Some women we interviewed said that they prefer looking for work through the firms because it is easier for those women who do not have their own information networks. On the other hand, finding work through the firms is difficult for women who have children because the firms do not want to find work for women with children. One of the women who could not find work because she had an 8 year old child argues that there should be crèches like in Europe. Otherwise all that is done is useless and the firms can not solve this problem. Also the firms look for experience and training in care work which many of these women lack. So the majority of women continue looking for work through their own networks.

The women claim that care work is related to a "person's moral values" rather than training. They give examples from the households where they provide elder care; they say that the household members treat their elderly or ill relatives very badly, without any affection, without concern. So one's own morality towards elderly makes a difference and not vocational training. They claim that they get job satisfaction because they treat the elderly with love and care. They also differentiate between domestic work and care work. Care work is less demanding but needs love and care. Domestic work is exhausting but does not necessarily require affection from the worker.

Attitudes Towards Domestic and Carework By Families, Neighbours and Women Themselves

Between the two studies and especially after 2000, deepening of economic crises, redundancies mainly experienced by male breadwinners, increasing costs of children's education pushed women into the labour market more than before. In the revisit it was observed that neither the families, nor the husbands had a choice in opposing women working in paid employment. Especially for poor migrant women without any skills employment opportunity appears to be in domestic and carework legitimized by family and kin. Hence, we found some women sharing their household responsibilities with their husbands, e.g. fathers taking care of the children while "she is lucky that day" to find work.

Cultural Factors Effecting Work Relations

We can argue that the pattern we described as "fictive-family" is still valid, but that there is a growing trend towards formalisation. In the case of the PEAs, a more skilled and formal women's labour force is demanded. But what seems to be most striking is the growing number of firms that contract workers on a daily basis and provide no security or guarantees of any kind; the workers are under the rule of an eventually "good-willing boss", but this is not comparable to the "trust based contract" of the "fictive-family model". Both are part of the informal economy. Child care, elder care and the care of ill persons still follow the "fictive-family" pattern. Cleaning work seems to be open to even a greater level of exploitation.

In our work (Kalaycıoğlu and Rittersberger-Tılıç 2001: 55) we argued that institutionalisation of irregular casual jobs can only be obtained when such jobs are included in a regular system with a legal definition of social security and insurance coverage. This is the only way to create a difference in domestic and carework. Otherwise, the work relations, even if firms are controlled by İş-Kur, will take place within the scope of the informal sector. Our book forecasted that gradually the regularity of domestic work will increase. In fact, this came through very slowly in individual cases. One of the women interviewed defended that domestic work in Turkey should be organised as in USA where regularity in work relations dominates, as she had learned through the experiences of her relative living in the USA.

Conclusion

The market has become the determining social and economic institution with a neo-liberal turn. It has expanded its influence in a wide range of spheres. Structural adjustment to the global economy lead to a decline in the power of labour compared to capital.

Domestic wage labour, child and elder care services formerly predominantly provided by state institutions or having been caught up in the informal economy, started to become more and more a part of private service providing firms. The role of PEAs is important in this sense. These agencies have to be seen as attempts towards formalisation, i.e. asking for an obligatory work contract and social security. In return, however, these kinds of job opportunities are only accessible to persons with a certain educational level and/or vocational skills. Actually, domestic and care work traditionally have been typical for unskilled and cheap women labour in Turkey. Thus, these types of job arrangements are still not accessible to those women. They actually can not join the formal labour market. These jobs appear in the unprotected sector, as Özyeğin (2001) in her study on domestic labour and the urban middle class in Turkey argues while stressing the lack of social security. Özyeğin shows that there is a growing awareness for the need of such a protection and emphasises the need for regulating social security and work conditions (ibid. 281).

A new development in this sphere has to be seen in the emergence of informal domestic and care services firms in the informal economy, too. Thus, there still persists the "traditional" model of a patron-client or as we called it "fictive-family" relation, but in addition, we see the emergence of informal firms employing women sporadically and on an ad hoc basis to do domestic services. Women, working for such firms, seem to be even more exploited in the sense that they have extremely long working hours, no security, and very low incomes. The owners of these firms also do not engage in any kind of "personal"-"family" engagement with their workers. Thus, while women working in private households as cleaners, babysitters or caretakers of the elderly or ill could strongly rely on informal support networks and additional forms of payment and immaterial support from their employers, those who work for such firms cannot. Relatively seen, the old system had certain "advantages". However, it seems to be crucial to address the fact that neither the old informal (fictive-family), nor the new informal (domestic and care services firms) change the disadvantaged position of women's labour in domestic and care services. Trends towards formalisation, supported by the introduction of PEAs, only reach the skilled and educated women. Therefore, it can be concluded that class and gender inequalities are reproduced and reinforced. A solution can be seen in organising labour and specifically informal labour, reforming labour laws, as well as re-considering the role of the public instead of private institutions. Following Thomson's (2009) argument; domestic workers are not maids or servants but workers!

13

WOMEN AND TRADE UNIONISM IN TURKEY: THE IMPACT OF THE EUROPEAN UNION

Şerife Gözde Yirmibeşoğlu[1]

In the recent international arena, the most common economic developments owing to the globalization process, have been a rise in economic integration, growth in capital flow and an increase in international competition for capital. In some cases, the globalization process means integration into the European Union. As Manuel Castells argues, 'European integration is both a reaction to the globalization process and the most enhanced expression of globalization' (1998: 318). For ordinary people in Turkey, which has been negotiating its EU membership for decades, global economic integration is linked directly with the European integration.

Turkey's neo-liberal transformation began with the 24 January 1980 stabilization package. Although Turkey was quite successful in achieving its integration into globalization via neo-liberal policies in the 1980s, its speed diminished in the 1990s. The AKP entered the political arena in the early 2000s with great energy and declared itself a great actor in accelerating the neo-liberal transformation begun in the 1980s. Actually, the leaders administrating the AKP, Recep Tayyip Erdogan and Abdullah Gul, have been extremely active in this transformation, since they have not followed their former leader and teacher Necmettin Erbakan, who was mistaken by giving great emphasis to the East and by standing politically and ideologically against the West, when he became prime minister in 1996. As Kramer emphasizes, 'Erbakan never made a secret of the fact that he preferred good and close political Turkish ties with major Islamic "brother states" to a stronger western integration' (1996: 382). In contrast, his disciples Erdogan and Gul had learnt how to come to and maintain power before they joined the elections of 2002. Thus, 'instead of moving towards the East as Erbakan had done, they hit the road to the USA long before coming to power' (Uzgel 2009: 20). This was the major factor leading to the success of the AKP in two consecutive elections.

The result is the continuation of changes in Turkey's political and economic structures started in the 1980s with the boost of the military coup of the 12 September 1980. Turkey has been an ardent supporter of neoliberal policies, which have had a severe impact on trade unionism and the working class. Yaylagül clearly summarizes the disastrous effects of such policies (2006: 169):

> Trade unions have gradually lost their influence owing to neo-liberal policies. The real income of the workers has decreased relentlessly. High wages are shown to be the reason for unemployment. Despite the fact that the working class has been the constant loser, tax rates imposed by the capital have been reduced so as to increase profit rates.

It is impossible to ignore the devastating impact of such policies on workers and trade unions in Turkey. As a consequence, the current picture of trade unions is rather blurred as Turkey has been suffering in both the economic and political spheres for the past two decades. When the rights of the working class, the most vital part of the political and economical arena, are investigated, it is possible to observe that lately, this picture is becoming increasingly vague. In other words, trade union membership has been decreasing sharply since 1980 and thus, their power has been reduced. For instance, according to the statistics provided by the Ministry of Labour and Social Security, trade union membership has dropped 11% between 1995 and 2006 (MLSS 2007). This shows a great decline in the power of trade unions. This shows a great decline in power of trade unions. Mütevellioğlu and Işık clarify the current situation of the labour in Turkey (2009: 198):

> Since the last decades of the 20th century, labour, whose dependency on market structures has been deepened by the neo-liberal policies, has been transformed into a docile commodity. In addition, it is considered to be converted into a cheaper and more obedient factor of production.

Lately, there has been an increase in positive attitudes toward Turkey's EU membership due to changing dynamics of the international arena. The most common argument comes from the sizeable young population of

Turkey. As Berberoğlu explains, 'Turkey may be an advantageous market for Europe with its young and large population, and thus, it will be much easier for Europe to enter and invade the Turkish market' (1981: 277-291). Accordingly, the European Community has proposed improved relations in many fields; the advance of Turkey in its democratic structures and institutions has been the major topic. The weak structure of trade unions has been discussed by the EU, and Turkish governments have been warned about the issue.

Conditional requirements imposed on candidate states to comply with EU directives are a coercive measure that seeks to change the state policies and practices (Kelley 2004: 425). For instance, Turkey's acceptance in December 1999 as a candidate for full membership led to a new period during which EU membership became an important social mission for diverse segments of Turkish society. Since then, the Turkish government has put great emphasis on connections with the EU, gaining particular success in obtaining a negotiation date. Accordingly, the primary activity of the parliament has been to enact the necessary legislation or make the necessary changes in current legislation so as to conform to the EU criteria, as the goal has been to start membership negotiations. However, government compliance is composed of two stages in policy reforms: legislative change and institutional change. What is lacking in the example of Turkish compliance is institutional change, the cause of the present suffering of democratic structures. Turkey is expected to improve its institutional structure in order to perform effectively because the attempts to solely conform to legal norms are not satisfactory.

One of the most problematic institutional structures in Turkey is its trade unions, which have innumerable problems, the most important of which is the hegemony and severe interference of political powers. The second problem comes in the form of constraints arising from the 1982 Constitution and its succeeding Acts. The third important problem for the trade unions is an abrupt decrease in the number of their members because of the fragmentation and absolute silence of the working class (Yirmibeşoğlu 2009: 213). The reason for the reluctance and decline of trade unions is highlighted by a woman trade union leader, who participated in this study:

'There is a deterrence policy of the state, and the government is against trade unions. Regardless of whether they are in the public or private sector, workers are exposed to the domination of the state. There are various types of coercion such as being sacked, jailed and arrested. The government favours and protects the unions which support them. I was banned twice because of my struggle for trade unions. Although I was able to reach the highest level of my job as a public officer and was awarded by my ministry due to my high performance, I was sacked because of my activities in trade unions.'

In fact, it is well-known that one of the main constituents of social and economic development is the trade union movement, and there is a direct correlation between socio-economic development and freedom and trade unionism. Unfortunately, although Turkey, a developing country, has displayed great performance in many fields due to its efforts regarding EU membership, it has not succeeded in improving trade unions in the country. On the contrary, since the 1980s with the influence of the military coup and neo-liberal policies following the coup, Turkey has succeeded in limiting, diminishing and finally wiping out trade unions and putting them under the control of the government. Therefore, it has been more and more difficult for women to carve out a space in trade unions in Turkey.

This chapter aims at debating the low participation and secondary position of women in trade unions in Turkey, a country that has been striving for EU membership for decades, and at discussing the impact of neo-liberal policies on women in trade unions in Turkey by investigating the insincere attitude of the AKP government during EU accession negotiations. Within this scope, 16 women having relatively high positions, five of them elected presidents of trade unions, were interviewed. Nine of the trade unionist women were interviewed twice. Both a recent interview and an interview which took place ten years ago are included in the study in order to determine the changes in the situation of women in Turkish trade unions. All the trade unionist women were very willing to contribute to the study. They all expressed the value of such studies and their impact on women while participating in the public sphere. Most of them are professionals. Although they had extremely tight schedules, they allocated long hours to the interviews. The limitation of the study was that some of the women, generally the younger ones and the ones joining the high ranks of the trade unions relatively recently, were not able to answer some of the questions.

Trade Unions and Women in Turkey
The emergence of trade unionism in Turkey does not have a long histori-

cal background. On the contrary, trade unions are new institutional structures which constitute one of the major constraints on their development. Another problem is the legal limitations with which trade unions are faced. In addition to the restrictions stemming from the Constitution of 1982 and the succeeding laws, trade unions in Turkey are not united. In fact, they are severely fragmented. As a result, they are not able to demonstrate strength in terms of their organizational and political structure.

Thus, trade unions in Turkey present a desperate picture and discussing the situation of women in such structures is severely disappointing. In fact, the involvement of women in the public sphere in Turkey is still extremely low. In other words, Turkish women are still confined to the private sphere and the AKP government intends to strengthen this confinement by imposing its 'veiling deal' and by propagating the party's minimum three-child policy for each family. On the one hand, the AKP spends great effort toward EU membership because this is what the great majority of Turkish voters want. On the other hand, it spends great effort for the restriction of women to the home sphere due to its ideological background, reflected here in an explanation by Göle: 'Islamist movements want to have moral control over the public sphere through control of women's sexuality, limiting public encounters between the sexes' (1997: 58). The AKP tries to legitimize itself by claiming that its aim is not to establish Sharia or Islamic Law in the country, but to bring European standards by means of EU membership. However, the hypocrisy of the AKP is a major political question.

The participation of women in labour has been decreasing sharply. This is the major reason for their involvement in trade unions in Turkey; while their participation in labour was 80% in the 1950s, it dropped to 33% in the 1980s (Koray 1993: 47). There is great influence from the rising Muslim culture and neo-liberal policies in this abrupt drop, and the result is low representation of women in trade unions.

Problems of Women in Trade Unions in Turkey

Women in Turkey have not been able to integrate into trade unions yet, although there has been a slight increase in the number of women in trade union leadership. Those women are the initiators of the tough struggle in such institutions. The social depression following the globalization process has shown that women need trade unions in order to survive, a fact ignored by the political parties.

Avdeyeva points out a remarkably important characteristic about the relationship between the ideology of governing parties in parliaments and the creation of viable institutions on gender equality (2010: 204-212). She declares:

> There is significant interaction between ideology of the ruling parties in parliaments and the strength of women's movements on the level of institutional reform in EU accession countries. Women's movement advocates are not single actors on the domestic political arena: the impact of their activity depends on other political actors, most importantly the ideology of governing parties. Thus, parties in parliament moderate the impact of women's movement actors on the degree of government compliance with international requirements, specifically on the degree of institutional change in accession countries.

In the last decades, there has been influence from the women's movement on political parties in Turkey. The parties in power have put emphasis on increasing the number of women in the Parliament in order to show the public that they give importance to the existence of women in the public sphere, but this is only a quantitative increase. While investigating the success of women's movements in Turkey, Ecevit argues that it has been flourishing in many respects since the 1980s. On the other hand, when she discusses what they were not able to do, she declares that women in Turkey could not raise social support (2004). This is, as the literature expresses, directly related to the attitude and ideology of the parties in government (Costain 1992). To illustrate, today, the AKP expects Turkish women to be only mothers and wives, while the party assumes itself a liberal party fighting for women's rights and argues that it is a defender of women's rights.

Naturally, the question to be discussed is 'how will women with three or more children join the public sphere and reach high ranks?' Zoonen responds by declaring that mothers with young children are hard to find in upper-level politics because of both practical and cultural obstacles (2006: 292). As expected, the most obviously practical obstacle is motherhood. Therefore, the picture that can be drawn for the future of Turkish women will be a much darker one, in which there will be a large drop in the number of women in the labour force and thus, in trade unions. The unfortunate product of such policies based upon the ideology of the party in power, the AKP, will be a rise in the number of women confined to the private sphere.

Obviously, neo-liberal policies play an important role in this confinement. It is possible to go back to the 1980s to observe the origins of the neo-liberal reforms in Turkey (Öniş 2003: 517). The drastically apparent result of the neo-liberal policies adopted in Turkey, similar to the policies of the AKP governing the country since 2002, can be seen in the low participation of women in paid employment, the vital component of the public sphere (see chapter by Toksöz in this volume). One extremely important consequence of low participation of women in the labour force is the decline in their involvement in trade unions. Unfortunately, increasing the number of women in trade unions is a difficult task. Furthermore, the status of women is quite low in trade unionism in Turkey. In other words, women are mostly confined to the low ranks of the unions; they are not able to reach the decision-making levels due to several reasons.

During the globalization process, a subject which has become a primary issue in the international trade union movement is the equality, organisation and participation of women in trade unions (Erdoğdu 2006: 304). For example, in its Charter on Gender Mainstreaming in Trade Unions, the European Trade Union Confederation (ETUC) emphasized that 'representation and visibility of women at all levels of decision-making is far from proportionate' (2007a: 2). Recently, there is new attention at the EU level regarding action on all these matters. Nevertheless, in the context of establishing gender equality in the work sphere, a serious and organized effort concerning political power and trade unions does not exist in Turkey (Tenekeci 2010: 20). For instance, the government of the AKP routinely ignores such matters emphasized by the EU, as these matters contradict the AKP's ideology which emphasizes and perpetuates the secondary position and motherhood role of women.

Women in Turkey are restricted to the home sphere via their 'homemaker role' and thus, excluded from the labour force and trade unions by means of state policies emphasizing the motherhood of women in any occasion. In other words, the burden of their familial role in the private sphere has been the major constraint (see the chapter by Memiş, Öneş and Kızılırmak in this volume). We see a strong similarity over time when comparing the recent interviews with those ten years ago. It is interesting to observe that one of the women expressed exactly the same things she did ten years ago:

'When I define the working woman, I declare that she is an individual with two employers, two exploiters, and four shifts, that is, home, work, child and a hard job. My definition of four-shift work and my solution, such as more democracy at home and also the willingness of the husband at home, are clear. My solution is that the government should assess the needs of women more democratically by solving problems such as nurseries, breast feeding rooms and providing work security, so that having children should not be a problem any longer'.

There is a large variety of social science texts expressing the existence of structures and processes within society which systematically cause and perpetuate the oppression of women (Fine 2007; Rees 1992; Walby 1990). Discrimination against women and their exclusion is explained by a range of reasons, one of which is motherhood. Hence, there is an assortment of academic work focusing on the familial burden of women which constructs a major barrier to entering the public arena (Regan and Paskeviciute 2003; Nicolson 1996; Gilligan 1982). One of the interviewed women, who was extremely happy to be in the management of the union and who affirmed her active struggle for women in the union ten years ago, expresses the sad experience of her exclusion from the union during her pregnancy:

'Because of pregnancy, I was not very active in the union and my relationship with the union ended after the birth. I was not accepted to the list to join the management owing to my previous opposition about their attitude against women's issues. When you are not taken into the list, it is your end in the union. If you have a political position, they want to keep you out'.

Another woman who was able to reach the top positions and survive explains the difficulty of being a mother and a unionist:

'When women go to the union with their children, the men of the union complain; they are afraid that their wives also may want to join the union. They always tell me that they hope their daughter can be someone like me in the future. They never say they hope to have a wife like me'.

Historically, it has been difficult to organize women and gather them for action in trade unions due to the pressure of their dual work as a wage earner and homemaker. In addition, the traditional attitude of governments has not been supportive. In fact, recently, with the influence of neoliberal policies, the Turkish government has been proposing flexible work so that women can manage to reconcile their dual work.

Besides the awareness of women about the dual work as a main constraint, women are conscious of the detrimental impact of globalization constituting a major restriction against women. Women who were interviewed ten years ago were not aware of the negative impact of globalization and neo-liberal policies on women. Recent interviews show that they are now certainly aware of such detrimental influences, and that is the reason why today they define themselves undoubtedly as feminists:

'I am definitely a feminist. In my trade union, they are always telling us that we should never declare that we are feminists, but I announce that on every occasion. Therefore, I have to struggle more with the opposition of men'.

The structure of trade unions defines the position of women and it constitutes another major problem against women. The patriarchal ideology of the government in Turkey also has its reflection on trade unions and women face severe discrimination. Hence, women are not often admitted as managers or high-ranking officials in trade unions, but are accepted only as ornaments to show off as most of the interviewees highlight:

'I have participated in many congresses. There are a couple of women, but they have different positions. I mean women are there only to show that there are women in the gatherings. Women are expected to play the role of flower because that is what men want. They were not women who came there by struggling. That is the reason why you see a woman once and then you do not see her anymore at the meetings. I think they are invited because they have close relations with someone'.

Besides the negative attitude of men, women who participated in the study mentioned the similar attitude of women towards the candidacy of other women:

'If women supported each other, our job would be much easier. Even men sometimes support us, but not women. Women have never supported me. They supported men by claiming that those men were the friends of their husband'.

There is an exceedingly close relationship between the political parties and trade unions, both of which emphasize the dominance of patriarchy. Thus, it is impossible to carve out a space for women in either. There is severe interference from the political parties on trade unions in Turkey, which affects the participation and representation of women. They reflect their patriarchal ideology on trade unions. As a result, the probable outcome is a much lower participation of women in trade unions due to the ignorance of gender equality in the public sphere as a whole in Turkey. All the interviewees highlighted the patriarchal structure of trade unions and their relation with the political parties:

> 'There is the hegemony of political power on trade unions, which are severely patriarchal institutions. When a woman succeeds in the union and reaches a high level position, they always wonder about the reasons for her success and always believe that there is a trick behind her victory. They do their best to weaken her, but they never do such things to a man. When a woman frequently goes to the union, they try to find some insulting reasons for her visits'.

One of the reasons persistently linked with patriarchy is the power of the trade union in providing various financial resources to its leader, who has the power to abuse them. Lipset (1983) stresses the low prestige of union leaders in most countries because of this kind of abuse. Since there is the possibility to exploit the financial reserves of the union (and there have been such cases), the men of the union do not want to give up their positions to women. In Turkey, trade union leaders earn huge amounts of money and that is the reason why men of the union do not want to share their strong position with women. The relation between power and financial profit in union leadership is underlined by most women leaders:

> 'Trade unions are extremely patriarchal institutions. In our country, it started as a man's job and it still continues to be a man's job. There is profit in this job, and that is the reason why there is dominance. When there is profit, it is difficult to share power'.

There is no doubt that the structure of organizations is gendered. It is gendered in terms of the distribution of women and men and distribution of gendered practices. Accordingly, another major problem related to the patriarchy in trade unions, which has been pointed out by almost all the participants of the study, is sexual harassment. Studies and surveys have shown how sexual processes and organizational processes are intimately connected (Hearn and Parkin 2001: 13). Since this study aims at exploring the barriers against women in trade unions, extensively gendered organizations, sexual harassment comes onto the agenda of the interviewees even without asking any specific question about it:

> 'There has been no change in the rigidity of the glass ceiling in the last ten years. Because of the hegemony of the leadership, there are many obstacles against women. To illustrate, there is sexual harassment, which is a very irritating issue. When it happens, men blame women. Women either quit speaking or leave. Consequently, it is the woman who resigns, it is never a man. I have never seen a man punished because of sexual harassment. There is no direct punishment against a woman, but they exclude her by isolating her. When you protect that harassed woman, they similarly isolate you'.

Another punishment against women, 'the fear of reprisal from employers,' is emphasized in the 2007 ETUC survey, 'Women in Trade Unions: Bridging the Gap' (ETUC 2007b). This is also an extremely important problem for women and is emphasized by many of the interviewees:

> 'To be a candidate for the trade union administration is very risky in our country. If you are not taken into the list of administrators by the top managers, it is the end of your career in trade union. You cannot survive there anymore. You also cannot go back to your job because your boss will never take you back due to your activities in the union. That is the reason why most administrators in the union are quite old, because people want to receive their retirement rights before participating in the administration of the union. I have taken the risk. I know that I cannot go back to my job if my name is not on the list in the future, but I am a brave woman'.

Furthermore, the ETUC survey points to male domination of trade union activities as an impediment for women to join a union. The survey high lights that '[women] are afraid to engage in an activity that traditionally and historically has been led by the male gender'. In fact, roles attributed to the male gender emerge from gender ideology, and 'gender ideology in many cultures gives males the license to argue in direct, demanding and confrontational ways, with unmitigated rivalry' (Sheldon 1997: 227). Women, on the other hand, are taught to smile and to be polite and thus, are not recognized as leaders of organizations. This difference is highlighted by the participants of the study:

> 'When I started trade union activities and visited workplaces, I
> realized that I was not listened to while I was explaining the same
> things as my colleague, who was a man. Then, I started to raise my
> voice. The workers are familiar with a typical man of the trade
> union. This is a man with a moustache and a big belly. You gradu-
> ally learn how to make them listen to you. This is my unique con-
> cession. You are recognized after a while when you pay more atten-
> tion to your relationships with people. They understand that you
> are elected not because of your physical attributes such as beauty. If
> you do not raise your voice, you are destined to be lost and to be
> expelled'.

Finally, there is horizontal discrimination against women in Turkish trade
unions; it is believed that trade unions are places only for men. That is the
reason why they do not want to accept the existence of women in the
patriarchal structure of the union. and they do not want to change this
structure at all. For instance one of the interviewees claimed that even
physically, there is no space for women in trade unions:

> 'Most unions have toilets only for men. Their recreation rooms are
> like men's coffee houses in Turkey because of the backgammon and
> card games. The existence of women is never taken into account.
> They are not honest, and they want to sustain their hegemony'.

Impact of globalization and the European Union
The impact of globalization has been different in developing countries
when compared with the developed ones. However, the primary role of
women as homemakers is still universal. As Marling points out, 'gender
roles change as a result of globalization, but not essentially. Women are
still the principal providers of childcare' (2006: 100). The exaggerated
motherhood role of women in trade unions has provided a false image of
Turkish women in the international arena, as asserted by one of the interviewees:

> 'We have been going to the meetings abroad. Foreign unionists
> asked me once how my husband had sent me abroad, why I was not
> wearing traditional clothes and a veil and how many wives my hus-
> band had. The EU thinks that Turkish women cannot be trade

unionists. During an ILO meeting in the USA, once they told me that there could not be women trade unionist in Turkey. They added that I was a liar and Turkish women were not as I described. They believe that the only area that Turkish women work in is agriculture'

When asked about the changes in the past ten years, the interviewed women claimed that there had not been a visible change in the involvement and position of women in trade unions in Turkey during this time. Although they generally applauded the improving power of the women's movement in the country, almost all of them declared that there has been no change in the status of women in trade unions:

'I have not noticed any improvement in the last ten years. When they feel that you will succeed and you will have a high position, they construct barriers and they try to convince you by insisting that a woman cannot maintain such a high level and cannot deal with men. They keep on telling that you are a woman, you are married, you are a mother, you cannot join the meetings of the union at night, you cannot come and you cannot sit together with men during the meetings. They never want us to rule, so they try to stop us when they see our supporters.'

To solve such problems in the participation and representation of women, gender equality has been on the agenda of the EC since its foundation. For instance, Zippel emphasizes 'the emergence of sexual harassment policy in the United States and its journey across the Atlantic, where it was adopted initially by the EU, and later in many European countries' (2006). Besides its focus on equal rights and equal treatment for women and men, the EU has also rewarded equal work by men and women with equal pay. These beginnings have since been strengthened by gender mainstreaming initiatives, which aim to evaluate the gender implications of policy-making across all EC activities (Millns 2007: 218). Furthermore, the EU has employed mainstreaming as its major policy approach to promoting gender equality.

The law on equal treatment is a vital principle and an effective tool in combating overt sex discrimination, but it is not a sufficient measure to ensure sex equality (Rees 2001: 245). Two problematic areas, organisation and equal opportunities for women and men, have been on the agenda recently in Turkey. Today, it is difficult to declare that there are strong civil society associations in Turkey, and that women are advancing towards a high level of participation in them. Principally, the EU has recently underlined that the Turkish government should support trade unions and make the necessary changes in the legal structure in order to provide them with democratic rights. Unfortunately, this advice of the EU has not received much respect since the current party in government, the AKP, is not willing to fortify the trade unions in the country. On the contrary, the AKP is keen on diminishing the power of the already weakened unions.

Similarly, although the EU gives significantly more importance to the rights of women in Turkey than the rights of workers, the government of the AKP does not seem to give emphasis to the issue. In fact, the AKP government has shown great performance since it came into power by changing Turkey's legal structures so that they conform to European standards. However, women, who need urgent support and trade unions, extremely important constituents of democracy, are completely ignored by this so-called ardent supporter of the EU, the AKP, because the pressure of the EU regarding both issues has been weaker when compared with others.

The 2007 ETUC survey outlines the factors preventing women from joining trade unions (Sechi 2007: 16-17). The barriers stated in the survey are completely in parallel with those found in this study. Initially, according to the results of this study, the reason mentioned most often is the lack of time women have as a result of family commitments. Similarly, the ETUC survey emphasizes that 'women's time is at a premium due to the compromise between work and family commitment to trade union activities' (2007). Another factor mentioned is the failure to understand the importance of trade union membership. The explanation of the interviewed women matches exactly the statements of the ETUC survey:

'There is an inaccurate image of organizations in our culture. We are supplied with a mistaken picture of organizations. In fact, the organisation is our second home. Now, I am telling women to state the name of their organisation as they would state the name of their lover. I realize that we only register with organizations and thus, we are not able to integrate into them after becoming a member. We pay our membership fee, but we do not become active members. We do not climb the stairs to the high positions.'

The EU adopted the Action Program to Promote Gender Equality (2001), which is a program structured in three strands: awareness raising activities with a view to reinforcing the Community dimension of the promotion of gender equality; analysis and evaluation of gender issues in EU policies and measures; and finally, development of the capacity of players to promote gender equality effectively. In spite of the successful programs implemented by the EU, Turkey has been reluctant to take such gender equality programs into account. In fact, Turkey has remained completely ignorant of such programs, especially in the last few years. The statement of an interviewed woman displays this unwillingness of the AKP quite clearly:

'I never expect kindness from the AKP. They always run after their own interests. Otherwise, they never give people anything. The actions of this government are only for show. I do not believe that EU membership will have a contribution because the current mentality does not want to see women, does not respect women. The EU conformity laws have not had a positive impact. Who cares about women? The ideology of the current government is clear: if you join the trade union, you are sacked'.

Equal treatment is not adequate in and of itself. It requires support by positive action and positive discrimination. When applied alone, equal treatment facilitates only the participation of middle-class and upper-class women in the work sphere by means of equal opportunities. Moreover, it sustains the persistence of already existing class-based inequalities among women. Positive action policy, on the other hand, involves the determination of barriers against women in work sphere and ways to remove such barriers. Therefore, positive action policy is based on the positive discrimination policy. The interviewed women touched upon this issue and one of them claimed:

'Quotas for women are generally helpful, but they are not adequate to promote the participation of women in unions and their ability to reach high-ranked positions. If there is not a feminist perspective, nothing will help'.

Unfortunately, part-time employment has been promoted in the recent policies of the EU. The interviewees of this study underlined the unfavorable impact of part-time work on workers in general in Turkey and on women workers in particular. While they were arguing against the 1982 Constitution and the Labour Act and Social Security Act enacted after the Constitution, they emphasized the current promotion of part-time and flexible work by stating that the class consciousness of workers was deliberately eradicated after 1980. Moreover, they added that women are increasingly restricted to the home sphere because of such policies:

> 'I believe nothing will change after EU membership. The number of women working at home without social security will increase. Women's labour will become cheaper and the exploitation of women by the government will rise due to part-time and flexible work'.

Therefore, an important conclusion is that the women who joined this study were aware of the detrimental effects of neo-liberal policies on women. A change in their approach towards those policies was found during the interviews. Unlike the approach displayed ten years ago, today women are conscious of the negative results of neo-liberalism such as part-time and flexible work.

Conclusion

To sum up, this study has found that there are both similarities and differences in the attitudes and opinions of women in trade unions in Turkey over the last ten years. The major reasons for their low involvement in trade unions and their exclusion from high-ranking positions remain the same: women's roles as mothers and patriarchy in trade unions. The interviewers stated the same arguments as they did in the past. They declared that men do not want to accept the existence of women in the unions and overemphasize the familial roles of women thereby deterring women from entering high positions in the unions. Moreover, the women interviewed point to the hegemony and the domination of the parties in power on the country's trade unions.

During the interviews, it was found that there are also important changes in the approach and gender awareness of the women in trade unions, even though the women announced that there has been no change in the last ten years. First, they express that they are feminists much more comfortably than ten years ago. They sometimes declare it even without being asked. They have become aware of the link between the domination of the political parties and patriarchy with regards to trade unionism. They connect the discrimination of women in trade unions to this relationship. They have discovered the function attributed to women by men in the union: flowers of the union representing only beauty. Furthermore, they are well aware of how the connection between trade union leadership and power leads to easy access of the financial resources of the union. They believe this is the reason that men do not want them to have important roles in the union and try to discourage them. A major difference is that they now state sexual harassment as a main impediment; in the past, this was a topic ignored by the interviewed women. Another difference is that the number of women who can answer the women-based questions from a feminist perspective is much higher, which means they display a greater gender awareness. They mostly agree that EU membership will not help unless the patriarchal ideology of the political parties and the social structures change.

The solutions prescribed by the women are meaningful. Initially, they argue that the September 12 laws should be abolished. In addition, they want the political parties to stop interfering in trade unions in Turkey. They believe that women will not be successful otherwise. They propose the establishment of a women's secretariat and a women's bureau. They add that there should be a separate budget for the education of women in trade unions and the quotas for women should start from the lowest level. They propose that there should be a reduction in the membership fee of women. They emphasize that they want to see more women in trade unions, but they should be the women who do not contribute to the domination of men and that is the reason why they highlight gender awareness education for women. They believe in the positive contribution of education seminars carried out by academic institutions. They also suggest solutions regarding sexual harassment, which is a principal problem in trade unions (Toksöz and Erdoğdu 1998: 101).

To conclude, the participation of women in trade unions in Turkey has been decreasing and their path to reach high-ranking positions is still difficult. The most noticeable culprit for the secondary role of women in trade unions is the neo-liberal policies adopted after 1980 in Turkey. Moreover, the governments, particularly the AKP government, have been successful in enacting laws to conform to EU standards, but they have been extremely reluctant to establish the institutional changes proposed by the EU. As a result, women in trade unions in Turkey suffer more due to such policies and the silence of the EU.

ENDNOTES

Chapter 1

1 Orloff (1993) 'Gender and the social rights of citizenship: State policies and gender relations in comparative perspective', American Sociological Review, 58, 3, 303-328., Lewis (1992) 'Gender and the development of welfare regimes' Journal of European Social Policy, 3, 159-73.; Jensen (1997) 'Who cares? Gender and welfare regimes', Social Politics, 4, 2, 182-187. Walby (2005) 'Gender mainstreaming: Productive tensions in theory and practice', Social Politics, 12, 3, 1-25.

Chapter 2

1 For a more detailed discussion, see Buğra (2007) and Buğra (2008: 157-178).

2 Despite the introduction of the Green Card system in 1992 to assure poor people means tested access to health services, a survey conducted in the aftermath of the economic crisis of 2001 indicated that about one-third of the population was without any health insurance (World Bank/SIS, 2005).

3 Conditional Cash Transfers are small but regular cash benefits provided to poor people with children on the condition that the children are sent to school and the smaller ones go through health check-ups and get immunisation.

4 Law no. 5510 on Social Security and General Health Insurance. See Official Gazette, 16 June 2006 http.//rega.basbakanlik.gov.tr/eskiler/2006/06/20060616-1.htm.

5 Office of the Prime Minister, Directorate General of Press and Information (18 March 2003), the Program of the 59th Government. http://www.byegm.gov.tr/icerikdetay.aspx?Id=59 (Accessed 8 March 2010.) Also relevant, AKP Party Program 5.8 (2 February 2007), Family and Social Services. http://eng.akparti.org.tr/english/partyprogramme.html#5.8 (Accessed 8 March 2010.)

6 For an in-depth analysis of the policies targeting the disabled in Turkey see Yilmaz (2010).

7   See, Official Gazette, 26 May 2008 for law n.5763 http://rega.basbakanlik. gov.tr/eskiler/2008/05/20080526-5.htm For more recent legislation introduced to encourage female employment, see Official Gazette, 25 May 2010 http://www .resmi-gazete.org/tarih/20100525-12.htm

8   The inadequacy of child care has been highlighted both by women's organisations and international organisations such as the World Bank as a deterrent to female employment. See KEIG (2008) and World Bank (2009). See also Buğra and Yakut-Cakar (2010).

9   Although means-tested assistance by the central government and the municipalities have grown through time, the magnitude of assistance does not exceed 0.4 per cent of the GDP (Yakut-Cakar and Yilmaz, 2009) and the poorest 20 per cent of the population only receives 3.8 percent of all social transfers (TurkStat 2009).

10   See, http://www.tgtv.org/web/guest/hakkimizda

11   http://www.egitimedestek.meb.gov.tr/index.php. (Last accessed 7.06.2010.)

12   http://www.ntvmsnbsc.com/news/412171.asp. (Last accessed 7.06.2010.)

13   When, in a poor Eastern town where candidates from right-wing parties have historically had little chance in elections, the local welfare administrators began to distribute consumer durables as social assistance to the poor, the autonomous board supervising the electoral process intervened to stop the practice. Nevertheless, the decision of the board was not heeded by the provincial governor appointed by the ruling government and the governor was supported by the Prime Minister: Milliyet, 2 January 2009. Also important in revealing the dimensions of the Islamic political economy of charity in its relationship with political circles was a scandal that involved the irregular use of a substantial amount of donations by a prominent Islamic charity organisation Lighthouse (Deniz Feneri), which is informally affiliated with an organisation with the same name that is active in Germany. The scandal erupted in Germany and ended with several prison sentences. There is currently a court case on the same matter going on in Turkey, with hearings closed to the public. See, http://www.milliyet.com.tr/default.aspx?aType =HaberDetay&ArticleID=1068082 (last accessed 10.06.2010) and http://hurar-siv.hurriyet.com.tr/goster/haber.aspx?id=14131955&yazarid=148&tarih=2010 -03-17 (Laccessed 10.06.2010)

14   This argument is developed in Buğra and Candas (forthcoming).

Chapter 3

1   Some have also traced the historical roots of contemporary women's movements back to Ottoman society. See Çakır (1994). Durakbaşa (1998).

2   In this paper we have used the term 'veiling' to refer to all kinds of covering (including the headscarf) women use in religious connotations.

3   Anthias and Yuval-Davis, for instance, delineated five major ways through which

women's subjectivity and agency are produced by gender politics. They are included as biological reproducers of ethnic/national groups, as reproducers of national/ethnic boundaries, reproducers of ideologies, as signifiers of ethnic/national boundaries, and as participants in national, economic, political and military struggles. See Yuval-Davis, Nira & Anthias, Floya. (eds). Woman - Nation - State, (London: Macmillan, 1989).

4   It has been argued that the women's movement of the early Republic was somehow confined to 'legitimate' causes and effectively curtailed when it organized around a discourse that was not compatible with the Republic's national priorities in the early years. See: Toprak (1986 and 1988).

5   Some analysts have argued that despite the liberalisation processes in the 1980s, the state's power survived in a modified and distinct form and the state-citizen relationship was transformed from a civic model into a form of clientelism. See Önis (1992).

6   For a review of the history of Islamist, Kemalist, Kurdish women's movement and feminism in Turkey, and the interaction of these groups See Acar Feride and Altunok (2009). Available online: www.quing.eu/files/2009/Acar_Altunok_QUING_Paper_Budapest_revisedII.doc; also in a later study Toktaş, Şule and Diner (2010).

7   Both the Civil and Penal Codes were later amended, in 2001 and in 2004 respectively, taking on board the essence of the women's critique. See Anıl et al. (2005). Turkish civil and penal code reforms from a gender perspective: The success of two nationwide campaigns. İstanbul: Women for Women's Human Rights (WHHR)-New Ways.

8   The ratification of the Convention on Elimination of all Forms of Discrimination against Women (CEDAW) in 1986 helped make gender equality issues visible. See: Acar (2000.) and also Arat (2001).

9   Most women who are active in the movement prefer to call themselves 'conservative' and/or 'religious'. For purposes of this paper, these terms are used interchangeably to reflect the self-definitions as well as the substantive character of the movement.

10 Other identity based movements also appeared on the social and political scene in this period. Women came to be more and more symbols and actors of the Kurdish nationalist movement in the political struggle of this ethnic group in the 1990s and in 2000s. Within the Kurdish movement in the early phases, women's suffering from the direct and/or indirect consequences of state policies was emphasized more than the discrimination they faced from community-based patriarchal beliefs and practices. Some analysts argue that from the 1990s on, the experience women have gained in political activism led to increased autonomy of Kurdish women within the Kurdish nationalist movement. See Çağlayan (2007).

11 For a detailed expose of the changes in the Turkish political scene so far as the rise of the Islamist movement and parties go see inter alia, Heper (1997), Toprak (1995).

12 Jenny White notes how veiling and seclusion have been used as status symbols throughout history. Veiling, pale skin, soft skin and hands have signified a woman's well-being, value and her liberation from labouring activities. Such emancipation enabled her to attend to non-worldly, pure and sublime activities such as praying and child-raising. See White (2003), Acar (1991c).

13 Fatma Karabıyık Barbarosoğlu (a well-known religious woman sociologist)'s depiction of the ideal Muslim covered woman and her remarks on the transformation of the way this ideal is experienced by women in Turkey also elaborates on the issue. See, Şişman (2000).

14 For a discussion of this transition in terms of religion-market interaction and consumer choices, see Sandıkçı and Ger (2005 and 2009).

15 Several legislative attempts to design and create specific policy to regulate the use of the 'headscarf' in higher education (and public employment) have been made in the last several decades at the national level. Under different governments bylaws and dress regulations (1981 and 1986) for the higher education system were made, laws were promulgated (1988) and finally an amendment to the Constitution (2008) was passed. These attempts were all turned down by various courts at different levels of judiciary appeal. In 2008, the Constitutional Court turned down the AKP government's initiative to amend the Constitution in order to lift the ban on headscarves in universities. On that instance, the Court ruled that such an amendment would itself be unconstitutional since it conflicted with the "unalterable" provisions of the Turkish Constitution regarding the state's secular character and the principle of equal guarantee of protection of different kinds of freedoms. Some women carried their appeals to the international arena by applying to international legal and women's rights institutions with claims of human rights violations. On these cases, European Court of Human Rights (Leyla Şahin v. Turkey-application no. 44774/98) and the UN CEDAW Committee (Rahime Kayhan v. Turkey, 8/2005), both made decisions, on different grounds that stopped short of finding the complainant's claims to be rightful, thus strengthening the secular state's position in implementing the ban.

16 A study conducted in 2000 showed that the support for the lifting the ban in the universities was 66.6 %. See Çarkoğlu and Toprak (2010).

17 In spring 2007, it was partly for this reason that nomination of Abdullah Gül, whose wife uses the headscarf, for the Presidency, was protested by mass rallies in which secularist-Kemalist women constituted some of the most ardent participants. Capital City Platform is the most notable of these.

18 Some analysts have argued that the decisions made by the Constitutional Court and Council of State on banning of headscarf were reflections of the tendency to

"securitize" the issue. Accordingly, the Courts interpreted secularism as a "way of life" and the headscarf as a threat. See Tok (2009).

19 In a recent study it was argued that the 'headscarf' ban functions as a deterrent to women's employment and promotion in the commercial sector in Turkey. See Cindoğlu (2010a).

20 For instance, the increasing emphasis on motherhood and women's role within family by the Prime Minister Erdoğan in these public speeches clearly emphasizes this attitude. At a meeting with women's organizations when women activists expressed their concern on these issues and suggested that as Prime Minister he should underline the notion of gender equality more, Erdoğan stated that he does not believe in gender equality but that he rather advocates equality of opportunity. He elaborated that women and men are different in nature and they should complement one another. (http://yeni.habercem.com.tr/n-102543-kadinla-erkek-esit-olamaz.aspx.)

21 Ayşe Böhürler, a conservative female journalist and one of the founders of AKP, after the completion of her documentary ("Behind Walls: Women in Islamic Countries"), on the lives of Muslim women in thirteen countries in an interview expressed that Turkey has a unique place among these countries in that it is far more liberal and advanced in terms of women's rights and status and that she was happy to live in this country. (http://arsiv.sabah.com.tr/2006/10/03/cp/gnc112-20061001-102.html)

Chapter 4

1 The previous work of Sylvia Walby (1986, 1996, 1997) referring to private and public patriarchy -although developed for European countries, particularly the UK in the historical context of industrialisation- seems to be still relevant in analysing the situation of women in some developing countries including Turkey.

2 During 2000–2006, 61 per cent of 1,729,000 newly created non-agricultural jobs for males were informal in character. Looking at the picture from the female side, we observe that informal work accounts for 59 per cent of 701,000 new jobs in non-agricultural employment.

3 In 2005, 68 per cent of employed women and 44 per cent of employed men worked without any social security coverage. The bulk of informal work rests within agriculture. In this sector, almost all women and four-fifths of men have no social security coverage. Employment without social security covers 48 per cent of males and 43 per cent of females in trade, 47 per cent of women and 37 per cent of men in industry and 24 per cent of females and 22 per cent of males in services. Although the largest gender discrepancy is in agriculture, informal work is more common among females than among males in other sectors as well (TUIK, 2007a:121-122).

4   Table: Demographic Indicators in Turkey

	2005	2006	2025	2050
Total fertility rare (per woman)	2.19	2.18	1.97	1.79
Population increase rate (%)	1.26	1.24	0.74	0.30
Mid year population (thousand)	72 065	72 974	87 756	96 498

5   Estimated by the Social Structure and Gender Statistics Division of the TurkStat from 1994 Income Distribution Survey basic findings. (accessed May 2008), www.die.gov.tr/tkba/t206.xls

6   The reason for taking October 2007 instead of 2009 as the last year is the continuing revision of the Household Labour Force Surveys after the implementation of the Address Based Population Registration System in November 2007. Adjustments are to be made in the household labour force survey results by taking into account the number of the total population according to the new registration system.

7   In 2006, 78.5 percent of socially insured female workers in industry were in these sub-sectors (Toksöz 2007:32).

8   According to TurkStat HLFS during the period 1988–2007 the female population not included in the labour force increased by 8.9 million from 11,230,000 to 20,181,000, and in October 2007, 12,887,000 women remained outside the labour force were housewives. With a far distance in-between, this group is followed by others including students (1,623,000) and the retired (624,000). Apart from these groups 931,000 women are ready to work without looking for jobs. Their number exceeds the number of officially unemployed women.

9   In 2006, the urban rate of labour force participation was 15.5 per cent for married women, 35 per cent for singles, and 43.2 per cent for divorced women (TurkStat 2007b:36).

10   According to the 2002 Household Budget Survey, 72 per cent of children who have never enrolled in school are girls. (DPT, Annual Programme 2006:137)

11   According to SHCEK (Social Services and Child Protection Agency) data 236 elderly care facilities existing in Turkey have a capacity for servicing only 19,450 persons. Half of these facilities are run by the public sector. Given the rising proportion of the population over age 65, it is clear that there is a large service gap (from Turkonfed, 2007:32).

Chapter 5

1   Work and schooling are incompatible events in Turkey so that very few students are gainfully employed. Including them in our analysis would unduly increase the proportion without any income.

2   Until very recently, women (men) could retire with full benefits after 20 (25)

years of service. A series of amendments made to the social security law has increased the number of contribution years and established a minimum age for retirement. The most recent amendment aims to equalize the pension ages for men and women gradually at 65 years by 2048 (Süral, 2007).

3   Earnings from casual work are also included here.

4   Self-employment refers to employers and those engaging in own-account work.

5   The female-male earnings ratio at different parts of the distribution is calculated by first obtaining the male and female earnings distributions separately and then, taking the ratio of earnings at various parts of the distribution (and repeating the exercise for the two subcategories of labour market earnings).

6   Time-use surveys show vastly different time input to household production by sex in Turkey. See Kasnakoğlu and Dayıoğlu (2002) and TurkStat (2007).

7   In the examination of self-employment incomes, there is the added complication that earnings represent returns to capital as well as to labour, including that of unpaid family workers, the majority of whom are women.

8   In this exercise, we first obtain deciles based on labour market earnings (and its subcomponents) by pooling men and women in a single group and than observe the share of female workers in each decile.

9   The law governing survivor benefits was amended in October 2008 making it impossible for the new claimants to claim survivor benefits from multiple sources. The new law, however, still allows widowed women who might have labour income or retirement benefits to claim survivor benefits from their husbands but not from their parents.

10 The legal status of young men as dependants depends on their age and education-al status. However, young men, even as students, cannot be considered dependants if they are over 25 years of age and therefore, are not entitled to receive survivor benefits.

11 This view is consistent with bargaining models. See for instance Manser and Brown (1980) and McElroy and Horney (1981).

12 Household incomes are corrected for household size and composition using an adult equivalent scale. The scale we use in this paper is the modified OECD scale, which counts the first adult in the household as 1, additional adults as 0.5 and children younger than 14 years of age as 0.3 adults. The exercise in this section, therefore, involves the computation of adult equivalent incomes by dividing household income (which is inclusive of personal incomes of all individuals living within the household as well as imputed rents for those living in owner-occupied dwellings) by the number of adult equivalents and assigning this income to all individuals in the household.

13 Measured on the basis of half (or alternatively, two-thirds) of the median income, 19 (32) per cent of women with no personal incomes would be classified as poor

as opposed to 14 (23) per cent of women with earnings. The corresponding figures for women with non-labour income are 20 (31) per cent.

14 27 per cent of women with labour market earnings have non-labour income as well. Therefore, the deterioration in the position of such women may in part stem from non-labour income, which makes up, on average, 8.3 per cent of the total personal income received by such women.

15 Duygan and Güner (2006) also point to the presence of assortative mating in Turkey and discuss its income inequality implications.

16 The HDI compares countries on the basis of three achievements: longevity, knowledge and income. The UNDP has also developed a number of other measures such as the Human Poverty Index that considers vulnerability to death before age 40, illiteracy, and limited access to health services, safe water and nourishment as its main indicators; the Gender-related Development Index that adjusts HDI for gender gaps in the chosen indicators; and the Gender Empowerment Measure that considers economic participation, political participation and earnings. Our index, while it adopts the methodology of these indices, differs from them in the chosen indicators.

17 Changing the maximum value to the 90th percentile does not change the general findings in this section but works to slightly increase the gender gap in the overall composite index discussed in the text.

18 Adopting the formulation of the Gender Development Index (GDI) that penalizes gender differences in achievement, we have introduced weights that give more importance to lower achievements in computing separate indices for men and women in three dimensions identified in the text. An index that employs two indicators to measure achievement is, hence, computed as: $I= ((X1_{1-e} + X2_{1-e})/2)1/1-e$. For $e=2$, which is what is used for GDI and what we adopt, this formulation gives the harmonic mean of X1 and X2. For a full discussion see UNDP (2007) and Anand and Sen (1995).

Chapter 6

1 The authors would like to thank Saniye Dedeoglu and Adem Y. Elveren for their valuable input and suggestions on an earlier version of this study. Authors also wish to acknowledge the generous support provided by the Scientific & Technological Research Council of Turkey for this research (TUBITAK-109K127 coded research project). The usual disclaimer of errors and omissions applies.

2 Unpaid work covers a range of different activities from taking care of children and other household members in need, to cleaning, shopping, maintaining the house, doing volunteer work, helping other members in the community. In some developing countries, in areas where services are lacking, unpaid work includes activi-

ties such as collection of free goods like water and fuel from common lands vital for the household.

3 The method used is explained further in Section 3.

4 Why women's participation in paid work declines with industrialisation is explained by several factors: the gender biased nature of technology and machine based production in industry, higher wages earned by men turning women into dependent labourers at home, separation of unpaid and paid work places due to the nature of industry work unlike homebound agricultural work are among these factors, all of which are experienced both in advanced countries and developing countries.

5 There is a wide literature that reviews and criticizes SAPs and structural reforms from a feminist perspective as well as from other heterodox approaches to economics. These are not reviewed here because the issue is beyond the scope of this paper, yet, a detailed discussion can be found in a great depth in Çağatay and Ertürk (2004). The authors present an extensive overview of the current knowledge on the complex relationships between gender inequalities and liberalisation policies.

6 Randomly chosen 5,070 households were contacted for the survey. The response rate is quite high as 85.7 per cent corresponding to 4,345 households.

7 The data of urban areas include 8,102 adults (4,244 women and 3,858 men) living in 2,251 households.

8 The data used in this study were weighted by the 'factor' variable provided in the dataset.

9 Instead of actual age information, only the age group is available in the data.

10 EUROSTAT Activity Coding List is used for time use activity classification.

11 Economic activities and occupations are classified according to Statistical Classification of Economic Activities in the European Community, NACE Rev.1.1 and International Standard Classification of Occupations (ISCO-88) respectively.

12 For surveys see Deaton (1992), Browning, and Lusardi (1996) and Browning and Crossley (2001).

13 For a formal treatment and further discussion of this model see Apps and Rees (2001).

14 It is crucial to mention here that our 'life course' is a pseudo analysis, a synthetic construct built upon analysis of households at different stages in their own life course. Ideally, observations on selected households over time would be needed for a time based life course analysis; however, given that we have only a cross-section data available, life course analysis over time is not possible. Here, we assume that cohort effects are insignificant in Turkish society and so can be disregarded. The pseudo life course analysis methodology uses the data for households at dif-

ferent points in their own life courses and does not take into account the differences in characteristics of individuals because they are born at different times,
which can over/underestimate the effect of any factor at issue.

15   The main difference between total and urban areas is that total work of single
men is higher than that of single women: 7.9 and 7.0 hours respectively. However,
as in the total, the difference is not statistically significant in urban areas.

16   See Brines (1993) and Blair and Lichter (1991) among others.

17   If the urban population is analyzed as isolated, we observe an increase in paid
work of women and men in when they move from singlehood phase to second life
course phase and a decrease in paid work of men in when they enter to the third
phase having children. The significance levels also change when first phase and
second phase households are compared. This may be due to a very limited number of single working urban females (10 out of 37 urban single employed households) in the survey. On the other hand, the effect of having children seems to be
more drastic on the urban working household members; where we observe
declines by 18 per cent and 10 per cent in paid work, as well as 63.7 per cent and
108 per cent increase in unpaid work for women and men respectively.

Chapter 7

1   I am grateful to Nilüfer Cağatay for her vision and support for this project to
become a PhD thesis.

2   The phrase "quasi-adoption" is used to distinguish between the status of evlatlıks
and legally- adopted children, who acquire the legal rights, such as inheritance
rights, of biological children. Evlatlıks are not children who are legally-adopted at
the time of arrival to the quasi-adoptive family. The practice continues to exist,
but it is rare. Evlatlıks are also different from "foster children", who live with a family other than their biological family for a temporary period of time. Foster par-
enting (koruma aileciliği) is a form of child protection which was recently introduced into law in Turkey in 2000. The practice is not widespread.

3   In India and South Asia generally, the term "didi" is used to refer to paid as well as
unpaid non-family workers. In Haiti, the term rejevak is used to refer to unpaid
non-family workers, who are mostly children. In Nepal, Kamlari system refers to
50-60 years old practice where poor families provided daughters as domestic servants in exchange for cash. In China , amah is a similar practice. The antebellum
period in the US, mammies served the same purpose. Perhaps this list is not complete. Others may exist.

4   Prof. Ferhunde Ozbay has initiated the first and only other study on evlatlıks in
Turkey. See references for her studies.

5   Relative poverty line is defined in relation to the overall distribution of income or
consumption in a country; for example, the poverty line could be set at 30 percent

of the country's mean income or consumption. Absolute poverty line is the standard monetary measure based on the cost of basic food needs of a household (i.e., the cost a nutritional basket considered minimal for the healthy survival of a typical family), to which a provision is added for non-food need.

6 Eventhough, this treatment may be similar for girls across class lines, being an evlatlık and facing such treatment have layers of differences.

7 Full list of Nussbaum's and other authors' capabilities list are discussed in Hande Toğrul unpublished dissertation manuscript

8 According to formal statistics housewives constitute a total of 13.2 million women in Turkey as of 2004. (Turkish State Institute of Statistics (DIE) www.die.gov.tr , gender statistics page www.die.gov.tr/tkba/tkba_tr.htm).

9 Toledo (1990) argues the crucial differences between the Western slave system and Ottoman slave system.

10 During the field study I organized one focus group where seven pseudo mothers were gathered for a dialogue.

Chapter 8

1 Harun Arıkan pins down the concept as Turkey being a different, difficult and more problematic case for the EU. When Turkey is an awkward candidate, the EU underlined an open ended accessing negotiation after which the outcome cannot be guaranteed (Arikan 2006).

2 The new Labour Law adopted in 2003 reinforced existing provisions such as prohibiting discrimination on the basis of gender and introduced some improvements for women workers by prohibiting discriminatory practices owing to marital status or family responsibilities such as prohibiting dismissal on grounds of pregnancy. It brought for the first time provisions against recognition of sexual harassment at the workplace.

3 Later in February 2007, this attempt of the women's groups turned into the establishment of a women's NGO (Initiative for Women's Work and Employment – KEIG) dealing specifically with female employment issues.

4 The survivor's benefit is for eligible dependants include a spouse, children under age 18 (age goes up to 20 if in pre-secondary education, age 25 if in university), a son aged 18 or older who is disabled and unemployed; an unmarried, widowed or divorced daughter of any age. In the latter case, she must be without insured employment and not receiving any social security benefits in her own right. Unequal treatment of male and female dependants reflects the existing traditional gender roles and ideology and supports women's dependency over men.

5 The Flying Broom (Uçan Süpüge) is a women's organisation which writes periodical reports to CEDAW examining the progress in women's issues.

6 In the current legislation, women workers regulated by Article 78 of the Labour

Law may take an additional six months of unpaid leave after the compulsory period of sixteen weeks of paid maternity leave. The proposed law extends this leave (sixteen weeks paid + 6 months unpaid) to twelve months but it must equally be shared between the woman worker and the husband who is a worker or civil servant. The current Law regulating Civil Servant No: 657, Article 108 grants that upon her request, a female civil servant may be granted a further twelve months of unpaid leave following her maternity leave. In the proposed law, this twelve months leave is shared by women and men. Therefore, this law converts women's six months unpaid maternity leave into parental leave and grants men with an extra six months of unpaid leave for care of children.

7   The discussion of the draft law took place under the roof of Parliament, specifically in the EU Harmonisation Commission, Health, Family, Work and Social Affairs Commission and Planning and Budgeting Commission, in 2005. When preparing their reports all three commissions discussed the draft with the bureaucrats of the General Directorate for Women's Status, experts from different NGOs (trade unions, Turkish Doctors' Union), and bureaucrats from various other Ministries. All commission reports supported the draft which gives each spouse a six-month period of unpaid parental leave.

8   In the recommendations of TİSK's Women's Employment Summit in 2006, there was no mention of parental leave, indicating the reluctance of employers to support the legislation. Following this Summit, women's groups in February 2006 published a common press release, stating that parental leave should be included in the national legislation and every private and public institution should take responsibility for the enforcement of the legislation.

Chapter 9

1   I am grateful to my advisor, Gülay Toksöz, for her invaluable support, and also would like to thank Adem Y. Elveren, Saniye Dedeoglu, Ferda Dönmez, Yiğit Karahanoğulları and Emel Memiş for their comments.

2   After this point "Reform" refers to the number 5510 Social Security and General Health Insurance Law in the rest of the text.

3   However, one should keep in mind that, the real number of women working at home as subcontractors in the manufacturing industry might be higher than the amount indicated in the statistics (Toksöz, 2007).

4   Care services are provided to the handicapped people who are in need of care in the public or private care centers or in their homes by this implementation provided that (total of all their incomes is considered) one month's share of the salary that goes to them is less than 2/3 of the net minimum wage.

5   Elson (2002) underlines the fact that the second sub-period of the neoliberal era –liberalisation of capital movement's era– has specific effects on the genders as

compared to the era characterized by the free movements of goods and services only. It is emphasized that especially in this period the budget got a lot of features which increase the gender inequalities.

6   Equal opportunity Commission for Women and Men is equipped with a set of important responsibilities and authorizations like presenting opinion on the stage legislations to the "standing committees" related with the equality of genders concerning the Constitution, international developments and responsibilities, preparing an evaluation report of the developments on gender equality at the end of each legislative year, examining the applications of claims on gender-based discrimination and passing them to the related institutions whenever necessary.

7   With the other pillar of the Reform three different social security institutions operating since 1949, 1965 and 1971, respectively, were brought together under a single roof, and main service, supervision and advisory units were re-structured.

8   The findings of a questionnaire based survey by Yıldırak et al. (2003) covering 1,236 female agricultural workers from 9 provinces are quite illuminating: (i) 41.4% of female workers are at age 20 or under. (ii) 54.2% of female workers are illiterate. (iii) 67.5% of female workers got married while they were under age 19 and 79.6% of these marriages were through intermediaries. 19.9% of married women have no civil marriage contract. (iv) 40.3% of female workers have given birth at least 6 times. (v) 66.8% of female workers are not covered by any social security scheme and 18.1% have green cards; 24.4% have never been to a doctor and 46.8% do not visit doctors for financial constraints. (vi) 58.5% of female workers contribute to family budget at least by 26%. (vii) 81% of female workers are not content with their employment for unfavourable working conditions and low pay. (viii) 46.4% of female workers would prefer to remain at home as housewives rather than working in agriculture. (ix) 64.7% of female workers would not marry an agricultural worker if they had a second life.

9   According to the TurkStat data for February 2010, about 1.9 million of 5.9 million employed women are unpaid family workers.

10 According to February 2010 data, while 3.3 million of 5.9 million employed women (56%) are employed informally, 5.5 million of 15.3 million male workers (36%) are employed in the informal sector (TurkStat, 2010).

11 A field work in Kenya shows that the health care reforms such as the introduction of a contribution rate, and user fees widen the gender inequalities by decreasing the number of women benefiting from health services even though they are insured (Nanda 2002). Similarly, a time-use study on South Africa shows that the deterioration of public infrastructure (drinking water, shelter, transportation etc.) increases the pressure on women's unpaid labour (Kizilirmak and Memis 2009).

12 Dünşen reports that according to the report prepared by the Human Rights Commission of Lesbian, Gay, Bisexual, Transvestite, Transexual Association

(LGBTT), 11 hate crimes were committed based on sexual orientation and sexual identity in the first 10 months of 2007.

Chapter 10

1   Gender Empowerment Measure evaluates the extent to which men and women are able to actually participate in economic and political life and take part in decision-making and measures progress in advancing women's standing in political and economic forums.

2   We must, however, acknowledge some initiatives in developing countries that are aimed at bridging this gap in reform policies. See, for instance, Mexico's health reform experience which successfully integrated a gender perspective (Langer and Catino 2006).

3   Ağrı and Iğdır are located in the North Eastern Anatolia region which experience harsh winter conditions.

4   SGK estimates that coverage under the formal social security system has increased to 83% of the population (SGK 2010). When the percentage of Green Card beneficiaries which amounts to 13 % of the population is added, the coverage rate increases to 96 %.

5   See the edict dated 18 September 2009 for detailed information on these fees and discounts (Official Gazette, 2009).

Chapter 11

1   Introduction of the private pension schemes is to referred to as 'privatisation of social security.'

2   For example, in France, it is shown that working 5 years less within "life-long career" curtails pension benefits by 50 per cent (Veil 2002, cited in Frericks and Maier 2007).

3   Women constitute of majority of the part-time jobs. For instance, women constitute 80-95 percent of part-time jobs in Italy, Germany, Canada, the U.K. and the U.S. (Bardasi and Gornick 2008).

4   For instance, using unisex mortality tables decreases the gender gap 5.5 percent at the retirement age 60 and more than 8 percent at the retirement age 65 in Poland (Balcerzak-Paradowska et. al. 2003) and decreases the gender gap from 4 - 11 per cent depending on different age categories in Turkey (Elveren 2008b). On the other hand, there are some countries that do not use gender specific tables in favor of women such as The Netherlands and Denmark.

5   See Turner (2006) for a detailed discussion on the fairness of raising the retirement age.

6   Indeed, simulations showed that topping up benefits in DC schemes by means of an MPG can be highly beneficial in reducing poverty among retired women

(World Bank 1994). For instance, in Chile while 35 percent of men benefit from the minimum pension, that rate is 60 percent for women (Mesa-Lago 2008). James et. al. (2003) showed that for Chile, a minimum pension guarantee raises women's benefits from 32 percent to 39 percent of average male benefits in the lowest education group.

Chapter 12

1 The authors would like to thank Saniye Dedeoglu and Adem Y. Elveren for their valuable input and suggestions on an earlier version of this study. Authors also wish to acknowledge the generous support provided by the Scientific & Technological Research Council of Turkey for this research (TUBITAK-109K127 coded research project). The usual disclaimer of errors and omissions applies.

2 TurkStat, address based population registration system population census results, 2009, Number 15, 25 January 2010

3 This market is also joined by foreign care workers: The role and position of foreign domestic workers is another major issue which however can not be elaborated in the frame of this article (Kaska, 2005/6).

4 Thomson (2009: 290) mentions a global network supporting the need of a growing awareness about the lack of rights and labour protection of (foreign) domestic wage workers; see: www.domesticworkerrights.org.

5 For details see ILO, 2010: 27-28.

6 In July 2010: 1 Euro was equal to 1.9 TL.

7 In one of the firms which are controlled by PEAs, the firm does not ask for commission but gives the women a room in the premises of the firm for spending and interacting with other workers in their spare time. This firm claims that they are a non-profit organisation but also has a role as an NGO and helping the workers morally and financially.

Chapter 13

1 I am grateful to my mother Zeliha Çağlayan Süerdem, my professor Feride Acar and my sister and colleague Filiz Elmas for their invaluable support and encouragement they shared my whole life. I would like to thank my colleagues Nergis Mütevellioğlu, Yıldırım Koç and Yaşar Seyman for their precious comments and assistance.

BIBLIOGRAPHY

Abadan-Unat, Nermin, 'Social Change and Turkish Women', in N. Abadan-Unat (ed), *Women in Turkish Society* (E.J. Brill-Leiden, 1981).

Acar, Feride and Gülbanu Altunok, 'Paths, Borders and Bridges: Impact of Ethnicity and Religion on Women's Movement in Turkey', the QUING Conference, Budapest, (2009).

Acar, Feride and Ayşe Güneş-Ayata, 'Gender and Cultures of Education in the Turkish Secondary Education System', in D. Kandiyoti and A. Skatanber (eds), *Fragments of Culture: The Everyday of Modern Turkey* (Rutgers University Press, 2002).

Acar, Feride, 'Turkish Women in Academia: Roles and Careers', *METU Studies in Development* 10(4), (1983), pp. 409-446.

Acar, Feride, 'Turkey in The First CEDAW Impact Study', in M. McPhedran (ed), *York University and the International Women's Rights Project* (2000).

Acar, Feride, 'The True Path Party, 1983-89', in M. Heper and J. Landau (eds), *Political Parties and Democracy in Turkey* (I.B. Tauris, 1991a).

Acar, Feride, 'Women in Academic Science Careers in Turkey', in V. Stolte-Heiskanen, F. Acar, N. Ananieva, D. Gaudart (eds), *Women in Science: Token Women or Gender Equality?* (Berg Publishers, 1991b).

Acar, Feride, 'Women in the Ideology of Islamic Revivalism in Turkey: Three Islamic Women's Journals' in R. L. Tapper (ed), *Islam in Modern Turkey* (IB Tauris, 1991c).

Acar, Feride, "Women and Islam in Turkey", in Ş. Tekeli (ed), *Women in Modern Turkish Society: A Reader* (Zed Books, 1995).

Acar, Feride, 'Turgut Özal: Pious Agent of Liberal Transformation', in M. Heper and S. Sayari (eds), *Political Leaders and Democracy in Turkey* (Lexington Books, 2002).

Acar-Savran, Gülnur, 'Feminist Sosyal Hak Taleplerinin Mantığı Üzerine', *Feminist Politika*, 6 (2010).

Adaman, Fikret, Ayşe Buğra and Ahmet İnsel, 'Societal Context of Labour Union Strategy: The Case of Turkey', *Labour Studies Journal* 34(2) (2009), pp. 168-188.

Adaman, Fikret, *Social Protection in the Candidate Countries: Country Study Turkey*, (Berlin: GVG, 2003).

Addabbo, Tindara (2003) 'Unpaid work by gender in Italy', in A. Picchio (ed), *Unpaid Work and the Economy* (Routledge, 2003).

Aisbett, Emma, 'Why are the Critics so Convinced that Globalization is Bad for the Poor?', NBER Globalization and Poverty Conference, 2004.

Akdağ, Recep, 'Foreword', *Entre Nous* 65 (2007).

Alkire, Sabina, 'Why the Capability Approach?', *Journal of Human Development and Capabilities* 6/1 (2005), pp. 115-133.

Anand, Sudhir and Amartya Sen, 'Gender Inequality in Human Development: Theories and Measurement', Occasional Paper No. 19, UNDP, 1995.

Anıl, Ela, et al., *Turkish civil and penal code reforms from a gender perspective: The success of two nationwide campaigns*, (Women for Women's Human Rights (WHHR)-NewWays, 2005).

Ansal, Hacer, 'Küreselleşme, Sanayide Teknolojik Modernizasyon ve Kadın İstihdamı', in F. Özbay (ed), *Kadın Emeği ve İstihdamındaki Değişmeler* (IKGV, 1998).

Antonopoulos, Raina, 'The Right to a Job, the Right Types of Projects Employment Guarantee Policies from a Gender Perspective', The Levy Institute Working Papers, no.516, 2007.

Antonopoulos, Raina, 'The Unpaid Care Work–Paid Work Connection', The Levy Institute Working Papers, no.541, 2008.

Antonopoulos, Rania and Emel Memis, 'Time and Poverty from a Developing Country Perspective', The Levy Institute Working Papers no. 600, 2010.

Antonopoulos, Rania and Indira Hirway, *Unpaid Work and the Economy: Gender, Time Use and Poverty in Developing Countries*, (Palgrave Macmillan, 2010).

Apps, Patricia F., and Ray Rees, 'Household Saving and Full Consumption over the Life course', IZA Discussion Paper no. 280, 2001.

Arat, Necla, *Kadın Sorunu*, (Say Yayınları, 1986).

Arat, Yeşim, *Religion, Politics and Gender Equality in Turkey: Implications of A Democratic Pradox, Final Research Report for the Project Religion, Politics and Gender Equality*, (UNRIDS, 2009).

Arat, Yeşim, 'The Project of Modernity and Women in Turkey', in S. Bozdoğan and R. Kasaba (eds), *Rethinking Modernity and National Identity in Turkey* (University of Washington Press, 1990).

Arat, Yeşim, *Rethinking Islam and Liberal Democracy: Islamist Women in Turkish Politics*, (State University of New York Press, 2005).

Arat, Yeşim, 'Contestation and Collaboration: Women's Struggles for Empowerment in Turkey', in R. Kasaba (ed), *The Cambridge History of Turkey Volume 4: Turkey in the Modern World* (Cambridge, 2008).

Arat, Yeşim, 'Democracy and Women in Turkey: In Defense of

Liberalism', *Social Politics* 6/3 (1999), pp. 370-387.

Arat, Yeşim, 'Women's Rights as Human Rights: The Turkish Case', *Human Rights Review*, 3/1: (October –December 2001).

Arat, Zehra, 'Educating the Daughters of the Republic', in Z. Arat (ed), *Deconstructing Images of the Turkish Woman* (St. Martin's Press, 1998).

Arıkan, Harun, *Turkey and the EU: An Awkward Candidate for EU Membership?*, (Ashgate, 2006).

Aslop, Ruth, 'Whose Interests? Problem in Planning for Women's Practical Needs', *World Development* 21/3 (1993), pp. 367-377.

Avdeyeva, Olga, "States' Compliance with International Requirements, Gender Equality in EU Enlargement Countries', *Political Research Quarterly* 63/1 (2010), pp. 204-212.

Ayata, Ayşe and Fatma Tütüncü, 'Party Politics of the AKP and the Predicaments of Women at the Intersection of the Westernist, Islamist and Feminist Discourses in Turkey', *British Journal of Middle Eastern Studies* 35/3 (2008), pp. 363-384.

Ayata, Sencer, 'Patronage, Party, and State: The Politicization of Islam in Turkey', *The Middle East Journal*, 50/1 (1996), pp. 40-56.

Bacchi, Carol Lee, *Women, Policy and Politics: The Construction of Policy Problems*, (Sage, 1999).

Bajtelsmit, Vickie L., Alexandra Bernasek and Nancy A. Jianakoplos, 'Gender differences in defined contribution pension decisions', *Financial Services Review* 8/1 (1999), pp. 1-10.

Balcerzak-Paradowska, Bozena, Agnieszka Chlon-Dominzcak, Irena Kotowska, Anna Olejniczuk-Merta, Irena Topinska and Irena Woycicka, 'The Gender Dimensions of Social Security Reform in Poland', in E. Fultz, M. Ruck and S. Steinhilber (eds), *The Gender Dimensions of Social Security Reforms in Central and Eastern Europe Case Studies of the Czech Republic, Hungary and Poland*, (ILO Subregional Office for Central and Eastern Europe, 2003).

Bardasi, Elena and Janet C. Gornick, 'Working for Less? Women's Part-Time Wage Penalties Across Countries', *Feminist Economics* 14(1) (2008), pp. 37-72.

Bardasi, Elena and Stephen P. Jenkins, 'The Gender Gap in Private Pensions', University of Essex ISER Working Paper no. 29, 2004.

Barnett, Kathleen and Caten Grown, *Gender Impacts of Government Revenue Collection: The Case of Taxation* (Commonwealth Secretariat, 2004).

Barrientos, Armando, 'Latin America: Towards a Liberal-Informal Welfare Regime', in I. Gough and G. Wood (eds), *Insecurity and Welfare Regimes in Asia, Africa and Latin America* (Cambridge, 2004).

Başlevent, Cem and Özlem Onaran, 'The Effect of Export-Oriented Growth on Female Labour Market Outcomes in Turkey', *World Development*, 32/8 (2004), pp.1375-1393.

Baxter, Janeen, 'Patterns of change and stability in the gender division of household labour in Australia 1996-1997', *Journal of Sociology* 38/4 (2002), pp. 399-424.

Becker, Gary S., A Treatise on the Family, (Harvard University Press, 1981).

Beijing Declaration, *Fourth World Conference on Women-Action for Equality, Development and Peace* Beijing, China, September 1995.

Beneria, Lourdes, 'Towards a greater integration of gender and economics', *World Development* 23/11 (1995), pp.1838-1850.

Beneria, Lourdes, *Gender, Development, and Globalization: Economics as if People Mattered*, (Routledge, 2003).

Berberoğlu, Berch, 'Turkey: The Crisis of the Neo-Colonial System', *Race & Class* 22/3 (1981), pp. 277-291.

Berktay, Fatmagül, 'Türkiye Solunun Kadına Bakışı, Değişen Bir şey Var mı?', in Ş. Tekeli (ed), *Kadın Bakış Açısından 1980'ler Türkiye'sinde Kadın* (İletişim, 1990).

Bernasek, Alexandra and Stephanie Shwiff, 'Gender, Risk and Retirement', *Journal of Economics Issues* 35/2 (2001), pp. 345-356.

Bertranou, Fabio M., 'Pension Reform and Gender Gaps in Latin America: What are the Policy Options', *World Development* 29/5 (2001), pp. 911-923.

Bibi, Sami and Rim Chatti, 'Gender Poverty in Tunisia: Is There a Feminization Issue?', ERF Working Paper no. 512, 2010.

Bittman, Michael, 'Now that the future has arrived: a retrospective of Gershuny's Theory of Social Innovation', Social Policy Research Centre Discussion Paper no. 110, 1999.

Bittman, Michael and Nancy Folbre, *Family Time: The Social Organisation of Care*, (Routledge, 2004).

Bittman, Michael, Nancy Folbre, Paula England, Liana Sayer and George Matheson, 'When does gender trump money? Bargaining and time in household work', *American Journal of Sociology* 109/1 (2003), pp.186-214.

Blair, Sampson Lee and Daniel T. Lichter, 'Measuring the Division of Household. Labour: Gender Segregation of Housework Among American Couples', *Journal of Family Issues* 12/1 (1991), pp. 91-113.

Bode, Ingo, 'Disorganized Welfare Mixes: Voluntary Agencies and New Governance Regimes in Western Europe', *Journal of European Social Policy* 16/4 (2006), pp. 346-359.

Booth, Christine and Cinnamon Bennett, 'Gender Mainstreaming in the European Union', *The European Journal of Women's Studies* 9/4 (2002), pp. 430-446.

Bora, Aksu, *Kadınlar Sınıfı; Ücretli Ev Emeği ve Kadın Öznelliğinin İnşası*, (İletişim, 2010).

Bora, Aksu, 'Türk Modernleşme Sürecinde Annelik Kimliğinin Dönüşümü', in A. İlyasoğlu and N. Akgökçe (eds), *Yerli Bir Feminizme Doğru* (Sel Yayıncılık, 2001).

Boratav, Korkut, 'Bir Çevrimin Yükseliş Aşamasında Türkiye Ekonomisi', in S. Sönmez and N. Mütevellioğlu (eds), *Küreselleşme, Kriz ve Türkiye'de Neoliberal Dönüşüm* (İstanbul Bilgi Üniversitesi Yayınları, 2009).

Boratav, Korkut, *Türkiye İktisat Tarihi: 1908-2007*, (İmge, 2010).

Boserup, Ester, *Women's Role in Economic Development*, (Allen & Ulwin, 1970).

Bozkuş, Cihan and Adem Y. Elveren, 'An Analysis of Gender Gaps in the Private Pension Scheme in Turkey', *Ekonomik Yaklaşım* 19/69 (2008), pp. 89-106.

Brines, Julie, 'The Exchange Value of Housework', *Rationality and Society* 5/3 (1993), pp. 305-340.

Browning, Martin and Annamaria Lusardi, 'Household Saving: Micro theories and Micro Facts', *Journal of Economic Literature* XXXIV (1996), pp. 1797-1855.

Browning, Martin and Thomas F. Crossley, 'The Life course Model of Consumption and Saving', *Journal of Economic Perspectives* 15 (2001), pp. 3-22.

Bryan, Mark L. and Almudena Sevilla-Sanz, 'Does housework lower wages? Evidence for Britain', *Oxford Economic Papers* (first published online: June 6, 2010)

Buğra, Ayşe, 'Immoral Economy of Housing in Turkey' *International Journal of Urban and Regional Research* 22/2 (1998), pp.303-317.

Buğra, Ayşe, 'Poverty and Citizenship: An Overview of the Social Policy Environment in Republican Turkey', *International Journal of Middle East Studies* 39/1 (2007), pp. 33-52.

Buğra, Ayşe and Aysen Candaş, 'Change and Continuity under an Eclectic Social Security Regime: The Case of Turkey', *Middle Eastern Studies* (forthcoming).

Buğra, Ayşe and Burcu Yakut-Cakar, 'Structural Change, Social Policy

Environment and Female Employment: The Case of Turkey', *Development and Change* 41/3 (2010), pp. 517-538.

Buğra, Ayşe and Sinem Adar, 'An Analysis of Social Protection Expenditures in Turkey in a Comparative Perspective', Bogazici University Social Policy Forum Working Paper, 2007.

Buğra, Ayşe and Çağlar Keyder, *New Poverty and Changing Welfare Regime of Turkey*, (UNDP, 2003).

Buğra, Ayşe and Çağlar Keyder, 'The Turkish Welfare Regime in Transformation', *Journal of European Social Policy* 16/3 (2006), pp. 211-228.

Buğra, Ayşe, *Kapitalizm, Yoksulluk ve Türkiye'de Sosyal Politika*, (İletişim, 2008).

Buvinic, Mayra and Geeta Rao Gupta, 'Female-Headed Households and Female-Maintained Families: Are They worth Targeting to Reduce Poverty in Developing Countries', *Economic Development and Cultural Change* 45/2 (1997), pp. 259-281.

Cağatay, Nilüfer and Korkut Ertürk, 'Gender and globalization: a macro-economic perspective', International Labour Office Working Paper no.19, 2004.

Cam, Erdem, 'Uluslarası Çalışma Örgütü Sözleşmeleri Çerçevesinde, Özel İstihdam Büroları ve Çeşitleri', *Çimento İşveren* (2008), pp. 20-31.

Cassels, Andrew, 'Health Sector Reform: Key Issues in Less Developed Countries', *Journal of International Development* 7/3 (2006), pp. 329-347.

Castells, Manuel, *End of Millennium*, (Oxford: Blackwell, 1998).

Cindoğlu, Dilek and Gizem Zencirci, 'Withering the Counter Hegemonic Potential of the Headscarf: Public Sphere, State Sphere and the Headscarf Question in Turkey', *Middle Eastern Studies* 44/5 (2008), pp. 791-806.

Cindoğlu, Dilek, *'Başörtüsü Yasağı ve Ayrımcılık: Uzman Mesleklerde Başörtülü Kadınlar'* (The Headscarf Ban and Discrimination:

Headscarved Women In Professional Jobs),(TESEV Yayınları, 2010).

Cindoğlu, Dilek, *Headscarved Women in Professional Jobs: Revisiting Discrimination in 2010*, (TESEV Publications, 2010).

Clark, David A., 'The Capability Approach: Its Development, Critique and Recent Advances', Global Poverty Research Group Working Paper no. 03, 2005.

Coltrane, Scott, 'Research on household labour: Modeling and measuring the social embeddedness of routine family work', *Journal of Marriage and Family* 62/4 (2000), pp.1208-1233.

Costain, Ann, *Inviting Women's Rebellion: a Political Process Interpretation of the Women's Movement*, (John Hopkins University Press, 1992).

Çağatay, Nilüfer, 'Gender Budgets and Beyond: Feminist Fiscal Policy in the Context of Globalization', *Gender and Development* 11/ 1 (2003), pp. 15-24.

Çağlayan, Handan, *Analar, Tanrıçalar ve Yoldaşlar*, (İletişim, 2008).

Çakır, Serpil, Osmanlı *Kadın Hareketi* (The Ottoman Women's Movement)' (Metis Yayınları, 1994).

Çarkoğlu, Ali and Binnaz Toprak, *Türkiye'de Din, Toplum ve Siyaset* (Religion, Society and Politics in Turkey), (TESEV Yayınları, 2010).

Çalışma ve Sosyal Güvenlik Bakanlığı, *Aile ve İş Yaşamının Uyumlaştırılması Çalışma Grubu Raporu, Yenileşme ve Değişim için Türkiye'de Sosyal Diyaloğu Güçlendirme Projesi*, (Avrupa Birliği Koordinasyon Dairesi Başkanlığı, 2007).

Da Roit, Barbara, 'Changing Intergenerational Solidarities within Families in a Mediterranean Welfare State: Elderly Care in Italy', *Current Sociology* 55/2 (2007), pp. 251-269.

Dayıoğlu, Meltem and İnsan Tunalı, 'Falling Behind While Catching Up: Changes in the Female-Male Wage Differential in Urban Turkey, 1988 to 1994', mimeo, 2003.

De Mesa, Alberto Arenas and Veronica Mentecinos, 'The Privatisation of Social Security and Women's Welfare: Gender Effects of the Chilean Reform', *Latin American Research Review* 34/3 (1999), pp. 7-37.

Deaton, Angus, *Understanding Consumption*, (Clarendon Press, 1992).

Dedeoglu, Saniye, *Women Workers in Turkey, Global Industrial Production in Istanbul*, (I.B. Tauris Academic Studies, 2008).

Defever, Mia, 'Health Care Reforms: the unfinished agenda', *Health Policy* 34/1 (1995), pp. 1-7.

Demirel, Ahmet, Zuhal Kayaalp Bilgin and Murat Kocaman, *Çalışmaya Hazır İşgücü Olarak Kentli Kadın ve Değişimi* (KSSGM,1999).

Dion, Michelle, 'Women's Welfare and Social Security Privatisation in Mexico', *Social Politics* 13/3 (2006), pp. 400-426.

DPT (State Planning Organisation), 'Annual Program', DPT, 2006.

Dünşen, Şevket Murat, 'Sınırların İhlali: Transgender Kimliklere Yönelik Şiddetin Kurumsal Kaynakları', Hacettepe Üniversitesi Sosyal Bilimler Enstitüsü Antropoloji Anabilim Dalı, Yüksek Lisans Tezi, 2010.

Durakbaşa, Ayşe, 'Kemalism as Identity Politics in Turkey', in Z. Arat (ed), *Deconstructing Images of the Turkish Woman* (St. Martin's Press, 1998).

Duygan, Burcu and Nezih Güner, 'Income and Consumption Inequality in Turkey: What Role Does Education Play?', in S. Altuğ and A. Filiztekin (eds), *The Turkish Economy: The Real Economy, Corporate Governance and Reform and Stabilization Policy* (Routledge, 2006).

Eardley, Tony, Jonathan Bradshaw, John Ditch, Ian Gough and Peter Whiteford, 'Social Assistance Schemes in OECD Countries: Volume I Synthesis Report', Department of Social Security Research Report no. 46, 1996.

EC (European Commission), 'Adequate and sustainable pensions. Joint report by the Commission and the Council', no. 7163/03, ECOFIN 76, SOC 115, 2003.

Ecevit, Yıldız, 'Türkiye'de Kadın Hareketi ve Ulusal Kadın Politikası', Uçan Süpürge Kadın ve Politika: Değişen ve Değiştiren Kadınlar Semineri, 2004.

Ecevit, Yıldız, 'Kentsel Üretim Sürecinde Kadın Emeğinin Konumu ve Değişen Biçimleri', in Ş. Tekeli (ed), *Kadın Bakış Açısından 1980'ler Türkiyesinde Kadınlar* (İletişim, 1990).

Elson, Diane, 'Gender-aware Analysis and Development Economics', *Journal of International Development* 5/2 (1993), pp. 237-247.

Elson, Diane, 'The Economic, the Political and the Domestic: Business, States and Households in the Organisation of Production', *New Political Economy* 3/2 (1998), pp. 189-208.

Elson, Diane, 'International Financial Architecture: A view from the kitchen', *Fema Politika*, (2002), pp. 26-32.

Elson, Diane, 'Unpaid Work: Creating Social Wealth or Subsidizing Patriarchy and Private Profit?', University of Massachusetts, Amherst, PERI, 2005.

Elson, Diane, *Budgeting for Women's Rights: Monitoring Government Budgets for Compliance with CEDAW*, (UNIFEM, 2006).

Elson, Diane, 'Social Reproduction in the Global Crisis', UNRISD Conference on Social and Political Dimensions of the Global Crisis, 2009.

Elson, Diane and Nilufer Cagatay, 'The Social Content of Macroeconomic Policies', *World Development* 28/7 (2000), pp. 1347-1364.

Elson, Diane, 'Labour Markets as Gendered Insitutions: Equality, Efficiency and Empowerment Issues', *World Development*, 27/3, (1999), pp.611-627.

Elveren, Adem Y., 'Assessing Gender Inequality in the Turkish Pension System', *International Social Security Review* 61/2 (2008), pp. 39-58.

Elveren, Adem Y. and Sara D. Hsu, 'Gender Gaps in the Individual Pension

System in Turkey', University of Utah Department of Economics Working Paper no. 6, 2007. Elveren, Ali Haydar, 'Bireysel Emeklilik Sisteminin Makro Ekonomik Etkileri', *İşveren Dergisi* 41/8 (2003a), p. 23.

Elveren, Ali Haydar, 'Individual Pension System', interview at NTV, http://ntv-msnbc.com.tr/news/241266.asp, 2003b.

Elveren, Ali Haydar, 'Bireysel Emeklilik Sistemi: İşleyişi ve Gelişmeler', Avrasya Sigortacılık Toplantısı, TSRSB Yayın no. 1, 2005.

Elveren, Mehmet Ali and Adem Y. Elveren, 'The Transformation of Welfare Regime in Turkey and the Individual Pension System (in Turkish)', *Mülkiye* 34/266 (2010), pp.243-258.

England, Paula, 'Emerging Theories of Care Work', *Annual Review of Sociology* 31/1 (2005), pp. 381-399

Eraydin Ayda and Asuman Turkun Erendil, *Yeni Üretim Süreçleri ve Kadın Emeği*, (KSSGM, 2000).

Ercan, Hakan and İnsan Tunalı, 'Labour Market Segmentation in Turkey', in T. Bulutay (ed), *Main Characteristics and Trends in the Turkish Labour Market* (TurkStat, 1998).

Erdoğdu, Seyhan, *Küreselleşme Sürecinde Uluslararası Sendikacılık*, (İmge, 2006).

Eren, Erdal, Yiğit Karahanoğulları, Aziz Konukman, Mustafa Şahin and Aşkın Türeli, 'Türkiye'de İşgücü, İstihdam ve Ücretler', mimeo, 2010.

Esping-Andersen, Gosta, *Three Worlds of Welfare Capitalism*, (Polity Press, 1990).

Esping-Andersen, Gosta, *Social Foundations of Post-Industrial Societies*, (Oxford, 1999).

Esping-Andersen, Gosta, 'A new gender contract', in G. Esping-Andersen, D. Gallie, A. Hemerijck and J. Myles (eds), *Why we need a New Welfare State* (Oxford, 2002).

ETUC Charter on Gender Mainstreaming in Trade Unions, 2007a.

ETUC Survey on Women in Trade Unions: Bridging the Gap, 2007b.

EuroStat, Online Database on Population and Social Conditions – Living Conditions and Social Protection. Available from: http://epp.eurostat.ec.europa.eu/portal/page/portal/living_conditions_and_social_protection/data/database, 2009.

Even, William E. and David A. Macpherson, 'When Will the Gender Gap in Retirement Income Narrow?', http://129.3.20.41/eps/lab/papers/0404/0404006.pdf, 2003.

Ferreira, Francisco H.G. and David Alejandro Robalino, 'Social Protection in Latin America: Achievements and Limitations', World Bank- Latin America and the Caribbean Region Policy Research Paper no. 5305, 2010.

Ferrera, Maurizio, 'The 'Southern Model' of Welfare in Social Europe', *Journal of European Social Policy* 6/1 (1996), pp. 17-37.

Fine, Ben, *Women's Employment and the Capitalist Family*, (Routledge, 2007).

Floro, Maria S., 'Women's well-being, poverty, and work intensity', *Feminist Economics* 1/3 (1995), pp. 1-25.

Flying, Broom, 4th and 5th CEDAW Shadow Report, (CEDAW, 2005).

Frericks, Patricia and Robert Maier, 'The gender pension gap: effects of norms and reform policies', in C. Arza and M. Kohli (eds), *Pension Reform in Europe Politics, policies and outcomes* (Routledge, 2007).

Frericks, Patricia, Robert Maier and Willibrord de Graaf, 'European Pension Reforms: Individualization, Privatisation and Gender Pension Gaps', *Social Politics* 14/2 (2007), pp. 212-237.

Fukuda-Parr, Sakiko, 'The Human Development Paradigm: Operationalizing Sen's Ideas on Capabilities', *Feminist Economics* 9/2-3 (2003), pp. 301-317.

Fultz, Elaine and Silke Steinhilber, 'Social security and gender equality: Recent experience in Central Europe', *International Labour Review* 143/3 (2004), pp. 249-273.

Fuwa, Makiko, 'Macro-Level Gender Inequality and the Division of Household Labour in 22 Countries', *American Sociological Review* 69/6 (2004), pp.751-767.

Gauthier, Anne H., Timothy T. Smeeding and Frank F. Furstenberg, 'Are Parents Investing Less Time in Children? Trends in Selected Industrialized Countries', *Population and Development Review* 30/4 (2004), pp.647-671.

Geist, Claudia, 'The Welfare State and the Home: Regime Differences in the Domestic Division of Labour', *European Sociological Review* 21/1 (2005), pp. 23-41.

Gershuny, Jonathan, *Changing Times: Work and Leisure in Postindustrial Society*, (Oxford, 2000).

Gilligan, Carol, *In a Different Voice: Psychological Theory and Women's Development*, (Harvard University Press, 1982).

Gimenez, Daniel M., 'Gender, Pensions and Social Citizenship in Latin America', ECLAC no: 46, 2005.

Ginn, Jay and Sara Arber, 'Moving the Goalposts: The Impact on British Women of Raising their State Pension Age to 65', in J. Baldock and M. May (eds), *Social Policy Review no. 7* (Social Policy Association, 1995).

Ginn, Jay, 'European Pension Privatisation: Taking Account of Gender', *Social Policy & Society* 3/2 (2004), pp. 123-134.

Göle, Nilufer, 'Toward an Autonomization of Politics and Civil Society in Turkey', in M. Heper and A. Evin (eds), *Politics in the Third Turkish Republic* (Boulder: Westview, 1994).

Göle, Nilüfer, 'Secularism and Islamism in Turkey: The Making of Elites and Counter-Elites', *Middle East Journal* 51/1 (1997), p. 58.

Göle, Nilufer, *The Forbidden Modern: Civilization and Veiling*, (University of Michigan Press, 1996).

Göle, Nilüfer, 'Secularism and Islamism in Turkey: The Making of Elites and Counter-Elites', *Middle East Journal* 51/1 (1997), pp. 46-58.

Göle, Nilufer, 'Islam in Public: New Visibilities and New Imaginaries', *Public Culture* 14/1 (2002), pp. 173-190.

Göle, Nilüfer, *Modern Mahrem: Medeniyet ve Örtünme*, (Metis, 2008).

Gonzales-Block, Miguel Angel, 'Comparative Research and Analysis Methods for Shared Learning from Health Sector Reforms', *Health Policy* 42/3 (1997), pp. 187-209.

Gough, Ian, 'Social Assistance in Southern Europe', *South European Society and Politics* 1/1 (1996), pp. 1-23.

Gough, Ian, 'Social Assistance Regimes: A Cluster Analysis', *Journal of European Social Policy* 11/2 (2001), pp. 165-70.

Green, Andrew, 'Reforming the Health Sector in Thailand: The Role of Policy Actors on the Policy Stage', *International Journal of Health Planning and Management* 15/1 (2000), pp. 39-59.

Gülalp, Haldun, 'Globalization and Political Islam: The Social Bases of Turkey's Welfare Party', *International Journal of Middle East Studies* 33/3 (2001), pp. 433-448.

Gülçubuk Bulenr, Haydar Sengul, Nilay Aluftekin, Nuray Kizilaslan and Mustafa Kilic, 'Tarimda Istihdam, Sosyal Guvenlik Uygulamaları ve Kirsal Yoksulluk', Ziraat Muhendisligi VI. Teknik Kongresi, 2005.

Gündüz-Hoşgör, Ayşe and Jeroen Smits, 'Variation in the employment status of women in Turkey', *Women's Studies International Forum* 31/2 (2008), pp.104-117.

Günlük-Şenesen, Gülay and Şemsa Özar, 'Gender Based Occupational Segregation in the Turkish Banking Sector', in E. M. Çınar (ed), *The Economics of Women and Work in the Middle East*, (Research in Middle

East Economics, 2001).

Hamzaoğlu, Onur, 'TÜSİAD-AKP-Sağlık: Patronlar Hükümetleri (miz)in Maskesini Düşürdü (TÜSİAD-AKP-Health: Bosses Took (Our) Governments' Mask off)', *Toplum ve Hekim* 19/4 (2004), pp. 242-7.

Hartmann, Heidi, 'The unhappy marriage of Marxism and. Feminism: Towards a more progressive union', Capital and Class 3/2 (1979), pp.1-33.

HDR (Human Development Report), Overcoming Barriers: Human mobility and development, New York: UNDP, 2009.

Hearn, Jeff and Wendy Parkin, *Gender, Sexuality and Violence in Organizations, the Unspoken Forces of Organisation Violations*, (Sage, 2001).

Heper, Metin,' Islam and Democracy in Turkey: Toward a Reconciliation', *Middle East Journal*, Vol. 51, Issue 1 (1997), pp. 32-45.

Hersch, Joni, and Leslie S. Stratton, 'Housework, Fixed Effects, and Wages of Married Workers', *Journal of Human Resources* 32/2 (1997), pp.285-307.

Hinz, Richard P., Asta Zviniene and Anna-Marie Vilamovska, 'The New Pensions in Kazakhstan: Challenges in Making the Transition', The World Bank SP Discussion Paper no. 0537, 2005.

Hobsbawm, Eric, *The Age of Extremes: A History of the World*, 1914-1991, (Abacus, 1995).

Hochschild, Arlie R. and Anne Machung, *The Second Shift*, (Avon Books, 1989).

Hook, Jennifer, 'Care in Context: Men's Unpaid Work in 20 Countries, 1965-1998', *American Sociological Review* 71/4 (2006), p. 639-660.

Hook, Jennifer, 'Gender inequality in the welfare state: Task segregation in housework, 1965-2003', *American Journal of Sociology* 115/ 5 (2010), pp.1480-1523.

HSBS (Health Seeking Behavior Study), Reproductive Health Program of Turkey, 2007.

Huber, Eevlyne, John D. Stephens, David Bradley, Stehanie Moller and François Nielsen, 'The Welfare State and Gender Equality', Luxemburg Income Study Working Paper no. 279, 2004.

HUIPS, Turkey Demographic and Health Survey 2008, http://www.hips.hacettepe.edu.tr/tnsa2008/analiz.shtml, 2008.

Human Development Report, *Overcoming Barriers: Human mobility and development*, (UNDP, 2009).

Ilkkaracan, Ipek and Raziye Selim, 'The Gender Wage Gap in the Turkish Labour Market', *Labour* 21/3 (2007), pp. 563-593.

İlkkaracan, Pınar, 'How Could Adultery Derail Turkey's Aspiration to Join the European Union', in R. Parker, R. Petchesky and R. Sember (eds), *Sex Politics: Reports from the Front Lines* (Sexuality Policy Watch, 2007).

ILO, *Social security and health insurance reform project, Social Secuirty Final Report, ILO/TF/Turkey/R.60*, (ILO, 1996).

ILO, *Global Employment Trends for Women*, (ILO, 2009).

ILO, *Report IV (1) Decent Work for Domestic Workers*, (ILO, 2010).

Işık, Oğuz and Melih Pınarcıoğlu, *Nöbetleşe Yoksulluk: Gecekondulaşma ve Kent Yoksulları: Sultanbeyli Örneği*, (İletişim, 2001).

IWPR (Institute for Women's Policy Research), 'Why Privatizing Social Security Would Hurt Women', IWPR Publication # D437RB, 2000.

İlyasoğlu, Aynur, *Örtülü Kimlik*, (Metis, 2000).

Jackson, William A., 'Capabilities, Culture and Social Structure', *Review of Social Economy* 63:1 (2005), pp. 101 - 124.

Jaggar, Alison M., 'Socialist Feminism and Human Nature', in J. P. Sterba (ed), *Morality in Practice 2/e* (Wadsworth, 1988).

Jaggar, Alison M., 'Reasoning About Well-being: Nussbaum's Methods of Justifying Capabilities', *Journal of Political Philosophy* 14/3 (2006), pp. 301-322.

James, Estelle, Alejandra Cox Edwards and Rebeca Wong, 'The Gender Impact of Pension Reform: A Cross Country Analysis', *Journal of Pension Economics and Finance* 2/2 (2003), pp. 181-219.

Jawad, Rana, *Religion and Social Welfare in the Middle East: A Lebanese Perspective*, (The Policy Press, 2009).

Jefferson, Therese and Alison Preston, 'Australia's "Other" Gender Wage Gap: Baby Boomers and Compulsory Superannuation Accounts', *Feminist Economics* 11/2 (2005), pp. 79-101.

Jelin, Elisabeth, 'Migration and Labour Force Participation of Latin American Women: The Domestic Servants in the Cities', *Signs* 3/1 (1977), pp. 129-141.

Jensen, Jane, 'Who cares? Gender and welfare regimes', *Social Politics*, 4/2 (1997), pp. 182-187.

Jessop, Bob, 'The Changing Governance of Welfare: Recent Trends in Primary Functions, Scale, and Models of Coordination', *Social Policy and Administration* 33/4 (1999), pp. 343-359.

Joekes, Susan, 'A gender- Analytical Perspective on Trade and Sustainable Development', United Nations Conference on Trade and Development, 1999.

Kabeer, Naila, 'Globalization, Labour Standards, and Women's Rights: Dilemmas of Collective (In)Action in an Interdependent World', *Feminist Economics* 10/1 (2004), pp. 3-35.

Kabeer, Naila and Rachel Sabates-Wheeler, 'Gender Equality and the extension of social protection', ILO Social Security Policy and Development Branch ESS Paper no.16, 2003.

Kabeer, Naila and Sarah Cook, 'Editorial Introduction: Re-visioning Social Policy in the South: Challenges and Concepts', *IDS Bulletin* 31/4

(2000), pp. 1-10.

Kadıoğlu, Ayşe, *Cinselliğin İnkarı: Büyük Toplumsal Projelerin Nesnesi Olarak Türk Kadınları, Bilanço 98, 75 Yılda Kadınlar ve Erkekler*, (Türkiye Ekonomik ve Toplumsal Tarih Vakfı, 1998).

Kadıoğlu, Ayşe, 'Civil Society, Islam and Democracy in Turkey: A Study of Three Islamic Non-Governmental Organizations', *The Muslim World* 95 (2005), pp. 23–41.

Kadıoğlu, Ayşe, *Cumhuriyet İradesi Demokrasi Muhakemesi* (Metis, 1999).

Kalaycıoğlu, Sibel, 'Elderly Care, Perceptions of Ageing and Social Inclusion in Turkey', in İ. Tufan (ed), *Proceedings Book of the 2nd International Symposium on Social and Applied Gerontology in Turkey* (GEROYAY, 2007).

Kalaycıoğlu, Sibel ve Helga Rittersberger-Tılıç, *Evlerimizdeki Gündelikçi Kadınlar: Cömert "Abla"ların Sadık "Hanım"ları*, (Su Yayınları, 2001).
Kalaycıoğlu, Sibel, Ulaş Tol, Önder Kucukural and Cengiz Kurtulus, *Yaşlılar ve Yaşlı Yakınları Açısından Yaşam Biçimi Tercihleri*, (*Living Arrangements of Elderly and Their Relatives*), (TÜBİTAK-TUBA-UNFPA, 2003).

Kandiyoti, Deniz, 'Emancipated but Unliberated? Reflections on the Turkish Case', *Feminist Studies* 13/2 (1987), pp. 317-338.

Kandiyoti, Deniz, 'Women and Turkish State: Political Actors or Symbolic Pawns?', in N. Yuval-Davis and F. Anthias (eds), *Women-Nation-State* (Macmillan, 1989).

Kandiyoti, Deniz, *Cariyeler, Bacılar, Yurttaşlar*, (Metis, 1997).

Kara, Orhan, 'Occupational gender wage discrimination in Turkey', *Journal of Economic Studies* 33/2 (2006), pp. 130-43.

Karamessini, Maria, 'Continuity and Change in the Southern Europen Social Model', *International Labour Review* 47/1 (2008), pp. 43-70.

Karshenas Massoud and Valentine M. Moghadam, 'Female Labour Force

Participation and Economic Adjustment in the MENA Region', in M. Cinar (ed), *The Economics of Women and Work in the Middle East and North Africa* (Elsevier Science Research in Middle East Economics, 2001).

Kaşka, Selmin, 'The New International Migration and Migrant Women in Turkey: The Case of Moldovan Domestic Workers', in A. Icduygu and K. Kirisci (eds), *Land of Diverse Migrations* (Istanbul Bilgi University Press, 2009).

Kasnakoğlu, Zehra and Meltem Dayıoğlu, 'Measuring the Value of Home Production in Turkey', in T. Bulutay (ed), *New Developments in National Accounts* (TurkStat, 2002).

Kasnakoğlu, Zehra and Meltem Dayıoğlu, 'Female Labour Force Participation and Earnings Differentials between Genders in Turkey', in J. M. Rives and M. Yousefi (eds), *Economic Dimensions of Gender Inequality: A Global Perspective*, (Praeger, 1997).

KEIG (Women's Labour and Employment Initiative) 'Kadın Örgütleri Basın Açıklaması (Press Release of Women's Groups on the Women's Employment Summit organised by TİSK)', 2006.
KEIG, 'Kadın Emegi ve Istihdami Toplantisi Program Metni', (KEIG, 2007).

KEIG, 'Sosyal Sigortalar ve Genel Sağlık Sigortası Yasa Tasarısı Kadınlara Nasıl Bir 'Sosyal Güvenlik' Vaat Ediyor?', Report Prepared by KEIG, 2008. http://www.keig.org/yayinlar/SSGSS_10mart2008_web. pdf

Kelley, Judith Green, 'International Actors on the Domestic Scene: Membership Conditionality and Socialization by International Institutions', *International Organisation* 58 (2004), p. 425-457.

Kılıç, Azer, 'The Gender Dimension of Social Policy Reform in Turkey: Towards Equal Citizenship', *Social Policy & Administration* 42/5 (2008), pp. 487-503.

Kızılırmak, Burca, 'Labour Market Participation Decisions of Married Women: Evidence from Turkey', in A. Deshpande (ed), *Globalization and Development: A Handbook of New Perspective* (Oxford, 2008).

Kızılırmak, Burça ve Emel Memiş, 'The Unequal Burden of Poverty on Time Use', The Levy Institute Working Paper no. 572, 2009.

Koray, Meryem, *Çalışma Yaşamında Kadın Gerçekleri*, (BASİSEN Eğitim ve Kültür Yayınları, 1993).

Korczyk, Sophie M., 'Women and Individual Social Security Accounts in Chile, Australia, and the United Kingdom', http://www.aarp.org/research/legis-polit/ssreform/aresearch-import-265-2003-09.html, 2003.

Korpi, Walter, 'Faces of Inequality: Gender, Class, and Patterns of Inequalities in Different Types of Welfare Sates', *Social Politics* 7/29 (200), pp. 127-191.

Kramer, Heinz, 'Turkey under Erbakan: Continuity and Change towards Islam', *Aussenpolitik* 47/4 (1996), p. 379-388.

KSGM (General Directorate on the Status of Women), *Women and Health*, (KSGM, 2008).
Kuhlmann, Ellen and Ellen Annandale, 'Bringing Gender Back to the Heart of Health Policy, Practice and Research', in E. Kuhlmann and E. Annandale (eds), *The Palgrave Handbook of Gender and Healthcare* (Palgrave Macmillan, 2010).

Kutzin, Joseph, 'Experience with Organizational and Financing Reform of the Health Sector', WHO SHS Paper no. 8, 1995.

Langer, Ana and Jennifer Catino, 'A Gendered Look at Mexico's Health Sector Reform', *The Lancet* 368/9549 (2006), pp. 1753-5.

Leibfried, Stephan, 'Towards a European Welfare State?', in Z. Ferge and J. E. Kberd (eds), *Social Policy in a Changing Europe* (Westview Press, 1993).

Lewis, Jane, Marry Campbell and Carmen Huetra, 'Patterns of Paid and Unpaid Work in Western Europe: Gender, Commodification, Preferences and the Implication for Policy', *Journal of European Social Policy* 18/1 (2008), pp. 21-31.

Lewis, Jane, 'Gender and Welfare State Change', *European Societies* 4/4 (2002), pp. 331-357.

Lewis, Jane, 'Work/family reconciliation, equal opportunities, and social policies: the interpretation of policy trajectories at the EU level and the meaning of gender equality', *Journal of European Public Policy* 13/3 (2006), pp. 420-437.

Lewis, Jane, 'Gender and Welfare Regimes: Further Thoughts', *Social Politics* 4/2 (1997), pp. 160-177.

Lewis, Jane, 'Gender and the development of welfare regimes', *Journal of European Social Policy* 2/3 (1992), pp. 159-73.

Lie, John, 'From Agrarian Patriarchy to Patriarchal Capitalism: Gendered Capitalist Industrialization in Korea' in V. M. Moghadam (ed), *Patriarchy and Economic Development* (Clarendon Press, 1996).

Lim, Linda, 'Women's Work in Export Factories: The Politics of a Cause', in I. Tinker (ed), *Persistent Inequalities* (Oxford, 1990).

Lindio-McGovern, Ligaya, 'Domestic Workers in Rome Labour Export in the Context of Globalization: The Experience of Filipino', *International Sociology* 18/3 (2003), pp. 513-534.

Lipset, Seymour Martin and William Schneider, *The Confidence Gap: Business, Labour and Government in the Public Mind*, (John Hopkins University Press, 1983).

Lipton, Michael and Martin Ravallion, 'Poverty and Policy', in J. Behrman and T.N. Srinivasan (eds), *Handbook of Development Economics 3* (Elsevier, 1995).

Lister, Ruth, *Citizenship: Feminist Perspectives*, (Palgrave Macmillan, 2003).

Lister, Ruth, 'Citizenship: Toward a feminist synthesis', *Feminist Review* 57/1 (1997), pp. 28-48.

Longo, Patrizia, 'Revisiting The Equality/Difference Debate: Redefining Citizenship for the New Millennium', *Citizenship Studies* 5/2 (2001), pp. 269-283.

Luttrell, Cecilia and Caroline Moser, 'Gender and Social Protection', Overseas Development Institute Report, 2004.

Makinen, Tiina, 'Public or private? International comparison of the structure and level of pension income', The ISA XV World Congress of Sociology, 2002.

Manning, Nick, 'Turkey, The EU and Social Policy', *Social Policy & Society* 6/4 (2007), pp. 491-501.

Manser, Marilyn and Murray Brown, 'Marriage and Household Decision Making: A Bargaining Analysis', *International Economic Review* 21/1 (1980), pp. 31-44.

Marling, William H., *How "American" Is Globalization*, (Johns Hopkins University Press, 2006).

McElroy, Marjorie and Mary Jean Horney, 'Nash-Bargained Household Decisions: Towards a Generalization of the Theory of Demand', *International Economic Review* 22/2 (1981), pp. 333-49.

MDG (Millennium Development Goals) Report Turkey, http://www.undp.org.tr/publicationsDocuments/TR%202010%20MD G%20Report_EN.pdf, 2010.

Meissner, Martin, Elizabeth W. Humphreys, Scott M. Meis and William J. Scheu, 'No exit for wives: Sexual division of labour and the cumulation of household demands', *Canadian Review of Sociology and Anthropology* 12/4 (1975), pp. 424-439.

Merçil, İpek, 'Islam ve Feminizm', in Z. Direk (ed), *Cinsiyetli Olmak: Sosyal Bilimlere Feminist Yaklaşımlar* (Cogito, 2007).

Mesa-Lago, Carmelo, 'Social protection in Chile: Reforms to imrove equity', *International Labour Review* 147/4 (2008), pp. 377-402.

Millns, Susan, 'Gender Equality, Citizenship, and the EU's Constitutional Feature', *European Law Journal* 13/2 (2007), p. 218-237.

Mingione, Enzo, 'Labour market segmentation and informal work', in H.

D. Gibson (ed), *Economic transformation, democratization and integration into the European Union Southern Europe in a comparative perspective* (Palgrave MacMillan, 2002).

Ministry of Health, 'Family Practice Pilot Project By law 25867', 2005. Ministry of Health, 'Ministry Circular on Maternal Deaths', General Directorate of Primary Care Services, 2008.

Ministry of Health, By-law on the Payments to and Terms of Contract with the Ministry of Health Personnel who would be working within the framework of Family Medicine Practice, no. 2010/1237, December 24, 2010.

MLSS (Ministry of Labour and Social Security), www.csgb.gov.tr, 2007.

Moghadam, Valentine M., 'Women, Work and Economic Restructuring: A Regional Overview', in M. Cinar (ed), *The Economics of Women and Work in the Middle East and North Africa* (Elsevier Science Research in Middle East Economics, 2001).

Moghadam, Valentine M., *Modernizing Women Gender and Social Change in the Middle East*, (Lynne Rienner, 2003).

Molyneux, Maxine, 'Beyond the Household Debate', *New Left Review* 116 (1979).

Molyneux, Maxine, 'Mobilization without emancipation? Women's interests, the state, and revolution in Nicaragua', *Feminist Studies* 11/2 (1985), pp. 227–54.

Moser, Caroline O. N., 'Gender Planing in The Third World: Meeting Practical and Strategic Gender Needs', *World Development* 17/1 (1989), pp.1799-1825.

Mülkiyeliler Birliği, 'Sosyal Güvenlik Reformu Üzerine Mülkiyeliler Birliği Görüşü', http://www.mülkiye.org.tr, 2006

Mütevellioğlu, Nergis and Işık, Sayım, 'Türkiye Emek Piyasasında Neoliberal Dönüşüm', in N. Mütevellioğlu and S. Sönmez (eds), *Küreselleşme, Kriz ve Türkiye'de Neoliberal Dönüşüm* (İstanbul Bilgi

Üniversitesi Yayınları, 2009).

Nanda, Priya, 'Gender Dimensions of User Fees: Implications for Women's Utilization of Health Care', *Reproductive Health Matters* 10/20 (2002), pp. 127-134.

Narlı, Nilüfer, 'The Rise of the Islamist Movement in Turkey', *Middle East Review of International Affairs* 3/3 (1999), pp. 38-48.

Neyzi, Ali H., *Evlatlık Bir Kızın Gizli Güncesi "Pafe"*, (Evrim Bilimsel Eğitim Araçları A. Ş., 1985).

Nicolson, Paula, *Gender, Power and Organisation*, (Routledge, 1996).

Nussbaum, Martha C., *Women and Human Development: The Capabilities Approach*, (Cambridge, 2000).

Nussbaum, Martha, *Sex & Social Justice*, (Oxford, 1998).
O'Connor, Julia S, 'Gender, Class and Citizenship in the comparative analysis of welfare state regimes: theoretical and methodological issues', *The British Journal of Sociology* 44/3 (1993), pp. 501-518.

OECD, 'Source OECD Employment and Labour Market Statistics', 2008

Official Gazette, 'Tedavi Katılım Payının Uygulanması Hakkında Tebliğ', no, 27353, sıra no: 12, 18 September 2009.

Orloff, Ann S., 'Gender and the Social Rights of Citizenship: The Comparative Analysis of Gender Relations and Welfare States', *American Sociological Review* 58/3 (1993), pp. 303-328.

Ostner, Ilona and Jane Lewis, 'Gender and the Evaluation of European Social Policies', in S. Leibfried and P. Pierson (eds), *European Social Policy: Between Fragmentation and Integration* (the Brookings Institute, 1995).

Özbay, Ferhunde, 'Gendered Space: A New Look at Turkish Modernisation', *Gender & History* 11/3 (1999), pp. 555-568.

Özler, Şule, 'Export Orientation and Female Share of Employment: Evidence from Turkey', *World Development* 28/7 (2000), pp. 1239-1248.

Öncü, Ayşe, 'Turkish Women in the Professions: Why So Many?', in N. Abadan-Unat (ed), *Women In Turkish Society* (E.J. Brill: Leiden, 1981).

Öncü, Ayşe, 'Politics of the Urban Land Market in Turkey: 1950-80', *International Journal of Urban and Regional Research* 12/1 (1988), pp. 38-64.

Önder, İzzettin, 'Sağlıkta Dönüşümün Ekonomi Politik Değerlendirmesi (Political Economic Analysis of Transformation in Health)', *Toplum ve Hekim* 21/3 (2006), pp. 219-229.

Öniş, Ziya, 'The political economy of the Islamic resurgence in Turkey: the rise of the Welfare Party in perspective', *Third World Quarterly* 18/4 (1997), pp. 743-766.

Öniş, Ziya, 'Neo-liberal Küreselleşmenin Sınırları: Türkiye Açısından Arjantin Krizi ve IMF'ye Karşılaştırmalı Bir Bakış', in A. K. Köse, F. Şenses and E. Yeldan (eds), *İktisadi Kalkınma, Kriz ve İstikrar* (İletişim, 2003).

Öniş, Ziya, 'Redemocratization and Economic Liberalisation in Turkey: The limits of state autonomy', *Studies in Comparative International Development*, Summer 92, Vol. 27, Issue 2 (1992).

Özar, Şemsa and Mustafa Şahin, 'Women, Citizenship and the Social Security System in Turkey: Exclusion and Dependency', mimeo, 2009.

Özar, Şemsa, 'Some Observations on the Position of Women in the Labour Market in the Development Process of Turkey', *Boğaziçi Journal* 8/1-2 (1994), pp. 21-43.

Özbay, Ferhunde, 'Kadınların Eviçi ve Evdışı Uğraşlarındaki Değişme', in Ş. Tekeli (ed), *Kadın Bakış Açısından 1980'ler Türkiye'sinde Kadınlar* (İletişim, 1990).

Özbay, Ferhunde, *Evlatlık institution in Turkey: Are they slaves or daughters?*, (Bogazici University Press, 1999).

Özbay, Ferhunde, 'Evlerde el kızları: Cariyeler, evlatlıklar, gelinler', in L. Davidoff and A. Durakbaşı (eds), *Feminist Tarih Yazımında Sınıf ve Cinsiyet* (İletişim, 2009).

Özdalga, Elizabeth, *The Veiling Issue, Official Secularism and Popular Islam in Modern Turkey*, (Curzon Press, 1998).

Özyeğin, Gül, *Baskalarının Kiri*, (İletişim, 2001).

Parrenas, Rhachel Salazar, 'Migrant Filipina Domestic Workers and the International Division of Reproductive Labour Source', *Gender and Society* 14/4 (2000), pp. 560-580.

Pateman, Carole, 'The Patriarchal Welfare State', in A. Gutmann (ed), *Democracy and the Welfare State* (Princeton University Press, 1988).

Pateman, Carole, *The Disorder of Women Democracy, Feminism and Political Theory*, (Stanford University Press, 1989).

Pearson, Ruth, 'Gender Issues in Industrialization', in T. Hewitt, H. Johnson and D. Wield (eds), *Industrialization and Development* (Oxford, 1992).

Pearson, Ruth, 'Nimble Fingers' Revisited: Reflections on Women and Third World Industrialization in the Late Twentieth Century', in C. Jackson and R. Pearson (eds), *Feminist Visions of Development* (Routledge, 2002).

Pierson, Paul, 'New Politics of the Welfare State', *World Politics* 48/2 (1996), pp. 143-179.

Rees, Teresa, 'The Feminization of Trade Unions', in T. Rees (ed), *Women and the Labour Market* (Routledge, 1992).

Rees, Teresa, *Mainstreaming Equality in the European Union: Education, Training and Labour Market Policies*, (Routledge, 1998).

Rees, Teresa, 'Mainstreaming Gender Equality in Science in the European Union: the ETAN Report', *Gender and Education* 13/3 (2001), pp. 243-260.

Regan, Patrick M. and Aida Paskeviciute, 'Women's Access to Politics and Peaceful States', *Journal of Peace Research* 40/3 (2003), pp. 287-302.

Robeyns, Ingrid, 'Sen's capability approach and gender inequality: selecting relevant capabilities', *Feminist Economics* 9/2-3 (2003), pp. 61-92.

Robeyns, Ingrid, 'The Capability Approach: A Theoretical Survey', *Journal of Human Development* 6/1 (2008), pp. 93-114.

Sainsbury, Diane, 'Taxation, family responsibilities, and employment', in D. Sainsbury (ed), *Gender and welfare regime* (Oxford, 1999)..

Sainsbury, Diane, 'Gendering dimensions of welfare state', in J. Fink, G. Lewis and J. Clarke (eds), *Rethinking European welfare Transformations of Europe and social policy* (Sage, 2001).

Sak, Güven and Ozan Acar, '22 Temmuz 2007 Seçimlerinin Ardından İkinci Nesil Reform Sürecinin Özellikleri Raporu', www.tepav.org, 2007.

Saktanber, Ayşe and Gül Çorbacıoğlu, 'The Veil: Debating Citizenship, Gender and Religious Diversity', *Social Politics* 15/4 (2008), pp. 514-538.

Saktanber, Ayşe, *Living Islam: Women, Religion and the Politicization of Culture in Turkey*, (I.B. Tauris, 2002).

Sandıkçı, Özlem and Güliz Ger, 'Aesthetics, Ethics and Politics of the Turkish Headscarf' in Susanne Küchler and Daniel Miller (eds) *Clothing as Material Culture:* 61–82, (Berg 2005).

Sandıkçı, Özlem and Güliz Ger, 'Veiling in Style: How Does a Stigmatized Practice Become Fashionable?', *Journal of Consumer Research*, November 17 (2009).

Saraceno, Chiara, *Social Assistance Dynamics in European Welfare States*, (Policy Press, 2002).

Schor, Juliet B., *The Overworked American: The Unexpected Decline of Leisure*, (Basic Books, 1991).

Seguino, Stephanie, 'Accounting for Gender in Asian Economic Growth', *Feminist Economics* 6/3 (2000), pp.27-58.

Sen, Amartya K., *Commodities and Capabilities*, (Oxford, 1985).

Sen, Amartya K., 'Development and Capabilities Expansion', *Journal of Development Planning* 19 (1989), pp. 41-58.

Sen, Amartya, *Inequality Re-examined*, (Oxford, 1992).

Sen, Amartya K., *Development As Freedom*, (Knopf Press, 1999).

Sen, Amartya K. and Martha Nussbaum, (eds), *The Quality of Life*, (Calerondon Press, 1993).

Sen, Gita, Piroska Ostlin and Asha George, 'Unequal, Unfair, Ineffective and Inefficient, Gender Inequality in Health Care: Why It Exists and How We Can Change It', Final report to the WHO Commission on Social Determinants of Health, 2007.

SGK (Social Security Institution), www.sgk.gov.tr, 2007.

SGK, www.sgk.gov.tr, 2010.

Sheldon, Amy, 'Talking Power: Girls, Gender Enculturation and Discourse', in R. Wodak (ed), *Gender and Discourse* (Sage, 1997).

Sirman, Nükhet, 'Feminism in Turkey: A Short History', *New Perspectives on Turkey* 3/1 (1989), pp. 1-34.

Sirman, Nükhet, 'Kadınların Milliyeti', in *Modern Türkiye'de Siyasi Düşünce Cilt 4* (İletişim, 2002).

Smeeding, Timothy M. and Susanna Sandstrom, 'Poverty and Income Maintenance in Old Age: A Cross-National View of Low-Income Older Women', in A. Stark, N. Folbre and L. B. Shaw (eds), Explorations Gender and Aging: Cross-National *Contrasts Feminist Economics* 11/2 (2005), pp. 163-198.

Soyer, Ata, 'Alternatifimiz Var (Mı?)', *Toplum ve Hekim* 21 (2006), pp. 256-258.

Ståhlberg, Ann-Charlotte, Agneta Kruse and Annika Sundén, 'Pension Design and Gender: Analyses of Developed and Developing Countries', in N. Gilbert (ed), *Gender and Social Security Reform: What's Fair for*

Women?(Transaction Publishers, 2006).

Stahlberg, Ann-Charlotte, Marcela Cohen Birman, Agneta Kruse and Annika Sunde, 'Retirement income security for men and women', International Social Security Association Technical Report no. 23, 2004.

Standing, Hilary, 'Gender Equity and Health Sector Reforms in Low and Middle-Income Countries', in E. Kuhlmann and E. Annandale (eds), *The Palgrave Handbook of Gender and Healthcare* (Palgrave Macmillan, 2010).

Standing, Hilary, 'Frameworks for understanding gender inequalities and health sector reform: an analysis and review of policy issues', Harvard Center for Population and Development Studies Working paper series No. 99.06, 1999.

State Planning Organisation and World Bank, 'Social and Economic Benefits of More and Better Job Opportunities for Women in Turkey', www.worldbank.org.tr, 2009.

Steinhilber, Silke, *The Gender Implications of Pension Reforms. General Remarks and Evidence from Selected Countries*, (UNRISD, 2006).

Strauss, John and Duncan Thomas, 'Human Resources: Empirical Modeling of Household and Family Decisions', in J. Behrman and T.N. Srinivasan (eds), *Handbook of Development Economics* (Elsevier, 1995).

Süral, Nurhan, 'Legal Framework for Gender Equality at Work in Turkey', *Middle Eastern Studies* 43/5 (2007), pp. 811-824.

Şahabettinoğlu Murat, Deniz Uyanık, Nil Ayhan, M. Akif Bakır and Anlı Ataöv, *Çocukların Temel Eğitime Katılmasının Sosyoekonomik Engelleri ve Destekleri*, (TurkStat, 2002).

Şahin, Şule and Adem Y. Elveren, 'Assessing the Minimum Pension Guarantees for the Private Pension System in Turkey', *International Social Security Review* 64/3 (2011).

Şahin, Şule and Adem Y. Elveren, 'A Minimum Pension Guarantee Application for the İndividual Pension System in Turkey: A Gendered Approach', *Journal of Women, Politics & Policy* (forthcoming).

Şenol, Nevin, Ceren İşat and Aysun Sayın, 'Equal Opportunities For Women and Men: Monitoring Law and Practice in Turkey', Open Society Institute Network Women's Program, www.soros.org/women, 2005.

Şenses, Fikret, *Structural Adjustment Policies and Employment in Turkey*, (METU Economic Research Center, 1996).

Seshi, Cinzia, 'Women in Trade Unions: Bridging the Gap', ETUC Survey, 2007.

Şişman, Nazife, *Kamusal Alanda Başörtülüler: Fatma Karabıyık Barbarosoğlu ile Söyleşiler*, (Timaş Yayınlar, 2000).

Şişman, Nazife, 'Müslüman Kadın Kimliği', in Kamusal Alanda Başörtülüler, *Fatma Karabıyık Barbarosoğlu ile Söyleşiler*,(Timaş Yayınları, 2000).

Talaş, Cahit, 'Sosyal Güvenlik Meselemiz', İçtimai Siyaset Konferansları Vol. VII, 1955.

Tansel, Aysıt, 'Wage-employment, Earnings and Returns to Schooling for Men and Women in Turkey', *Economics of Education Review* 13/4 (1994), pp. 305-320.

Tansel, Aysıt, 'Public-Private Employment Choice, Wage Differentials and Gender in Turkey', Yale University Economic Growth Center Discussion Paper no. 797, 1999.

Tekeli, Şirin, 'Women in Turkish Politics', in N. Abadan-Unat (ed), *Women in Turkish Society* (E.J.Brill, 1981).

Tekeli, Şirin, 'Emergence of Feminist Movement in Turkey', in D. Dahlerup (ed), *The New Women's Movement: Feminism and Political Power in Europe and USA* (Sage, 1986).

Tekeli, Şirin, 'Women in Changing Political Associations of the 1980s', in A. Finkel and N. Sirman (eds), *Turkish State, Turkish Society* (Routledge, 1990).

Tenekeci, İlknur, *Sekiz Kadın Sekiz Dünya Sendikacı Kadınlar Anlatıyor*, (Petrol-İş Yayını, 2010).

TEPAV, 'Türkiye'nin Rekabet Gücü İçin Sanayi Politikası Çerçevesi', www.tepav.org, 2007.

Theobald, Sally, Rachel Tolhurst and Helen Elsey, 'Introductory Comments: The Background and Structure of the Resource Pack', in S. Theobald, R. Tolhurst and H. Elsey (eds), 'Sector Wide Approaches: Opportunity and Challenges for Gender Equity in Health' (Gender and Health Group, Liverpool School of Tropical Medicine, 2002).

Thomson, Marilyn, 'Workers not Maids: Organizing Household Workers in Mexico', *Gender & Development* 17/2 (2009), pp. 281-292.

TİSK (Confederation of the Unions for Turkish Employers), 'Women's Employment Summit Proceedings Concluding Comments', TİSK, 2006a.

TİSK (Confederation of the Unions for Turkish Employers), 'Social Policy, Employment, EU Acquis Communautaire and Turkey: The Report of the Commission on EU Directives', TİSK, 2006.

Tok, Gül Ceylan, 'The Securitization of the Headscarf Issue in Turkey: 'The Good and Bad Daughters' of the Republic', *The International Studies Association of Ritsumeikan University: Ritsumeikan Annual Review of International Studies*, Vol. 8 (2009), pp. 113-137.

Toksöz, Gülay, *Women's Employment Situation in Turkey*, (ILO, 2007).

Toksöz, Gülay, 'Neoliberal Piyasa ve Muhafazakar Aile Kıskacında Türkiye'de Kadın İşgücü', in S. Sönmez and N. Mütevellioğlu (eds), *Küreselleşme, Kriz ve Türkiye'de Neoliberal Dönüşüm* (İstanbul Bilgi Üniversitesi Yayınları, 2009).

Toksöz, Gülay and Seyhan Erdoğdu, *Sendikacı Kadın Kimliği*, (İmge Kitabevi, 1998).

Toktaş, Şule and Çağla Diner, 'Waves of Feminism in Turkey: Kemalist, Islamist and Kurdish Women's Movements in an Era of Globalization', *Journal of Balkan and Near Eastern Studies*, Vol. 12, No. 1 (2010), pp. 41-57.

Toktaş, Şule and Dilek Cindoğlu, 'Modernization and Gender: A History

Of Girls' Technical Education In Turkey Since 1927', *Women's History Review* 15/5 (2006), pp. 737–749.

Toprak, Binnaz et al., *Being Different in Turkey: Religion, Conservatism and Otherization, Research Report on Neighborhood Pressure*, (Open Society Foundation and Bogazici University, 2009).

Toprak, Binnaz, 'Islam and the Secular State', in Çiğdem Balım et al. (eds), *Turkey: Political, Social and Economic Challenges in the 1990s*, (E. J. Brill, 1995).

Toprak, Zafer, 'Cumhuriyet Halk Fırkasından Önce Kurulan Parti: Kadınlar Halk Fırkası' (The Party Formed Before the Republican People's Party: Women's People Party), *Tarih ve Toplum* 51/9, (Mart 1988).

Toprak, Zafer, *1935 İstanbul Uluslararası Feminizm Kongresi ve Barış*, (Düşün Mart 1986).

Tunalı, İnsan and Cem Başlevent, 'Married Women's Participation Choices and Productivity Differentials: Evidence from Urban Turkey', Koç University working paper, 2009.

Tunalı, İnsan, 'Female Part Time Employment in Turkey: Statements and Comments, Independent Expert Report', http://pdf.mutual-learning-employment.net/pdf/norway%2005/TR_Tunali.pdf, 2005.

Turkish National Maternal Mortality Study, Hacettepe University Institute of Population Studies, 2005.

TURKONFED, *İş Dünyasında Kadin Raporu*, (TURKONFED, 2007).

TurkStat, *Statistical Yearbook of Turkey*, (TurkStat, 2006).

TurkStat, 'Zaman Kullanım Anketi Sonuçları 2006', News Bulletin TurkStat, 2007.

TurkStat, *Household Labour Force Statistics* 2005, (TurkStat, 2007a).

TurkStat, *Household Labour Force Statistics* 2006, (TurkStat, 2007b).

TurkStat, *Database on Household Labour Force Statistics*, TurkStat, 2008.

TurkStat, 'Gelir ve Yaşam Koşulları Araştırması Sonuçları 2006-2007', Newsletter No: 221, 2009.

TurkStat, 'Household Budget Surveys', TurkStat, 2010.

Turner, John A., 'Social Security Privatisation Around the World', http://www.aarp.org/research/legis-polit/ssreform/inb106_intl_ss.html, (accessed May 2008), 2005.

Turner, John A., 'Work at Older Ages: Is Raising the Early Retirement Age an Option for Social Security Reform', SSRN, 2006.

TUSIAD, *Türkiye'nin Fırsat Penceresi, Demografik Dönüşüm ve İzdüşümü*, (TUSIAD, 1999).

UN, *World Survey on the Role of Women in Development: Globalization, Gender and Work*, Report of the Secretary-General, 1999.

UNDP, Human Development Report, 2007/2008. New York: Palgrave Macmillan, Technical note 1, 2007.

Uzgel, İlhan, 'AKP: Neoliberal Dönüşümün Yeni Aktörü' in İ. Uzgel and B. Duru (eds), *AKP Kitabı Bir Dönüşümün Bilançosu* (Phoenix Yayınevi, 2009).

Van Ginneken, Wouter, 'Extending social security: Policies for developing countries', ILO Social Security Policy and Development Branch Extension of Social Security Paper no. 13, 2003.

Veil, Mechthild, *Alterssicherung von Frauen in Deutschland und Frankreich*, (Hans-Boeckler-Stiftung, 2002).

Verloo, Mieke, 'Displacement and Enpowerment: Reflections on the Concept and Practice of the Council of Europe Approach to Gender Mainstreaming', *Social Politics* 12/3 (2005), pp. 344–365.

Walby, Sylvia, *Patriarchy at Work*, (University of Minnesota Press, 1986).

Walby, Sylvia, 'The 'Declining Significance' or the 'Changing Forms' of Patriarchy?', in V. M. Moghadam (ed), *Patriarchy and Economic Development* (Clarendon Press,1996).

Walby, Sylvia, *Gender Transformations*, (Routledge, 1997).

Walby, Sylvia, *Theorizing Patriarchy*, (Blackwell Publishers, 1990).

Walby, Sylvia, 'The European Union and Gender Equality: Emergent Varieties of Gender Regime', *Social Politics* 11/1 (2004), pp. 4-29.

Walby, Sylvia, 'Gender Mainstreaming: Productive Tensions in Theory and Practice', *State & Society* 12/3 (2005), pp. 321-343.

Watson, John and Mark McNaughton, 'Gender Differences in Risk Aversion and Expected Retirement Benefits', *Financial Analysts Journal* 63/4 (2007), pp. 52-62.

White, Jenny B., *Islamist Mobilization in Turkey: A Study in Vernacular Politics*, (University of Washington Press, 2002).

White, Jenny B., 'State Feminism, Modernization, and the Turkish Republican Woman', *Feminist Formations* 15/3 (2003), pp. 145-159.

White, Jenny, *Money Makes Us Relatives: Women's Labour in Urban Turkey*, (Routledge, 2004).

WHO http://www.euro.who.int/en/what-we-do/health-topics/ health-determinants/gender/gender-definitions (accessed 25 August 2010), 2010.

Wilber, Charles K. and Kenneth P. Jameson, *The Political Economy of Development and Underdevelopment, 5th ed.* (McGraw Hill, 1992).

Williamson, John B. and Sara E. Rix, 'Social Security Reform: Implications for Women', Center for Retirement Research at Boston College, 1999.

Wolf Diane L., 'Daughters, Decisions and Dominations: An Empirical and Conceptual Critique of Household Strategies', in N. Visvanathan, L.

Duggan, L. Nisonoff and N. Wiegersma (eds), *The Women, Gender & Development Reader* (Zed Books, 1997).

World Bank, 'Turkey Labour Market Study', Report No. 33254-TR, 2006.

World Bank, 'Female Labour Participation in Turkey: Trends, Determinants and Policy Framework', Report No: 48508-TR, 2009.

World Bank, 'Turkey: Expanding Opportunities for the Next Generation', Report No: 48627-TR, 2010.

World Bank/SIS (State Institution of Statistics), 'Turkey: Joint Poverty Assessment Report', Report No. 29619-TU, 2005.

Yakut-Çakar, Burcu and Volkan Yılmaz, 'Social Assistance in Turkey: On the Margins of Redistributive Justice', Annual International Conference "Beyond Social Inclusion: Towards a More Equal Society?, Loughborough University, UK, 2009.

Yaylagül, Levent, *Kitle İletişim Kuramları, Egemen ve Eleştirel Yaklaşımlar*, (Dipnot Yayınevi, 2006).

Yazıcı, Berna, 'Social Work and Social Exclusion in Turkey: An Overview', *New Perspectives on Turkey* 38/Spring (2008), pp. 107-134.

Yeldan, Erinç, *Küreselleşme Sürecinde Türkiye Ekonomisi*, (İletişim, 2001).

Yıldırak, Nurettin, Bülent Gülçubuk, Sema Gün, Emine Olhan and Mehmet Kılıç, *Türkiye'de Gezici ve Geçici Kadın Tarım İşçilerinin Çalışma ve Yaşam Koşulları ve Sorunları*, (Tarım İş Sendikası, 2003).

Yılmaz, Volkan, 'The Political Economy of Disability in Turkey's Welfare Rejime', MA thesis, Bogazici University Ataturk Institute of Modern Turkish Studies, 2010.

Yirmibeşoğlu, Gözde, *Trade Unionism in Turkey: Self-understanding of Labour Union Türk-İş*, (VDM Verlag, 2009).

Young, Brigitte, 'Disciplinary Neoliberalism in the European Union and Gender Politics', *New Political Economy* 5/1 (2000), pp. 77-98.

Young, Iris Marion, 'The Limits of Dual Systems Theory', in L. Sargent (ed), *Women and Revolution* (South End Press, 1981).

Young, Iris Marion, *Justice and the Politics of Difference*, (Princeton University Press, 1990).

Young, Iris Marion, 'Structural Injustice and the Politics of Difference', in A. S. Laden and D. Owen (eds), *Multiculturalism and Political Theory* (Cambridge, 2007).

Zippel, Kathrin, *The Policies of Sexual Harassment: a Comparative Study of the United States, the European Union and Germany*, (Cambridge, 2006).

Zoonen, Liesbet Van, 'The Personal, the Political and the Popular; a Woman's Guide to Celebrity Politics', *European Journal of Cultural Studies* 9/3 (2006), p. 287-301.

2004/7 Sayılı Başbakanlık Genelgesi: Personel Temininde Eşitlik İlkesine Uygun Hareket Edilmesi, (The Prime Ministry Circular on Observing Gender Equality Principle During Recruitment), the Official Gazette, 10 February 2004.

THE CONTRIBUTORS

Feride Acar
Acar is Professor of Political Sociology and Gender and Women's Studies at the Middle East Technical University, (METU) Ankara, Turkey and a member of the UN Convention on the Elimination of Discrimination Against Women (CEDAW). She received her PhD from Bryn Mawr College, Pa., USA.

Tuba İnci Ağartan
Ağartan is an Assistant Professor of Health Policy and Management at Providence College, USA. She holds a PhD in Sociology from Binghamton University, USA.

Gülbanu Altunok
Altunok is a PhD candidate in Political Science at Bilkent University, Ankara, Turkey. She was a visiting researcher at the Department of Political Science at the University of California Berkeley between 2004 and 2005.

Cem Başlevent
Başlevent is an Associate Professor of Economics at Istanbul Bilgi University. He earned his PhD degree in Economics from Boğaziçi University in 2001.

Ayşe Buğra
Buğra is currently a professor at Ataturk Institute of Modern Turkish History and the founding director of the research center 'Social Policy

Forum' at Boğaziçi University, Istanbul. She earned her PhD in Economics at McGill University in 1981.

Meltem Dayıoğlu
Dayıoğlu is an Associate Professor of Economics at the Middle East Technical University. She earned her PhD in Economics from the Middle East Technical University in 1995.

Saniye Dedeoglu is Marie Curie Fellow at the Centre for Research in Ethnic Relations at the University of Warwick, UK, and Assistant Professor in the Department of Labour Economics at the University of Muğla, Turkey. She holds a PhD from the Department of Development Studies at the School of Oriental and African Studies (SOAS), University of London, and is the author of *Women Workers in Turkey: Global Industrial Production in Istanbul* (I.B.Tauris, 2007).

Adem Y. Elveren is Assistant Professor of Economics at Sütçü İmam University, Kahramanmaraş, Turkey. He holds a PhD in Economics from the University of Utah, and has also studied at Ankara University and Boston University.

Sibel Kalaycıoğlu
Kalaycıoğlu is an Associate Professor at the Department of Sociology at Middle East Technical University, Ankara. She recieved her PhD combined degree in Sociology and Social Anthropology in 1995 from University of Kent at Canterbury.

Burça Kızılırmak
Kızılırmak is an Associate Professor of Economics at Ankara University. She earned her PhD degree in Economics in 2002 from Ankara University.

Emel Memiş
Memiş is an Assistant Professor of Economics at Ankara University. She received her PhD in Economics at the University of Utah in 2007.

Umut Öneş
Öneş is Assistant Professor of Economics at Ankara University and among the Board of Directors of Political Psychology Research Center. He received his PhD at Brown University in 2009.

Helga Rittersberger-Tılıç
Rittersberger-Tılıç is an Associate Professor at the Department of Sociology, Middle East Technical University, Ankara. She earned her PhD in Sociology from Universität Gesamthochschule Essen in 1997.

Mustafa Şahin
Şahin is a Legislative Expert at the Grand National Assembly of Turkey and a PhD candidate in Labour Economics and Industrial Relations at Ankara University.

Şule Şahin
Şahin is a lecturer at the Actuarial Sciences in Hacettepe University, Ankara and a registered actuary. She earned her PhD degree in Actuarial Mathematics, Heriot-Watt University, Edinburgh.

Hande Toğrul
Toğrul is the Adult Program Director at The Inclusion Center for Community and Justice, Salt Lake City, Utah. She earned her PhD degree in Economics from the University of Utah in 2009 (completion of courses in 1998).

Gülay Toksöz
Toksöz is a Professor of Labour Economics at Ankara University. She earned her PhD from the Department of Political Sciences of Free University Berlin in 1990.

Şerife Gözde Yirmibeşoğlu
Yirmibeşoğlu is an Assistant Professor at Akdeniz University, Antalya, Turkey. She received her PhD degree in Political Science and Public Administration in 2007 from the Middle East Technical University.

INDEX

Accumulation regime 144
Agriculture 8, 19, 20, 23, 51, 56, 91, 93, 126, 146-48, 217, 227, 235
Aging population 10, 14, 138, 173
Aid for disabled individuals 144
Alevi 145
Antenatal care 161, 166-68, 170-71
Artisans 147, 163
Asia 21, 49, 53, 232
Autonomy 39, 45, 105, 108, 111, 113-14, 117-18, 120-21, 225

Bag-Kur 18, 163
Barcelona Council 127
Bargaining power 47, 49, 119, 199
Biological household 105, 111-16
Bozkuş, S. Cihan 179
Breadwinner 4, 7-8, 11-12, 15, 21, 49, 51, 58, 93, 134, 143, 151, 157, 165, 178, 180, 197, 202
Buğra, Ayşe 8-9, 19, 20-22, 24, 130, 142, 148, 189, 223-24

Capability 105-06, 108, 111, 114-15
Capabilities approach (CA) 11,
104-07, 111, 114-15
Capital accumulation 40, 144, 175, 180-81
Capital flows 144, 205
Care work 9-10, 14, 50, 59, 60, 62, 94, 127, 132, 136, 189-90, 193-94, 198, 200-03, 237
Care work market 190
Charity 8, 11, 18, 27-30, 39, 103-04, 109, 112, 114, 224
Child-alikes 103
Child care 6, 11, 27, 54, 62, 94, 127-28, 132-33, 135-38, 175, 191-92, 198, 202-03, 216, 224
Childcare services 62, 127, 192
Child health 168
Civil code 6, 34, 125, 155
Civil rights 141
Coalition of Women's Groups for Women's Work and Labour (KEIG) 30, 63, 133, 137, 147, 151, 156, 165-66, 224, 233
Commercialisation 8, 23, 164
Commodification 5, 13, 177-78, 193
Convention on the Elimination of

Discrimination against Women (CEDAW) 42, 63, 129, 132, 135, 142, 145, 225-26, 233
Conditional cash transfer 24, 27, 161-62, 166, 223
Confederation of Employers' Associations of Turkey (TİSK) 133, 138, 234
Conservative corporatist regime 15, 142
Constitution 130-31, 133, 140, 155, 207, 209, 219, 226, 235
Constitutional amendment 6, 125, 131
Contributory regime 143-44, 148
Crisis 19, 24, 26, 91, 141-42, 157, 223

Defined contribution (DC) 173, 176-77, 236-37
Democrat Party, the 38
Denial of sexuality 144
Dependants 11, 18-19, 50, 90, 94, 97, 125, 131, 142-43, 145, 148-50, 229, 233
Developing world 47-49, 89, 157, 159
Dignity 108, 111, 113-14, 117-118, 120-21
Division of labour 6, 10, 31, 37, 43, 47, 54, 60, 62-63, 71, 88-90, 94, 101, 142-43, 151, 157, 197
Domestic work 10-11, 110, 120, 147, 166, 190, 191, 193-95, 197-200, 202-04, 237
Domestic labour 6, 11, 14, 103-5, 108-9, 111, 114, 120, 145, 166, 194, 198, 200, 203
Domestic violence 38, 121, 129, 162

Double-shift 101
Dual-earner 10, 94-97, 101

Early Childhood Development (ECD) 27, 29
Earnings distribution 69, 70-72, 74-75, 85, 229
Earnings gap 70-73, 81
Economic Policy Research Foundation of Turkey (TEPAV) 53
Elderly care 27, 59, 62, 125, 193, 228
Elson, Diane 60, 87, 92, 144, 145, 153, 234-35
Empowerment 34, 42, 58, 111, 121, 155, 158-59, 172, 230, 236
Entitlement conditions 12, 142, 150-51
Erdogan, Recep Tayyip 11, 132, 205
Esping-Andersen, Gosta 4-5, 15, 175
European Trade Union Confederation (ETUC) 211, 215, 218
European Union (EU) 5-6, 11-12, 14, 17-18, 26, 50-51, 53, 63, 123, 125-28, 130-33, 137, 139, 141, 152, 155-56, 160, 162, 171, 174, 176, 193, 205-11, 216-21, 234-35
Euro Mediterranean Partnership (MEDA) 160
EU accession 12, 14, 26, 123, 125, 130, 139, 141, 193, 208, 210
EU directives 131-32, 207
Evlatlık 10-11, 103-121, 191-92, 232-33
Ethnicity 4, 6, 31, 34, 60, 112, 145, 153, 225
Export-led growth 9

Export-led industrialisation 48-9
External debt 144

Familialism 8-9, 18, 24-30
Female employment 8-9, 12, 19, 48, 51-52, 57-60, 63-64, 125-140, 143, 147, 165, 178, 224, 233
Female labour force participation 9-10, 12, 27, 30, 47, 49, 50-51, 55, 60-61, 63, 88, 130, 136-37, 139, 174, 190-91, 229
Female-male earning ratio 70-71, 229
Female participation 49, 52
Feminisation 57, 90
Feminisation of the labour force 57
Feminist 4, 9, 31-33, 36-38, 41-45, 127, 131, 133, 139, 145, 213, 219-21, 231
Feminism 36-37, 225
Fertility rate 54
Flexible work 135, 137, 139, 151, 212, 220
Foreign direct investment 9, 53, 144
Foreign capital 53
Functionings 105-8, 111, 114

Garment sector 57-58
Gendered institution 28, 60
Gendered system 191
Gender equality 6-9, 11-12, 31-46, 47-48, 50, 55, 63-64, 88, 91, 102, 125-140, 145, 155-56, 158-59, 160, 162, 172, 210-11, 214, 217-19, 225, 227, 235
Gender gap 10, 12-13, 48, 54-55, 62, 76-77, 84, 89, 173-187, 230, 236
Gender mainstreaming 13, 127, 155-56, 158-60, 162, 171-72, 211, 217
Gender relations 12, 37, 60, 63, 108, 119, 127, 130, 138-39, 149, 156, 189, 195, 223
Gender regime 5, 33-36, 128
Gender socialisation 60
General Directorate on the Status of Women (KSGM) 129, 160, 162, 172, 234
Gini coefficient 65, 74, 78, 80
Green Card 24-25, 144, 163, 167, 169, 223, 236-37
Gross Domestic Product (GDP) 22-23, 25, 176, 224
Göle, Nilüfer 36, 39-41, 43, 154, 209

Health care 13, 24, 149-50, 155-72, 178, 198, 235
Health Sector Reforms (HSRs) 155-56, 159, 168
Health Seeking Behavior Study (HSBS) 161, 167-69
Health surveys 83
Health Transformation Programme (HTP) 13, 155-56, 163, 193
Headscarf 9, 32-33, 38-45, 224, 226-27
Home-based piece work 58, 175
Homemakers 11-12, 35, 91, 93, 96-97, 125-26, 136, 139, 211-12, 216
Honour crimes 129, 145
Hot money 144
Household Budget Survey (HBS) 66, 71, 228
Household income 78-82, 84-86, 89, 113, 180, 197, 229
Housewifisation 87-88
Housing policy 22

Humiliation 111, 113, 121, 201

Import substituting industrialisation 20, 50, 52
Income distribution 10, 32, 52, 54, 65-86, 182, 228
Income inequality 65, 69-86, 230
Individual Pension System (IPS) 13, 173, 176-84
Industrialisation 9, 16, 20, 48-50, 52-53, 60, 63, 90-91, 227, 231
Inflation 150, 175
Informal activities 126
Informal enterprises 58
Informal sector 7, 14, 16, 129, 137, 143, 166, 175, 178, 189-204, 235
Insecure jobs 135
Institutionalised care 192
International Labour Organisation (ILO) 55, 63, 176, 189, 194, 217, 237
International Monetary Fund (IMF) 24, 52, 91, 152, 176
Islam 14, 28, 39, 40, 226
Islamic conservatism 9, 18, 20
Islamist movement 32, 209, 226
Islamist politics 33
Islamist women 9, 33, 38-45

Job accident 149-50
Joint Inclusion Memorandum (JIM) 26
Justice and Development Party (AKP) 6-7, 11, 24, 27-28, 30, 42, 45, 131-32, 141, 156, 160, 162-63, 168, 171, 205-6, 208-11, 218-19, 221, 223, 226-27

Kandiyoti, Deniz 37, 45, 51, 129
Kemalist 9, 32, 34, 37, 39, 42-43, 129, 225, 226
Kinship 21, 130, 193, 195, 199, 201
Kurdish 24, 37, 112, 145, 153, 225-26

Labour income 10, 66, 68, 74-80, 82, 84-86, 229-30
Labour-intensive 51-53
Labour law 6, 125-26, 131-34, 137, 139-40, 204, 233-34
Labour market 6-7, 9, 10-14, 15-16, 19, 22, 28, 47-48, 50, 54-55, 57, 59-61, 63-69, 74, 76, 79-86, 88-90, 93, 97-98, 102, 104, 126-32, 134-39, 150, 155, 165, 174, 182, 189-95, 197, 202-3, 229-30
Latin America 16-17, 21, 49
Latin Rim 130
Liberalisation 17, 23, 36, 43, 141, 144, 173, 225, 231, 235
Liberal residualist 15, 17
Life expectancy 13, 76, 134, 175, 180, 183-85

Mainstream 4, 13, 42, 158
Male breadwinner model 4, 7-8, 12, 15, 21, 143, 151, 157, 165, 202
Market-led 5, 128
Market Oriented 12, 17, 23, 179
Manufacturing 49, 51-54, 57-60, 91, 143, 234
Maternal health 159, 162, 167-68, 172
Maternal mortality 160-61, 170
Maternity insurance 149-50
Maternity leave 7, 136, 138, 234
Means-testing 19, 25, 143, 163, 165-66, 171
Migrant women 59-60, 191-93,

202
Micro-enterprises 72
Middle East 55, 109
Middle East and North Africa
(MENA) 48-50
Millennium Development Goals
(MDG) 155, 159-60, 172
Minimum pension guarantee
(MPG) 13, 182-85, 237
Mobility 117, 121
Modernisation 3, 126, 129
Modernity 35, 40
Muslims 40, 42, 109-10, 145, 209,
226, 227

Nation-state 34, 42, 144
Neoliberal policies 36, 52-53, 62,
64, 92, 206, 208, 212
Nimble fingers 59
Non-contributory regime 143-44,
148
Non-earner household 95
Non-Governmental Organisation
(NGO) 28-30, 41, 43, 138-39, 161,
163, 172, 233-34, 237
Non-labour income 10, 66, 74-80,
82, 84-86, 230
Non-muslim minorities 145
Nussbaum, Martha 107-8, 233

Occupational disease 149-150
OECD 20, 22-23, 126, 229
Old age 8, 18-19, 22, 25, 27, 152,
192
Old age pension/insurance 19, 147,
150-51
Open Method of Coordination 26
Orphan 11, 103, 110, 143, 146-47,
152
Ottoman (Empire) 34, 104, 109,

191, 224, 233
Out-of-pocket expenditure 165-66,
168-69

Özbay, Ferhunde 109-10, 191-92,
197, 234

Parental leave 126, 135, 137-38,
234
Parenthood 66, 87, 101, 138
Part-time work 137, 175, 191, 219
Paternalist protectionism 165
Patriarchal ideology 14, 213-14,
221
Patriarchy 9, 36, 37, 44, 47-48, 51,
54-55, 59-64, 90, 214, 220, 227
Pay-as-you-go (PAYG) 173-76,
184-85
Peasant 11, 19-20, 34, 103, 110,
144, 191-92
Penal code 6, 38, 42, 125, 155, 225
Pension benefit 174, 180, 236
Pension companies 177, 181, 183-
84
Pension reforms 174
Personal income 66-69, 78-82, 84-
86, 229-30
Policy-led 5, 128
Political Islam 32, 37, 41, 43
Political rights 35, 142
Polarisation 153
Positive discrimination 7, 140, 219
Poverty 3, 8-10, 17-18, 22-24, 26-
27, 29-30, 64, 65-66, 82-85, 87-88,
91, 105-6, 108-9, 119, 153, 159,
163, 175, 182, 193, 230, 232-33,
237
Preventive and curative services
168
Privatisation 14, 141, 144, 152-53,

164, 170, 173-76, 180, 185, 189, 236
Private employment agencies (PEA) 14, 133, 194
Private pension 12-14, 142, 152, 173-74, 176, 178, 180-81, 184-85, 236
Private sphere 14, 34, 37, 43, 131, 133, 193, 209-211
Pseudo-family 103, 105, 107, 112-14, 116-17, 119-120
Public expenditure 59, 62, 91
Public services 5, 9, 17, 59, 62, 128, 142, 144, 153
Public sphere 14, 33, 35-36, 44, 47, 61, 63, 132, 208-11, 214
Purchasing power 142

Quasi-adoption 11, 103, 232

Rational choice 87, 89-90
Redistribution 16, 28, 135, 145, 153, 182
Regular Contributions (RC) 179-80
Religion 31-34, 39, 121, 145, 153, 198, 225-27
Replacement rate 149-50, 174
Reproductive Health Program (RHP) 160-62, 168
Retirement 7, 12-14, 18-19, 67-68, 86, 131, 134, 145, 151-52, 173-77, 181, 229, 236
Retirement benefits 68-69, 75-76, 78, 180-81, 192, 229
Retirement earnings 180-81, 184-85
Retirement Fund (ES) 18, 163
Retirement income 14, 68, 75, 85, 174-75, 179-80, 183-85

Rural 8, 10, 13-14, 20-21, 23, 32, 34, 40, 59, 61-62, 92, 103, 109, 111-13, 126, 143, 147, 161, 166, 181, 185, 190, 192-93, 195, 200

Secularism 34, 37, 227
Secondary earners 175
Self-determination 110-11
Self-employment 67, 73-74, 130, 229
Sen, Amartya 83, 105, 107-8, 158-59, 230
Schooling 62, 74, 82-83, 107, 112, 228
Shariat/Sharia 34, 42, 209
Shopkeepers 147
Sickness 111, 149-150
Single-earner 94-97, 101
Singlehood 87-88, 97-101, 232
Small farmers 146-48
Social aid 8, 11, 142-44
Social assistance 11, 16-19, 22, 24, 26-30, 68, 143, 161, 224
Social benefits 12, 142-43, 149, 174, 179, 182
Social democratic 5, 15, 128
Social Health Insurance (SHI) 165-66
Social insurance 125, 143, 146-52, 164, 167, 182
Social Insurance and General Health Insurance Law, the 7, 12, 134, 141
Social Insurance Institution (SSK) 18, 163
Social policy 3-5, 11, 15-18, 22, 25-30, 127, 145
Social protection 8, 12, 15-19, 22, 24, 30, 53, 64, 130, 142-43, 150, 152, 165-66

Social rights 126, 141-42, 145, 150
Social risks 11, 148-49, 152-53
Social security 3, 7-8, 12-13, 17-25, 30, 53, 76, 84-85, 128, 130, 133-35, 141-54, 166-67, 173-74, 176-79, 184-85, 191, 193, 197, 200, 203-4, 206, 220, 227, 229, 233, 235, 236
Social Security Institution (SGK) 23, 148, 163-64, 166-67, 236
Social services 27, 29, 102, 130, 174
South European Model 15-16, 18-19
State feminism 37, 226
State Planning Organisation (DPT) 91, 229
Statistical discrimination 175
Structural Adjustment Program (SAP) 9, 52, 91-92, 189, 231
Subcontracting 25, 53, 57, 194
Survivor benefits 27, 68, 76-77, 86, 229
Symbolic pawns 3, 129

Tax incentives 177
Textile 56-57, 166, 190
Time-autonomy 121
Time poverty 87
Time use 10, 88-90, 92, 94, 97, 99-101, 229, 231, 235
Trade unions 14, 139, 205-221, 234
Treaty of Rome, the 127
Turkic republics 60
Turkish Employment Organisation (İş-Kur) 138, 193-94, 198, 200, 203
Turkish Foundation of Voluntary Organisations (TGTV) 28, 224

Turkish Industry and Business Association (TUSIAD) 54

Unemployment Insurance 16
United Nations (UN) 63, 142, 156, 159-60, 227
United Nations Development Programme (UNDP) 83, 129, 159, 230
Universalisation 5
Unpaid family worker 7, 51, 61, 68, 71, 94, 130, 133, 147, 229, 235
Unpaid work 10, 87-92, 94-102, 176, 182, 230-32
Unregistered work 190
Urban 8, 11, 20-21, 23-24, 32, 34, 36, 40-41, 51, 59, 61-62, 92, 103, 109, 111, 126, 129, 133, 147, 157, 181-82, 185, 189-92, 195, 200, 203, 228, 231-32
Urbanisation 40, 91, 192

Virginity 38, 43, 144
Vulnerability of women 10, 66, 68, 178

Wage gap 71, 98, 143
Welfare Party, the 39
Welfare regimes 5, 8-9, 11, 13-14, 15-30, 50, 104, 130, 138, 142-45, 149, 173, 177-78, 189
Welfare state 3-14, 16-17, 25, 28, 101, 120, 125-26, 128-32, 139, 143, 177, 182, 193
Welfare state-led 5, 128
Welfare clientelism 16
Well-being 11, 66, 84, 87, 103-21, 174, 226
Winter guesthouse 161, 170
Women's bargaining power 47, 49

Women's earnings 58, 66, 70, 81-82, 85
Women's movement 9, 31-33, 36-43, 45, 47, 129, 156, 210, 217, 224-25
Women's organizations 30, 42, 63-64, 139, 156, 163, 165, 172, 224, 228, 233
Women's welfare 8, 13, 101, 173
World Health Organisation (WHO) 156, 158, 172
World Trade Organisation (WTO) 51